T0230023

Lecture Notes in Computer Science 734

Edited by G. Goos and J. Hartmanis

Advisory Board: W. Brauer   D. Gries   J. Stoer

Jens Volkert (Ed.)

Parallel Computation

Second International ACPC Conference
Gmunden, Austria, October 4-6, 1993
Proceedings

Springer-Verlag

Berlin Heidelberg New York
London Paris Tokyo
Hong Kong Barcelona
Budapest

Series Editors

Gerhard Goos
Universität Karlsruhe
Postfach 69 80
Vincenz-Priessnitz-Straße 1
D-76131 Karlsruhe, Germany

Juris Hartmanis
Cornell University
Department of Computer Science
4130 Upson Hall
Ithaca, NY 14853, USA

Volume Editors

Jens Volkert
Institut für Informatik, Johannes Kepler Universität Linz
Altenbergerstr. 69, A-4040 Linz, Austria

CR Subject Classification (1991): D.1.3, D.2.6, F.2.1-2, D.3.2

ISBN 3-540-57314-3 Springer-Verlag Berlin Heidelberg New York
ISBN 0-387-57314-3 Springer-Verlag New York Berlin Heidelberg

Typesetting: Camera-ready by author
Printing and binding: Druckhaus Beltz, Hemsbach/Bergstr.
45/3140-543210 - Printed on acid-free paper

Preface

The Austrian Center for Parallel Computation (ACPC) is a co-operative research organization founded in 1989 to promote research and education in the field of software for parallel computer systems. The areas in which the ACPC is active include algorithms, languages, compilers, programming environments, and applications for parallel and high-performance computing systems.

The partner institutions of the ACPC come from the University of Vienna, the Technical University of Vienna, and the Universities of Linz and Salzburg. They carry out joint research projects, share a pool of hardware resources, and offer a joint curriculum in Parallel Computation for graduate and postgraduate students. In addition, an international conference is organized every other year. The Third International Conference of the ACPC will take place in Vienna in 1995.

The *Second International Conference of the ACPC* took place in Gmunden, Austria, from October 4 to October 6, 1993. The conference attracted many participants from around the world. Authors from 17 countries submitted 44 papers, from which 15 were selected and presented at the conference. In addition, 4 distinguished researchers presented invited papers. The papers from these presentations are contained in this proceedings volume.

The organization of the conference was the result of the dedicated work of a large number of individuals, not all of whom can be mentioned here. I would like, in particular, to acknowledge the efforts made by the members of the Program Committee and the referees. The organizational and administrative support from Alfred Spalt, Romana Schiller, Irmgard Husinsky and Bernhard Knaus was exceptionally valuable.

Finally, we gratefully acknowledge the following organizations which have supported the conference:

The Austrian Ministry for Science and Research
The Austrian Science Foundation (FWF)
The Governor of the Province of Upper Austria
The Mayor of Gmunden
Amt der O.Ö. Landesregierung
Kammer der Gewerblichen Wirtschaft für Oberösterreich
Linzer Hochschulfonds
Vereinigung Österreichischer Industrieller Landesgruppe O.Ö

Bacher Systems EDV GmbH (Vienna, A)
CRAY Research GmbH (Munich, D)
Digital Equipment Corp. (Vienna, A)
GE.PAR.D, Ges. f. Parallele Datenverarbeitung GmbH (Vienna, A)
IBM (Vienna, A)
Intel Corporation Ltd. (Swindon, U.K)
MasPar Computergesellschaft (Neubiberg, D)
nCUBE Deutschland GmbH (Munich, D)
Siemens Nixdorf Informationssysteme GmbH (Vienna, A)
Silicon Graphics GmbH (Vienna, A)

Linz, August 1993   Jens Volkert

Contents

Programming Environments

High-Performance Computing on a Honeycomb Architecture *

Borut Robič and Jurij Šilc

Institute Jožef Stefan, Laboratory for Computer Architectures
Jamova 39, 61111 Ljubljana, Slovenia
e-mail: borut.robic@ijs.si

Abstract. We explore time and space optimization problems involved in the mapping of parallel algorithms onto a honeycomb architecture. When a well-known mapping is used, mapped algorithms generally exhibit execution slow-down and require too large area. We design several optimization techniques and enhance the mapping process. Experimental results show more than 50 % saving in processor resources and 30 % saving in execution time, on average. Since computing performances are improved, also the applicability of the honeycomb architecture is wider.

1 Introduction

In sequential computation special purpose machines have no major advantage over general purpose machines, since the later can perform the same functions almost as fast as the former. This means that, in sequential computation, the universality can also be made efficient. In parallel computing, however, the question of whether efficient universality can be found has no clear answer yet, in spite of the fact that several models of realistic machines have been proposed and many parallel computers have been built. For example, systolic and wavefront VLSI processor arrays proved efficient in execution of decision-free algorithms which are characterized by having a dataflow pattern and computation order independent of the data values [1]. Yet, these algorithmically specialized arrays are not suitable for execution of many other algorithms that do not exhibit such a high regularity.

For this reason, a universal processor array, i.e. an array capable of executing arbitrary algorithms, was suggested in [2]. The array consists of cells (processing elements) which are arranged in rows, each pair of rows being separated by the communication bus (Fig. 1a). The bus enables cells to communicate with a host computer for algorithm down-loading and data I/O. Each cell has six immediate neighbors, and is connected to them by point-to-point links. The computation is data-driven, i.e. each cell is capable of testing for the presence of its operands and executing only the instructions for which all the necessary operands have arrived. The name *honeycomb* is suggested by Fig. 1b, where only cells are depicted. An

---

* This research is supported by the Ministry of Science and Technology of the Republic of Slovenia under grant P2-5092-106/93.

arbitrary parallel algorithm is written in a dataflow language, and mapped onto honeycomb architecture using a four-stage process. During the first stage the program is translated to a dataflow graph (DFG). The second stage, referred to as DFG-*mapping*, maps the DFG onto a potentially unbounded honeycomb. The third stage partitions the array into chips while the last stage down-loads the tasks to the cells of the array. This idea of direct mapping an arbitrary algorithm on a hexagonally connected VLSI array was introduced in [3] and improved in [4] where medium grained parallelism was used.

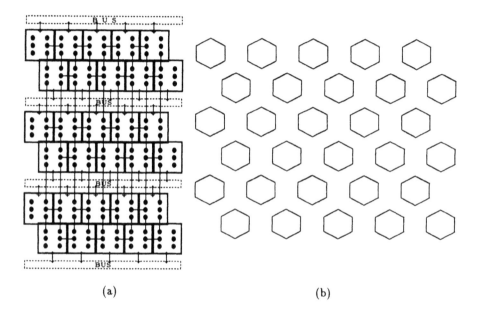

(a)   (b)

Fig. 1. Honeycomb architecture: (a) Implementation. (b) Scheme.

However, the universality of the array is not as attractive as it seems at first sight because not all mapped algorithms use the array efficiently. In particular, some may require a too large chip area, others may not execute fast enough. The mapping process may be improved by changing array architecture, thus making it more amenable to the mapping. In [5], for example, blocks of cells (characterized by tighter coupling) are created, and array connectivity is improved by addition of wires and switching elements between blocks. In [6] cells contain up to 16 nodes and two communication links connect every two adjacent cells. In this paper, we improve computing performance of the honeycomb by adding the optimization process to the DFG-mapping while keeping the basic cell architecture.

2 Mapping

The mapping process starts with the translation of a program, written in the dataflow language VAL, to a DFG. The translator was built utilizing Unix tools Lex and YACC [7]. Fig. 2 shows a simple **if-then-else** VAL program [8] and its translation to the DFG.

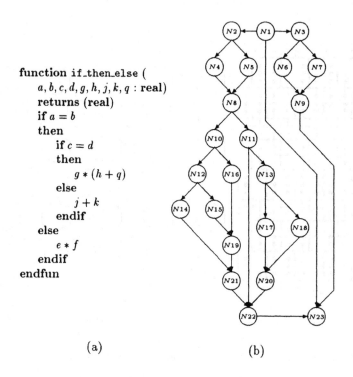

function if_then_else (
    $a, b, c, d, g, h, j, k, q$: **real**)
    returns (**real**)
    if $a = b$
    then
        if $c = d$
        then
            $g * (h + q)$
        else
            $j + k$
        endif
    else
        $e * f$
    endif
endfun

(a)   (b)

Fig. 2. if-then-else: (a) VAL program. (b) Its DFG.

2.1 DFG-mapping

The DFG is mapped onto theoretically unbounded honeycomb during the DFG-mapping stage. At this point, some fundamental constraints, imposed by technological characteristics of the architecture, are to be obeyed. In particular, each cell is connected to six adjacent cells, communicates with them simultaneously, and is capable of performing computational and routing tasks concurrently.

The DFG-mapping consists of three steps, referred to as layer construction, placement of the layers, and path construction.

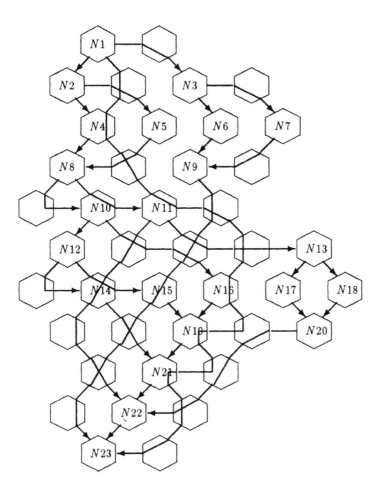

Fig. 3. if-then-else: Direct mapping.

During the first step, the set of vertices of DFG is partitioned into *layers*. Layer 0 consists of vertices accepting only external input data. A vertex is in layer $i > 0$, if one of its inputs comes from a vertex at layer $i - 1$, and none come from layers $k \geq i$. In order to construct layers, arcs that close loops are first detected applying depth-first traversal of DFG. These backward arcs are temporarily cut. This results is an acyclic subgraph of DFG whose vertices are then partitioned into layers according to labels obtained by topological sort. In the second step, each of the layers is placed on its own row of cells in the array. The placement is performed according to the associated labels, i.e. layer i is placed onto the i-th row. Next, the vertices in each row are permuted so that the paths which still remain to be built in the next step are expected to be short.

Vertices which are to be connected are arranged as much as possible one under another to allow the paths between them to be as vertical as possible. The final step of DFG-mapping determines how the arcs of DFG are represented by paths in the array. The paths are built in a heuristic piece-meal fashion moving from one cell to another. At each cell, a single communication link is added to one or more incomplete paths which go through it. The processing of the incomplete paths is performed according to their dynamically assigned priorities. This makes it possible to choose a suitable routing heuristic. However, situations still develop where a large number of paths have to be routed through a small area on the array. In such cases only the last decision in the routing process is changed instead of performing an extensive backtracking to search for other routings. If this does not solve the problem, a row or column of cells is simply added to the array. The result of DFG-mapping for `if-then-else` example is depicted on Fig. 3.

Clearly, the depth-first traversal of the DFG cuts the loops at the last possible moment and thus constructs many layers. Since each layer is placed onto its own row the mapped DFG is overstretched downwards across the array. Moreover, each arc of DFG that has been temporarily cut connects vertices whose label-difference is proportional to the length of the loop. The corresponding path in the array may thus be very long.

In summary, the mapped graph is exaggeratedly stretched downwards across the hosting array. It generally has vertical paths some of which connect cells of very distant rows. As a consequence, such DFG mappings exhibit two disadvantages. First of all, since time complexity of routing operation is not negligible [9], execution slow-down may occur as a result of remote communication between some cells (especially for cyclic DFGs). Secondly, DFG mappings may require a too large area.

2.2 Optimization

To evaluate the applicability of the proposed array, and to use it efficiently, one has to be able to map parallel algorithms onto it as optimally as possible. Hence, an optimization stage has to be designed.

Let μ be a mapping and G a DFG. The cost of a mapped graph $M = \mu(G)$ is $E(M) = \sum_p \ell(p)$, where the sum is taken over all paths of M which are mappings of arcs in G, and $\ell(p)$ is the number of cells along each such path without endpoints. The object is to find mapping μ^* which minimizes the cost E. Instead of a direct searching for μ^* an existing mapping μ_0 is fixed, and an additional transformation τ^* of $\mu_0(G)$ is searched to minimize the cost by a composed mapping $\mu = \tau^* \circ \mu_0$. For μ_0 the mapping of DFG-mapping from [3, 4] is used. Fig. 4 shows the result of applying such a transformation to the mapping on Fig. 3. The cost was reduced from $E = 40$ to $E = 9$.

Given some mapping M of a DFG we say that a transformation of M is *regular* if it moves a single vertex of M to an adjacent cell and rerouts all possible paths [10]. Generally, there are several regular transformations applicable to M. The neighborhood $\mathcal{N}(M)$ of M consists of all mappings obtained from

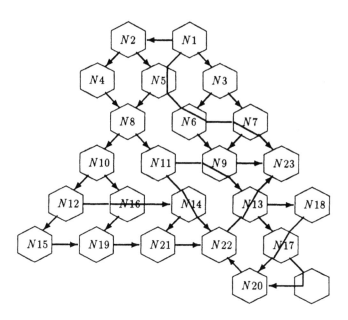

Fig. 4. if-then-else: "Optimal" mapping.

M by regular transformations. *Local search $\mathcal{LS}$*, which is a general method for designing approximation algorithms [11], starts at initial mapping $M = \mu_0(G)$ and searches for a mapping M' in $\mathcal{N}(M)$, so that $E(M') < E(M)$. As long as an improved mapping M' exists, the algorithm adopts it and repeats the search from it. When a local minimum is reached, the algorithm stops. Fig. 5 shows the result of applying $\mathcal{LS}$ to the if-then-else example. The cost was reduced from $E = 40$ to $E = 27$.

Probabilistic algorithms. Local search is a fast method but it generally gets trapped in a local optimum. To escape from local optima several probabilistic algorithms have been proposed in the past, including *simulated annealing $\mathcal{SA}$* [12], *threshold accepting $\mathcal{TA}$* [13], and *quenching $\mathcal{Q}$* [14].

$\mathcal{SA}$ has become a popular tool for solving a wide class of combinatorial optimization problems [12]. In our case the algorithm runs as follows. As in local search it starts at initial mapping $\mu_0(G)$. After some mapping M has been reached, another mapping M' is *randomly* chosen from the neighborhood $\mathcal{N}(M)$. If M' is better than M, it is accepted. If it is worse, however, it is accepted only with a certain probability. This enables the algorithm to escape from trapping into a local minimum. The acceptance probability depends on a time-dependent parameter T and on the decrease in E. Since T is slowly

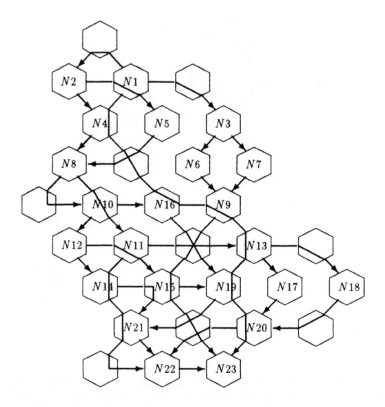

Fig. 5. if-then-else: $\mathcal{LS}$ mapping.

lowered during the running time, also the acceptance probability is lowered, making "bad" acceptances more and more improbable. The algorithm has been implemented with the following annealing schedule: T is lowered by a constant value (*temperature function*), at each T changes are attempted until a number of acceptances have occurred (*number of repetitions*), and the algorithm stops when sufficiently few acceptances are occurring at successive temperatures (*stopping criteria*). Fig. 6 shows the result of applying $\mathcal{SA}$ to the if-then-else example where the cost was reduced to $E = 24$.

A similar yet simpler algorithm is threshold accepting $\mathcal{TA}$. It was reported in [13] that the algorithm yields better results than $\mathcal{SA}$. Moreover, it was observed that with the same number of steps $\mathcal{TA}$ solutions were on the average better than $\mathcal{SA}$ solutions.

In our case, while $\mathcal{SA}$ accepts worse mappings with certain probabilities, $\mathcal{TA}$ accepts every new mapping M' which is "not much worse" than the old mapping M. To be more specific, after some mapping M has been reached, another mapping M' is randomly chosen from the neighborhood $\mathcal{N}(M)$. If M' is

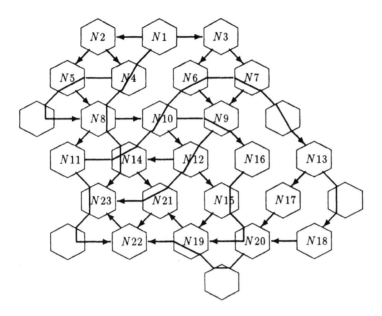

Fig. 6. if-then-else: $\mathcal{SA}$ mapping.

better than M, i.e. if $E(M') < E(M)$, it is accepted. If it is worse, it is accepted only if $E(M') - E(M) < t$, for some *threshold* $t > 0$. This enables the algorithm to escape from trapping into a local minimum. However, the acceptances of worse mappings become more and more rare because the threshold t is slowly lowered during the running time.

Deterministic modifications. The choice of a "good" neighborhood for the problem is usually guided by intuition. There is a trade-off between large and small neighborhoods, since large neighborhoods may provide better local optima but generally take longer to search [12]. If the neighborhoods are too small, the process may not be able to move around quickly enough to reach the minimum in a reasonable time. On the other hand, if the neighborhoods are too large, the process essentially performs a random search. In our case, the neighborhood $\mathcal{N}(M)$ as defined above (by regular transformations of M) is an adequate compromise. However, the neighborhood structure is not the only aspect that is free to be chosen so that the convergence speed of the algorithms is improved. In this paper we design two modifications of $\mathcal{SA}$ and $\mathcal{TA}$, which are still capable of escaping local minima but have improved convergence speed. Informally, after some mapping M has been reached, *deterministic* selection of the next mapping $M' \in \mathcal{N}(M)$ is performed instead of a random one. This selection is made by using "the most promising" transformation of M, i.e. such a regular transformation γ, that the greatest decrease in the cost E is expected after applying γ on M. We call γ the *guiding* regular transformation, and the modified algorithms *Guided Simulated Annealing* $\mathcal{GSA}$ and *Guided Threshold Accepting* $\mathcal{GTA}$.

$\mathcal{GSA}$ algorithm:

let M be initial mapping $\mu_0(G)$
choose an initial temperature $T > 0$
loop: construct guiding transformation γ
    $M' := \gamma(M)$
    $\Delta E := E(M') - E(M)$
    if $\Delta E < 0$
        then $M := M'$
        else if $random(0,1) \le e^{-\Delta E/T}$
            then $M := M'$
    if a long time no decrease in E
      or too many iterations
        then lower T
    if some time no change in E
        then stop
goto loop.

$\mathcal{GTA}$ algorithm:

let M be initial mapping $\mu_0(G)$
choose an initial threshold $t > 0$
loop: construct guiding transformation γ
    $M' := \gamma(M)$
    $\Delta E := E(M') - E(M)$
    if $\Delta E < t$
        then $M := M'$
    if a long time no decrease in E
      or too many iterations
        then lower t
    if some time no change in E
        then stop
goto loop.

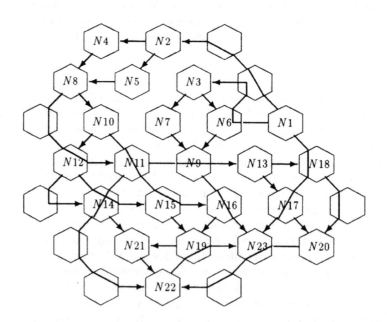

Fig. 7. if-then-else: $\mathcal{GSA}$ mapping.

Heuristic construction of the guiding regular transformation of M proceeds as follows. For each vertex v of M and each path p incident to v a physical force of attraction is assigned to v, having its magnitude proportional to $\ell(p)$ and direction from v to the next processor on p. Let $\overrightarrow{F}(v)$ be the vector sum of all such forces acting upon v, $F(v)$ its magnitude, and $d(v)$ one of six directions from v to adjacent processors which is closest to $\overrightarrow{F}(v)$. Now, let $v_1, v_2, \ldots$ be ordering of vertices of M, such that $F(v_i) \geq F(v_{i+1})$, for $i = 1, 2, \ldots$. Then the guiding regular transformation γ is described by a pair $(v_k, d(v_k))$, where k is the smallest index such that v_k can be moved in direction $d(v_k)$ to the adjacent processor rerouting all incident paths.

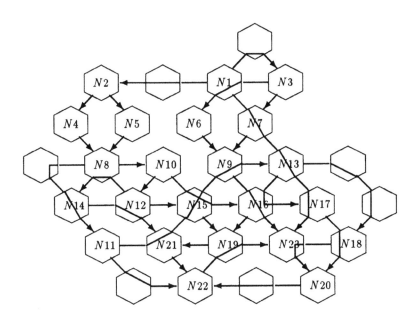

Fig. 8. if-then-else: $\mathcal{GTA}$ mapping.

Fig. 7 and Fig. 8 show the results of applying $\mathcal{GSA}$ and $\mathcal{GTA}$ to the if-then-else example, respectively. $\mathcal{GTA}$ returned $E = 23$ while $\mathcal{GSA}$ returned $E = 21$. Moreover, these results were obtained 3 to 5-times quicker compared to $\mathcal{SA}$.

3 Experimental Results

We obtained several experimental results utilizing *GraphCompactor*, a tool which we designed to perform optimization with algorithms $\mathcal{LS}$, $\mathcal{GTA}$, $\mathcal{GSA}$, and $\mathcal{SA}$ [15]. We considered fourteen DFGs from [3, 9, 16]. For each DFG probabilistic algorithms have been run 3 – 5 times with different annealing schedules. Algorithms $\mathcal{SA}$ and $\mathcal{GSA}$ were implemented with the following annealing schedule. Initial temperature is $T_0 = aE_0$, where E_0 is the cost of initial mapping and $a > 0$. At each temperature T_i changes are attempted until cn of acceptances have occurred, after which T_i is lowered to $T_{i+1} = bT_i$, where n is the number of nodes in graph, $0 < b < 1$, and $c > 0$. Algorithms stop when sufficiently few acceptances are occurring at successive temperatures. The annealing schedule for $\mathcal{GTA}$ algorithm was the same as above with threshold t instead of temperature T. We considered $0.1 \leq a \leq 0.2$, $0.8 \leq b \leq 0.9$, and $0.2 \leq c \leq 0.3$.

The quality of mappings $M = \mu(G)$ was evaluated by the following measures:

- *area* $A(M)$, i.e. the number of cells utilized by mapping M,
- *chip-size* $C(M)$, the number of cells in the smallest rectangle enclosing M,
- *maximum path length* $\widehat{\ell}(M)$, i.e. the number of cells on the longest path of the mapping M,
- *average path length* $\bar{\ell}(M)$, i.e. the average number of cells used to map an arc of G,
- *average execution time* $\omega(M)$ of the mapping M.

Table 1. Average relative improvement of the DFG-mapping (in %).

Algorithm	area A	chip-size C	max.path length $\widehat{\ell}$	avrg.path length $\bar{\ell}$	avrg.execution time ω
$\mathcal{LS}$	30	**32**	61	56	**23**
$\mathcal{GTA}$	43	**47**	80	75	**27**
$\mathcal{GSA}$	44	**46**	84	78	**38**
$\mathcal{SA}$	47	**51**	82	81	**36**
"optimal"	51	**61**	87	90	**46**

Table 1 shows average relative improvements of the DFG-mapping which were obtained by algorithms $\mathcal{LS}$, $\mathcal{GTA}$, $\mathcal{GSA}$, and $\mathcal{SA}$. The average reduction in the chip size C (i.e. processor resources) was between 32 % and 51 %, depending on the algorithm used. Note that at the same time the execution time ω was reduced by 23 % to 36 %. Generally, it is difficult to say how close to optimal the improvements are, since there is no efficient way of knowing what the best mapping for a specific DFG is. However, using interactive mode of our *Graph-Compactor* we were able to obtain "optimal" mappings, i.e. mappings having the energy E "close" to 0 (Table 1). Note that the results obtained automatically are near-"optimal".

4   Concluding remarks

Since the honeycomb data-driven array is capable of executing arbitrary algorithms, it can be connected to a host system to function as a slave processor to handle specialized computationally intensive tasks. In the paper, we have experimentally shown that the efficiency of the array may be considerably improved. As a result, the improved performance of the array makes its universality much more attractive. This makes possible to compare this pure data-driven architecture to other ones, especially the new hybrid data/control-driven architectures [17, 18].

In discussing the problem of mapping parallel algorithms onto honeycomb architecture we have shown that there is a lot of possibilities for improvement of initial mappings produced by the DFG-mapping from [3, 4]. In particular, these mappings exhibit execution slow-down and require too many cells (processing elements). We designed an optimization process and enhanced the DFG-mapping. The execution efficiency was thus considerably improved (more than 50 % saving in honeycomb space and 30 % saving in execution time, on average). The applicability of the array is therefore much wider, since larger parallel algorithms can be mapped onto it. For example, algorithm **Even process** [7] originally used 14 × 16 cells. After optimization, however, it was mapped onto an array consisting of 8 × 8 cells and executed twice faster. Similarly, the area and execution time for algorithm **Newton** [3] were reduced by 62 % and 43 %, respectively. For **Runge-Kutta** [16] these improvements are 50 % and 45 %.

Since electronic components will never be totally reliable, a possibility of production or run-time failures should also be considered. For that reason, all the algorithms mentioned above should take into account the presence of faulty cells in the array. Finaly, to speed up even these new optimization algorithms, the possibility of their parallelization should be analyzed.

References

1. Kung, S.Y.: *VLSI Array Processors*. (Prentice Hall, 1988).
2. Koren, I., Peled, I.: The Concept and Implementation of Data-Driven Array. *IEEE Computer* **20** (July 1987) 102–103.
3. Koren, I., Silberman, G.M.: A Direct Mapping of Algorithms onto VLSI Processing Arrays Based on the Data Flow Approach. *Proc. 1983 Int'l Conference on Parallel Processing*, August 1983, 335–337.
4. Mendelson, B., Silberman, G.M.: An Improved Mapping of Data Flow Programs on a VLSI Array of Processors. *Proc. 1987 Int'l Conference on Parallel Processing*, August 1987, 871–873.
5. Weiss, S., Spillinger, I., Silberman, G.M.: Architectural Improvements for Data-Driven VLSI Processing Arrays. *Proc. 1989 Conference on Functional Programming Languages and Computer Architecture*, September 1989, 243–259.
6. Mendelson, B., Koren, I.: Using Simulated Annealing for Mapping Algorithms onto Data-Driven Arrays. *Proc. 1991 Int'l Conference on Parallel Processing*, August 1991, I-123–I-127.
7. Koren, I., Mendelson, B., Peled, I., Silberman, G.M.: A Data-Driven VLSI Array for Arbitrary Algorithms. *IEEE Computer* **21** (October 1988) 30–43.
8. Mendelson, B., Koren, I.: Estimating the Potential Parallelism and Pipelining of Algorithms for Data Flow Machines. *Journal of Parallel and Distributed Computing* **14** (January 1992) 15–28.

Refined Local Instruction Scheduling Considering Pipeline Interlocks

Jörg Schepers
Siemens AG / ZFE ST SN 24
Otto-Hahn-Ring 6, W - 8000 München 83
phone: +49-89-636-48964, fax: +49-89-636-49767, e-mail: js@zfe.siemens.de

Abstract

We present a refined local instruction-scheduling algorithm for superscalar and superpipelined microprocessor architectures. The algorithm explicitly considers pipeline interlocks that may occur, for example on a floating-point pipeline, even among data-independent instructions. A refined attributed DAG representation is used for this purpose. The algorithm has been implemented for the MIPS R4000 microprocessor. Evaluation of the algorithm shows that optimal schedules are generated for almost all basic blocks. A significant performance gain is achieved for numeric applications as well as for general-purpose code.

1 Introduction

Modern superscalar and superpipelined microprocessors comprise several functional units and deep pipelines for a parallel execution of instructions. However, full utilization of the power of those architectures requires a sophisticated instruction sequencing. Hazard conditions have to be considered and pipeline interlocks may slow down execution time significantly if data dependencies occur in the instruction sequence. The objective of instruction scheduling is to find an instruction sequence with a minimal execution time which fulfills the semantics of the source program.

In this paper we present an efficient and almost always optimal algorithm for local instruction scheduling. Contrary to global instruction scheduling (like percolation or trace scheduling [Fish81, Nic85]) local instruction scheduling considers only instructions of one basic block at a time and computes an optimal sequence for them. From the theoretical point of view this optimization problem is NP-hard [Henn83]. Therefore, several heuristics have been developed which try to minimize the length of a schedule [Bern88, Bern89a, Gibb86, Good88, Hsu87, Proe91, Shie89]. However, we will show that this does not necessarily result in optimal execution times, especially if pipelines with complex interlock conditions have to be considered.

We propose another cost function for this optimization problem which directly corresponds to the number of machine cycles necessary for the execution of an instruction sequence. The scheduling algorithm itself is based on an enhanced DAG representation[1] of a basic block and considers delay cycles as well as pipeline interlocks. The algorithm is architecture-independent in a wide range; only the hazard and interlock conditions of a specific architecture must be known for DAG construction.

In the next section we will first discuss the disadvantages arising from approaches that only minimize the length of a schedule. We will then propose a new approach which overcomes these problems. In section 3 we describe a specific implementation of our algorithm for the MIPS R4000 microprocessor. We present results obtained from that implementation and some variants of our scheduling heuristic in section 4. Comparison with a branch&bound algorithm shows that we get optimal solutions for almost all basic blocks. The paper ends with an assessment and discussion of these results.

---

[1] Dependencies among instructions are internally represented as a directed acyclic graph (DAG).

9. Mendelson, B., Silberman, G.M.: Mapping Data Flow Programs on a VLSI Array of Processors. *Proc. 14th Annual Int'l Symposium on Computer Architecture*, June 1987, 72–80.

10. Robič, B., Kolbezen, P., Šilc, J.: Area Optimization of Dataflow-Graph Mappings. *Parallel Computing* **18**, 3 (1992) 297–311.

11. Papadimitriou, C.H., Steiglitz, K.: *Combinatorial Optimization: Algorithms and Complexity.* (Prentice Hall, 1982).

12. Johnson, M.E., ed.: Simulated Annealing (SA) & Optimization: Modern Algorithms with VLSI, Optimal Design, and Missile Defence Applications. *American Journal of Mathematical and Management Sciences* **8**, 3 & 4 (1988) 205–449.

13. Dueck, G., Scheuer, T.: Threshold Accepting: A General Purpose Optimization Algorithm Appearing Superior to Simulated Annealing. Tech. Rep. TR 88.10.011, IBM Scientific Center, Heidelberg, October 1988.

14. Lee, C., Bic, L.: Comparing Quenching and Slow Simulated Annealing on the Mapping Problem. *Proc. 3rd Annual Parallel Processing Symposium*, March 1989, 671–685.

15. Robič, B., Kolbezen, P., Šilc, J.: Graph Compactor for Mapping of Algorithms on VLSI Processor Arrays. *Proc. ISMM Int'l Workshop Parallel Computing*, September 1991, 198–200.

16. Mendelson, B., Silberman, G.M.: Private communication.

17. Iannucci, R.A.: A Dataflow / von Neumann Hybrid Architecture. Tech. Rep. TR-418, Lab. Computer Science, MIT, Massachusetts, May 1988.

18. Šilc, J., Robič, B.: Synchronous Dataflow-Based Architecture. *Microprocessing and Microprogramming* **27**, 1-5 (1989) 315–322.

2 Minimal Schedules

2.1 Soft-Delays

Instruction scheduling must be performed under consideration of data and control dependencies among instructions. Most scheduling algorithms are based on a representation of those dependencies by a directed acyclic graph (DAG) [Aho88]. Instructions are represented as nodes of the graph and are connected by a directed edge if an instruction has to be executed before another due to data or control dependencies. Fig. 1 shows a MIPS instruction sequence and the corresponding DAG representation which is labeled by the corresponding delay times of each instruction[2].

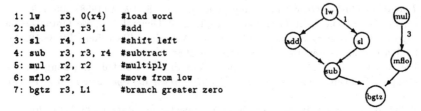

```
1: lw    r3, 0(r4)    #load word
2: add   r3, r3, 1    #add
3: sl    r4, 1        #shift left
4: sub   r3, r3, r4   #subtract
5: mul   r2, r2       #multiply
6: mflo  r2           #move from low
7: bgtz  r3, L1       #branch greater zero
```

Figure 1: Instructions of a basic block and the corresponding DAG

The example shows a load-use delay of one cycle between instruction ① and ③ and three pipeline interlock cycles between the mult-instruction ⑤ and the move_from_lo instruction ⑥ .
The difference of both delays is that a load-use delay must be explicitly guaranteed by insertion of noop-instructions, whenever necessary. However, delays, as for example between ⑤ and ⑥ , are caused by internal pipeline interlocks and have not to be explicitly considered in the instruction sequence.

Most of the list-scheduling algorithms or selection heuristics published in the last years are based on attributed DAGs as described above. However, these algorithms often minimize only the length of an instruction sequence, i.e. the total numbers of instructions (including noop-instructions). Hence, the following schedule must be accepted as an optimal solution, because noop-instructions can be omitted:

$$\text{lw, sl, add, sub, mul, mflo, bgtz} \qquad (1)$$

However, if we look closer to the number of machine cycles that are necessary to execute this schedule, we will find that it is no longer optimal. The pipeline will stall for three cycles between the mul- and mflo-instruction. Therefore, an optimal instruction sequence w.r.t. the number of execution cycles, i.e. without pipeline stalls, is

$$\text{mul, lw, sl, add, mflo, sub, bgtz.} \qquad (2)$$

It becomes obvious at this point that we also have to consider pipeline stalls explicitly if we want to compute schedules with a minimal number of execution cycles. In particular this becomes essential for modern superscalar and superpipelined microprocessor architectures with several deep pipelines, like the MIPS R4000 [Mips91] or the ALPHA processor [DEC92], where for example load-instructions have no explicit delay cycles. Those data-dependencies are detected dynamically by hardware and handled implicitly by pipeline interlocks whenever necessary. Consideration of execution times for multi-cycle instructions by means of node attributes in the DAG may help to identify critical paths with most interlocks. However, especially if several pipelines are used in a superscalar architecture, pipeline interlocks may also be caused by data-independent instructions. For example, data-independent floating-point instructions may interlock a floating-point pipeline due to resource

---

[2]For simplicity, the execution time of a multiply is assumed only with 3 cycles.

conflicts on pipeline stages. Therefore, an adequate scheduling algorithm considering *all* interlocks has to be used in order to generate most efficient schedules.

In the following we denote delay cycles caused by pipeline interlocks as so-called *soft-delay* cycles. In the schedule itself soft-delays are represented by special s_noop instructions which are handled just as noop-instructions by the scheduling algorithm, i.e. they will be replaced by independent instructions whenever possible. They are used to guarantee that the schedule length corresponds to the number of execution cycles of a basic block. In contrast to noop instructions, however, they will be deleted before code generation, so they are for internal use only. For example, schedule (1) is internally represented as

> lw, sl, add, sub, mul, s_noop, s_noop, s_noop, mflo, bgtz

and its length now corresponds to the number of execution cycles. Schedule (2) has not to be modified because no soft-delay cycles occur.

Our scheduling strategy is now to minimize the schedule length *including* s_noop instructions which will result in schedules with a minimal number of execution cycles. After a schedule has been fixed the s_noop instructions are removed from the schedule and additional code will be generated only for noop instructions.

2.2 Refined DAG Structure

In order to provide sufficient information for the scheduling algorithm we have to refine the standard DAG representation as shown in fig. 1. Especially, more detailed attributes concerning pipeline interlocks have to be defined.

Soft-delay cycles are caused either by explicit data dependencies (e.g. by a pair of load-use instructions) or by implicit resource conflicts (e.g. on the floating-point pipeline). The first ones can easily be detected and annotated as additional edge-attributes of the DAG. Hence, an edge becomes attributed by the number of delay-cycles as well as by the number of soft-delay cycles.

Soft-delays caused by resource conflicts may occur even among data-independent instructions. For example, independent floating-point instructions may cause interlocks due to conflicts on the floating-point ALU. Unfortunately, this scheme does not fit into the standard DAG representation because those conflicts are symmetrical and are not determined by data dependencies. For this reasons we define a new edge type, so-called resource-conflict edges (RCF edges), for the DAG. A RCF edge connects two instructions which use the same critical resource of a processor and thereby may cause pipeline interlocks if their execution overlaps. As dependency edges RCF edges are annotated with the number of delay and soft-delay cycles for each direction. In order to minimize the total number of edges in a DAG, RCF edges are only inserted if they indicate at least one additional delay cycle and do not overlap with directed edges. In the next section we will see that these new edges provide sufficient information for the scheduling algorithm to determine schedules with a minimal number of execution cycles and without introducing new, artificial dependencies.

An example for this refined DAG representation is shown in fig. 2. Dashed lines represent RCF edges and tuples denote the number of delays and soft-delays. The floating-point add- and abs-instructions are connected by a RCF edge, because they may cause interlocks due to conflicts in the floating-point pipeline.

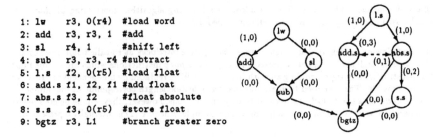

```
1: lw    r3, 0(r4)  #load word
2: add   r3, r3, 1  #add
3: sl    r4, 1      #shift left
4: sub   r3, r3, r4 #subtract
5: l.s   f2, 0(r5)  #load float
6: add.s f1, f2, f1 #add float
7: abs.s f3, f2     #float absolute
8: s.s   f3, 0(r5)  #store float
9: bgtz  r3, L1     #branch greater zero
```

Figure 2: Refined DAG representation

An optimal schedule for this example is given by

l.s, lw, abs.s, sl, add, add.s, s.s, sub, bgtz.

Under consideration of the additional information on soft-delays it can easily be computed by a refined scheduling algorithm. Several strategies based on this scheme are discussed in the next section.

3 The Scheduling Algorithm

Many scheduling algorithms for (super)pipelined microprocessors have been published in the last years; an overview of work in this area is given in [Kri90]. Two different approaches can basically be identified: list scheduling algorithms and selection heuristics similar to the Gibbons/Muchnick algorithm [Gibb86].

Both are based on an attributed DAG representation. Node attributes have to be computed in a first pass and scheduling is then performed under consideration of these attributes. Following this scheme we have to define some new or modified node attributes which also reflect informations about pipeline interlocks. We will then use this additional information in a scheduling algorithm which is a variant of the Gibbons/Muchnick algorithm.

3.1 Node Attributes

The node attributes of a DAG are used to decide locally which instruction should be scheduled next. Therefore, they have to provide information concerning the number of interlocks caused by this and all subsequent instructions. We define the following attributes for a node n of a DAG:

- **lock(n)**
  Is true if an instruction may cause delay or soft-delay cycles to at least one of its successors.

- **no_succs(n)**
  The number of data-dependent successors in the DAG. The more successors of an instruction exist, the higher is its priority to become scheduled because it "blocks" all its data-dependent successors.

- **height(n)**
  Specifies the maximum distance from the node to a leaf of the DAG. It is recursively defined over all pathes of dependency edges in the DAG as follows:

  Let $succ(n) := \{n' \mid (n, n') \text{ is a data-dependency edge of the DAG }\}$
  be the set of all data-dependent successors of n and

$d(n, n') :=$ the maximal number of delays and soft-delays between n and $n' \in succ(n)$ on data-dependency and RCF edges.

The height-value of n is then defined by

$$height(n) := \begin{cases} 0 & \text{if } succ(n) = \emptyset \\ \max_{n' \in succ(n)} (height(n') + d(n, n')) + 1 & \text{otherwise.} \end{cases}$$

Delays on pure RCF edges, i.e. between data-independent instructions, are not considered in the height-attribute because they do not necessarily increase the critical path length. They are handled in the scheduling algorithm separately.

− subnodes(n)
The total number of nodes that are reachable via data-dependency edges from n.

If again $succ(n)$ is the set of all data-dependent successors of n and

$$succ^*(n) := \bigcup_{n' \in succ(n)} succ^*(n')$$

is the closure of this relation, then we define $subnodes(n) := |succ^*(n)|$.

$succ^*(n)$ induces a subgraph with root n of the DAG and subnodes(n) states how many instructions must be scheduled after n.

− subcycles(n)
Similar to subnodes(n) this attribute corresponds to the complexity of the subgraph that is induced by $succ^*(n)$. It is defined by :

$$subcycles(n) := \sum_{n_1, n_2 \in succ^*(n)} d(n_1, n_2)$$

Hence, subcycles(n) is the sum of the maximum number of delay and soft-delay cycles that may occur after instruction n.

3.2 The Basic Algorithm

All these attributes may be used as local criteria in order to decide which instruction should be scheduled next. The basic schedule algorithm using these criteria is as follows:

 i. Start with an empty schedule and all DAG nodes unmarked.

 ii. Determine the candidate-set from the DAG, i.e. all nodes with all predecessors being marked.

 iii. If the candidate-set is empty $\Longrightarrow$ STOP.

 iv. Determine those candidates which could be scheduled now with a minimum number of additional delay or soft-delay cycles and put them into the ready-set.

 v. Use a selection heuristic to find that instruction from the ready-set which should be scheduled next.

 vi. Append to the schedule the necessary number of NOOP- and S_NOOP-instructions that have to be inserted before the selected instruction.

 vii. Append the instruction itself and mark the corresponding DAG node as scheduled.
    Continue at ii.

This basic algorithm offers a great degree of freedom when the next instruction of the schedule is to be determined in step v. Several criteria with different priorities may be used for this selection. By that, this algorithm provides a sound basis for implementation and evaluation of several scheduling heuristics.

3.3 Selection Heuristics

In our implementation we have evaluated four different heuristics based on the node attributes defined above. All variants follow the same idea: Try to find an instruction that causes no interlocks or delays now and that may become a bottleneck later, i.e. that prevents most other instructions from being scheduled. Two of these heuristics use the more simple attributes no_succs and height for this decision, the other two use the more complex attributes subnodes and subcycles. The first ones can be computed with a complexity of $\mathcal{O}(n)$, the latter ones only in $\mathcal{O}(n^2)$. Whether the more complex attributes result in better schedules will be shown in section 4.

The selection heuristic used in step v. of the basic algorithm checks successively for different criteria until one unique instruction remains. If no single instruction could be determined an arbitrary one of the last non-empty selection set is taken. The following heuristics have been implemented and evaluated:

Version 1:   a) Select nodes with lock = true.
                 b) Select nodes with maximum value for no_succs(n).
                 c) Select nodes with maximum height(n).

Version 2:   Same as version 1, but with b) and c) interchanged.

Version 3:   a) Select nodes with lock = true.
                 b) Select nodes with maximum value for subnodes(n).
                 c) Select nodes with maximum value for subcycles(n).
                 d) Select nodes with maximum height(n).

Version 4:   Same as version 3, but with b) and c) interchanged.

3.4 Implementation for the MIPS R4000

The complete local scheduling algorithm has been implemented in a testbed compiler for the MIPS R4000 microprocessor [Mips91]. The R4000 has an integer and a floating-point pipeline and may execute integer multiply and divide operations concurrently with other integer instructions. It has no explicit load-delay cycles, but the pipeline interlocks for two cycles if a read_after_write conflict occurs after a load-instruction. Furthermore, it has a branch-delay of one cycle and a lot of interlock conditions on the floating-point pipeline. Additional hazard-conditions have to be considered in the context of move_from_lo and move_from_hi instructions as well as for some floating-point operations.

All these architecture-specific scheduling constraints are considered during DAG construction and reflected in the DAG structure and its attributes. Thus, the scheduling algorithm itself is completely architecture-independent. Even the existence of an integer and a floating-point pipeline needs not to be handled explicitly, because we get the separation of integer and floating-point instructions for free under consideration of RCF edges. Heuristics, as for example alternating scheduling of integer and floating-point instructions, as proposed in [Warr90] for the IBM RS6000, are not necessary. Step iv. of the algorithm considers pipeline interlocks in the floating-point pipeline, implicitly, and schedules the next floating-point instructions not before those interlocks can be avoided.

In our implementation local instruction scheduling is performed after standard optimizations, such as strength reduction, common subexpression elimination, dead code removal etc., and also after code mapping and register allocation. It is directly followed by an algorithm for filling branch delays from other basic blocks.

3.4.1 Branch Delays

Branch delays do not fit into the normal execution order, because instructions at these positions are executed before the branch is taken. Therefore, they have to be handled explicitly in the scheduling algorithm. Furthermore, in our implementation we have also to consider branch delays which occur inside of basic blocks. Due to an inter-procedural dataflow analysis, which is performed before instruction scheduling, dataflow information is available for call-instructions, thus they do not necessarily terminate basic blocks. This increases the length of basic blocks significantly and leaves more room for optimizations. However, as a consequence we have now to fill branch delays inside as well as at the end of basic blocks.

This is done after the normal instruction scheduling for a basic block has been performed. If unfilled branch-delay slots remain, we first try to fill them with operations from the same basic block, i.e. with those ahead of the branch. If this is not successful, we postpone the problem until scheduling is completed for all basic blocks. Then we try to fill the remaining unfilled branch-delay slots at the end of basic blocks with an operation from its successor(s). By that, we also consider branches back to loop headers and convert them into special branch-likely instructions[3]. We are then allowed to fill the delay slot with the first operation of the branch target, which substantially improves the runtime behavior of small loops. In addition, we fill call-delay slots inside of basic blocks with the first instruction of the called function, if its code is locally available. By this method, we get nearly 70 % of the branch delays filled on average (see section 4).

4 Evaluation

The scheduling algorithm for the MIPS R4000 has been integrated in a testbed compiler tool for superscalar and superpipelined microprocessors. This tool also comprises a highly parameterized machine simulator that allows for a detailed simulation of the R4000 architecture at a low level, i.e. including cache misses, pipeline stalls etc. [Boe90]. The simulator produces a detailed output for each simulation run and was used for the dynamic evaluation of our test programs.

For static evaluation we have also implemented a branch&bound algorithm that computes an optimal schedule for each basic block. By that, we can assess the degree of optimality of the complete scheduling algorithm as well as of the different selection heuristics.

For all evaluations we have used a set of example programs covering different kinds of applications. Bubblesort, hashing, matmult, gauss and queens belong to the class of numerical programs which perform many arithmetic operations within loops and recursions. Beautify, check_style and dhrystone operate on complex data structures and perform also some input/output operations. Cat_hex, list_doc and lpr_format are input/output-intensive programs which format documents and operate only on simple data structures. We have used these programs for static evaluation as well as for dynamic evaluation on the simulator.

4.1 Static evaluation

For static evaluation we compare the schedule lengths of the example programs, i.e. the number of execution cycles including delays and soft-delays which can be determined statically. Figure 3 shows the results obtained from the four versions of the scheduling algorithm (see 3.3) compared with the schedules resulting from the original instruction sequence and the solution found by the branch&bound algorithm.

The measurements show that all heuristics result in nearly optimal schedules and shorten the schedule for more than 12 % on average. The improvements of the matmult program are much better, because its inner loop has been unrolled four times, which results in a very large basic block with high optimization potential. Also, the other numeric programs, especially hashing and gauss gain more from instruction scheduling than the others. Nevertheless, significant improvements are achieved for all examples, so the scheduling algorithm seems to be robust and suitable for any kind of code.

---

[3] This R4000 instruction nullifies the instruction in the branch delay slot, if the branch is not taken.

Program	Original Schedule	branch&bound Cycles	%	Version 1 Cycles	%	Version 2 Cycles	%	Version 3 Cycles	%	Version 4 Cycles	%
beautify	305	283	92.8	284	93.1	283	92.8	283	92.8	283	92.8
bubblesort	59	52	88.1	53	89.9	52	88.1	53	89.9	53	89.9
cat_hex	294	261	88.8	261	88.8	261	88.8	261	88.8	261	88.8
check_style	1630	1444	88.6	1445	88.7	1445	88.7	1445	88.7	1445	88.7
dhrystone	751	669	89.1	672	89.5	671	89.3	671	89.3	671	89.3
hashing	98	85	86.7	85	86.7	85	86.7	85	86.7	85	86.7
gauss	2166	1840	84.9	1863	86.0	1850	85.4	1851	85.5	1852	85.5
list_doc	445	404	90.8	405	91.0	405	91.0	405	91.0	405	91.0
lpr_format	565	504	89.2	506	89.6	505	89.4	505	89.4	505	89.4
matmult	217	170	78.3	170	78.3	170	78.3	170	78.3	170	78.3
queens	329	284	86.3	286	86.9	286	86.9	286	86.9	286	86.9

Figure 3: Static improvements of local instruction scheduling

A more detailed comparison of the four scheduling heuristics shows that they often result in the same instruction sequences. However, fig. 3 suggests that the schedules of version 1 are a little bit poorer than the others. This supposition has been proven by further measurements which can be summarized as follows: For 42 examples we got a total sum of 65.925 cycles for the original schedules. Version 1 decreases this sum to 58.091 cycles (88.1 %), version 2 to 57.907 cycles (87.8 %), version 3 to 57.961 cycles (87.9 %) and version 4 to 57.931 cycles (87.9 %). Thus, the best results are obtained from version 2 which prefers nodes on critical pathes before those with many successors in the DAG. Version 3 and 4 could not improve these results, although they use more complex information about the subgraphs of a node. So, from the pragmatical point of view, version 2 is most suitable because it uses only a simple node attribute that can be computed in $O(n)$ and generates the shortest schedules.

In the following we investigate in more detail the behavior of the scheduling algorithm with selection heuristic 2. From fig. 4 we see that from the static point of view the results are 99.7 % optimal on average. However, due to the exponential complexity of the branch&bound algorithm we have had to limit the number of recursions allowed for each basic block. If after 500.000 recursions no (provable) optimal solution has been found, the schedule generated by the scheduling heuristic has been taken if it was better than the branch&bound solution computed so far. Hence, we got for some basic blocks slightly suboptimal solutions but, nevertheless, more than 90 % of all scheduling cycles of the branch&bound solution could be proven to be optimal[4]. In addition, the comparison has been restricted only to those basic blocks, for which an optimal solution has been found. The 'pure'-column shows that this makes no difference and the heuristic is also 99.7 % optimal on these basic blocks, on average.

Program	Original Schedule	B & B Cycles[4]	Version 2 Cycles	Opt. Degree all	pure[5]	Branch Delays tot	fill	%	Load Delays tot	fill1	%	fill2	%
beautify	305	283	283	100.0	100.0	45	27	60.0	16	13	81.2	10	62.5
bubblesort	59	52	52	100.0	100.0	10	6	60.0	8	6	75.0	4	50.0
cat_hex	294	261	261	100.0	100.0	59	44	74.6	26	26	100.0	25	96.2
check_style	1630	1444	1445	99.9	99.9	254	181	71.3	226	169	74.8	141	62.4
dhrystone	751	669	671	99.7	99.7	85	69	81.2	105	69	65.7	63	60.0
hashing	98	85	85	100.0	100.0	14	11	78.6	10	9	90.0	6	60.0
gauss	2166	1840	1850	99.5	99.4	191	139	72.8	243	194	79.8	112	46.1
list_doc	445	404	405	99.8	99.7	102	71	69.6	28	26	92.9	18	64.3
lpr_format	565	504	505	99.8	99.8	82	61	74.4	64	52	81.2	43	67.2
matmult	217	170	170	100.0	100.0	13	12	92.3	14	14	100.0	14	100.0
queens	329	284	286	99.3	99.3	57	36	63.2	40	30	75.0	26	65.0
total	6859	5996	6013	99.7	99.7	912	657	72.0	780	608	77.9	462	59.2

Figure 4: Improvements for scheduling heuristic version 2

---

[4] From a total of 5996 cycles 5648 cycles could be computed by the branch&bound algorithm (94.2%).
[5] Restricted to basic blocks with an optimal branch&bound solution.

Additionally, fig. 4 gives statistics of the number of branch- and load-delay slots that could be filled by the scheduling algorithm. These values are at the upper bound of the range which could be expected for an architecture with two load-delay cycles (see [Henn90]). They are even better than the results from the new MIPS GCC2.00 [Mei92], that only succeeds in filling about 57 % of *one* load delay and 64 % of the branch delays.

From a theoretical point of view we can summarize that for the local optimization problem the scheduling algorithm presented here generates almost always an optimal solution and leaves only little room for further improvements. However, we have still to investigate the performance of the generated code in order to check whether these local optimizations also result in a significant global speed-up at runtime.

4.2 Dynamic Evaluation

The dynamic evaluation of the example programs has been performed on a simulator of the MIPS R4000 processor. The simulator allows for a detailed observation of all internal events, such as pipeline-slips and -stalls or cache-misses. The utilization of each pipeline stage can be visualized interactively and detailed statistics allow for an exact analysis of the runtime behavior.

Due to the complex simulation we have run all example programs with only small input data. For example, bubble_sort is performed only for 65 elements, the queens problem is solved for an 5x5 area and dhrystone iterates its inner loop only 200 times.

For each example program we have evaluated the total number of machine cycles used for its execution. In fig. 5 we compare the values obtained from the original instruction sequence and from the schedules generated by the four variants of the scheduling algorithm.

Program	Original	Version 1		Version 2		Version 3		Version 4	
	Cycles	Cycles	%	Cycles	%	Cycles	%	Cycles	%
beautify	49633	46327	93.3	46332	93.3	46327	93.3	46333	93.4
bubble_sort	43255	41177	95.2	39182	90.6	41177	95.2	41177	95.2
cat_hex	48785	45407	93.1	45407	93.1	45407	93.1	45407	93.1
check_style	94103	79524	84.5	79550	84.5	79555	84.5	79555	84.5
dhrystone	106299	95703	90.0	95350	89.7	95139	89.5	95132	89.5
gauss	46930	40946	87.2	40181	85.6	40181	85.6	40181	85.6
hashing	48769	40849	83.8	40849	83.8	40849	83.8	40849	83.8
list_doc	21899	18711	85.4	18719	85.5	18720	85.5	18719	85.5
lpr_format	124503	118020	94.8	118020	94.8	118020	94.8	118020	94.8
matmult	55896	39438	70.6	38311	68.5	38713	69.3	38236	68.4
queens	50857	47073	92.6	47081	92.6	47081	92.6	47077	92.6
total	690929	613175	88.7	608982	88.1	611169	88.5	610686	88.4

Figure 5: Simulation results for the example programs

The results confirm the static evaluation. Overall, the runtime improvements are more than 11 % on average and, hence, the same magnitude as evaluated statically. This indicates that the optimizations are, on average, fairly distributed over all basic blocks. Again, there are only slight differences among the four versions; only the performance of the code generated by version 1 is perceptibly worse.

Also the observation that numerical programs gain more from instruction scheduling than general-purpose code is confined by these simulation results.

A static evaluation has also been performed for the SPEC benchmarks, however, dynamical results could not be achieved due to their complexity and some restrictions of the simulator w.r.t. system calls. However, the static improvements are all in the same range as of our examples (88.5% - 89.1%), so that similar dynamic results can also be expected.

If our scheduling algorithm generates code which runs 11 % faster than the original one, the next question is how much of this speed-up is caused by explicit consideration of pipeline interlocks? We have investigated this question by implementing variants of the scheduling algorithm which consider none or only a few of the interlocks that may occur. This has been realized by different edge attributes of the DAG:

Variant a ignores all soft-delays, i.e. the soft-delay attributes of all edges in the DAG are valued by zero; only delays and hazard conditions are considered.

Variant b ignores all soft-delays except load-delays, however, only *one* load-delay is assumed.

Variant c same as variant b, but with two load-delay cycles.

The schedules have been computed using version 2 of the scheduling algorithm. The simulation results are summarized in fig. 6.

Program	Original Cycles	Version 2 Cycles	%	Variant a Cycles	%	Variant b Cycles	%	Variant c Cycles	%
beautify	49633	46332	93.3	47263	95.2	46385	93.5	4601	93.5
bubble_sort	43255	39182	90.6	42917	99.2	41393	95.7	40007	92.5
cat_hex	48785	45407	93.1	45402	93.1	45402	93.1	45407	93.1
check_style	94103	79550	84.5	79563	84.5	79613	84.6	79781	84.8
dhrystone	106299	95350	89.7	97812	92.0	95991	90.3	95946	90.3
gauss	46930	40181	85.6	44278	94.3	43211	92.1	42430	90.4
hashing	48769	40849	83.3	41733	85.6	41425	84.9	41437	85.0
list_doc	21899	18719	85.5	18719	85.5	18723	85.5	18721	85.5
lpr_format	124503	118020	94.8	118036	94.8	118022	94.8	118018	94.8
matmult	55896	38311	68.5	54530	97.6	50566	90.5	50566	90.5
queens	50857	47081	92.6	49493	97.3	49037	96.4	49098	96.5
total	690929	613175	88.7	639746	92.5	629768	91.1	627812	90.8

Figure 6: Simulation results with different interlocks considered

These results reveal an interesting fact: Most of the improvements are obtained from the scheduling algorithm itself. Even if interlocks and execution times of instructions are totally ignored, the heuristic generates code that is nearly 8 % faster than the original one. Consideration of load-delays improves the performance by only 1 % and surprisingly it seems not to be significant whether one or two load-delays are used. Only the consideration of *all* interlocks results in a performance gain of again 2 %, on average.

These results can be explained as follows: The optimization strategy of the scheduling algorithm, to prefer operations on critical pathes in combination with an efficient filling of branch-delays and the usage of branch_likely instructions, results in the most significant improvements. However, some of the examples (bubble_sort, matmult, gauss) are more sensitive to the consideration of load delays than the others. This is caused by their internal structure. In their (small) inner loops these programs operate on global variables which have to be accessed by load/store operations. Thus, they gain more from the consideration of load delays than the others. Consideration of *all* pipeline interlocks improves mainly the performance of computation-intensive programs like matmult, queens, gauss and hashing (2-5%). This effect can be traced back to the significantly smaller number of pipeline interlocks due to arithmetic operations. It shows that explicit consideration of all interlocks may results in a significant speed-up, especially for programs with many multi-cycle operations.

5 Conclusion

We have presented a refined local instruction scheduling algorithm which considers pipeline interlocks explicitly, even between data-independent instructions. The formal optimization problem is refined to the minimization of the total number of execution cycles of an instruction sequence, including soft-delay cycles caused by interlocks. All information about soft-delays are represented in an enhanced DAG structure, thus the scheduling algorithm itself is totally architecture independent and may be used for various architectures.

The algorithm has been implemented for the MIPS R4000 microprocessor. Static evaluation of several scheduling heuristics shows that for nearly all basic blocks optimal schedules could be found. Even a heuristic based on simple DAG-node attributes generates schedules which are 99.9 % optimal on average. The dynamic evaluation confirms these results; a performance gain of more than 11 % can be achieved.

References

[Abra88] Abraham, S; Padmanabhan, K.; *Instruction Reorganization for a Variable-Length Pipelined Microprocessor*; IEEE Intl. Conf. on Comp. Design, 1988, pp. 96-101

[Aho88] Aho, A.V.; Sethi, R.; Ullmann, J.D. *Compilers: Principles, Techniques, Tools*; Addison Wesley, 1988

[Ary85] Arya S. ; *An Optimal Instruction-Scheduling Model for a Class of Vector Processors*; IEEE Trans. on Comp., Vol. 34, No. 11, 1985, pp. 981-995

[Bern88] Bernstein, D.; *An Improved Approximation Algorithm for Scheduling Pipelined Machines*; Proc. of the Intern. Conf. on Parallel Processors; St. Charles, Aug. 1988

[Bern89a] Bernstein, D.; Gertner, I.; *Scheduling Expressions on a Pipelined Processor with a Maximal Delay of One Cycle*; ACM Trans. on Prog. Lan. and Sys.; Vol 11, No. 1, 1989, pp. 57-66

[Bern89b] Bernstein, D.; Rodeh, M.; Gertner, I.; *Approximation Algorithms for Scheduling Arithmetic Expressions on Pipelined Machines*; Journal of Algorithms, Vol. 10, 1989, pp. 120-139

[Bern89c] Bernstein, D.; Rodeh, M.; Gertner, I.; *On the Complexity of Scheduling Problems for Parallel/Pipelined Machines*; IEEE Trans. on Comp., Vol. 38, No. 9, 1989, pp. 1308-1313

[Boe90] Böckle, G., Trosch, S.; *A Simulator for VLIW Architectures*; Technische Universität München, TUM-I9031, SFB-Bericht 342/16/90 A, 1990

[Coff72] Coffman, E.G. Jr.; Graham, R.L.; *Optimal Scheduling for Two-Processor Systems*; Acta Informatica 1, 1972, pp. 200-213

[Dav86] Davidson, J.W. *A Retargetable Instruction Reorganizer* SIGPLAN Notices, Vol. 21, No.7, 1986, pp. 234-241

[DEC92] Digital Equipment Corporation; *ALPHA Product Information*; 1992

[Fish81] Fisher, J.A.; *Trace Scheduling: A Technique for Global Microcode Compaction*; IEEE Trans. on Comp., July 1981, pp. 478-490

[Gibb86] Gibbons, P.B.; Muchnick, S.S.; *Efficient Instruction Scheduling for a Pipelined Architecture*; Proc. SIGPLAN 86, SIGPLAN Notices, Vol. 21, No. 7, pp. 11-16

[Good88] Goodman, J.R.; Hsu, W.C.; *Code Scheduling and Register Allocation in Large Basic Blocks*; Proc. of the IEEE-ACM Supercomp. Conf., Orlando 1988, pp. 442-452

[Henn83] Hennessy, J.L; Gross, T.; *Postpass Code Optimization of Pipeline Constraints*; ACM Trans. on Prog. Lang. and Sys., Vol. 5, No. 3, 1983

[Henn90] Hennessy, J.L; Patterson, D.A.; *Computer Architecture A Quantitative Approach*; Morgan Kaufmann Publishers, 1990

[Hsu87] Hsu, W.C.; *Register Allocation and Code Scheduling for Load/Store Architectures*; Univ. of Wisconsin-Madison, Tech. Report No. 722, Oct. 1987

[Kri90] Krishnamurthy, S.M.; *A Brief Survey of Papers on Scheduling for Pipelined Processors*; SIGPLAN Notices, Vol. 25, No. 7, 1990, pp. 97-106

[Lam90]   Lam, M.S.; *Instruction Scheduling for Superscalar Architectures*; Ann. Rev. Comp. Sci., Vol. 4, 1990, pp. 173-201

[Mei92]   Meissner, M.; *Effectiveness of Filling Multiple Load-Delay Slots*; Usenet Discussion, comp.arch, 14.2.1992

[Mips91]   *MIPS R4000 Microprocessor User's Manual*; MIPS Computer Systems, 1991

[Nic85]   Nicolau, A.; *Percolation Scheduling: A Parallel Compilation Technique* ; Technical Report No. TR 85-678, Cornell University, Ithaca, N.Y., 1985

[Pad86]   Padua, D.A.; Wolfe, M.J.; *Advanced Compiler Optimizations for Supercomputers*; Comm. of the ACM, Vol. 29, No. 12, 1986, pp. 1184-1201

[Proe91]   Proebsting, R.A.; Fischer, C.N.; *Linear-time, Optimal Code Scheduling for Delayed-Load Architectures*; ACM SIGPLAN 91, Toronto, Canada, 1991, pp. 256-267

[Shie89]   Shieh, J.J.; Papachristou, C.A.; *On Reordering Instruction Streams for Pipelined Computers*; Proc. of the MICRO-22 Conf., Dublin, 1989

[Tie89]   Tiemann, M.D.; *The GNU Instruction Scheduler*; CS343 course report, Stanford University, 1989

[Warr90]   Warren, H.S. Jr.; *Instruction Scheduling for the IBM RISC System/6000 Processor*; IBM J. RES. DEVELP. Vol 34, No. 1, 1990, pp. 85-92

Microscopic and Macroscopic Dynamics

Wm. G. Hoover, C. G. Hoover, A. J. De Groot, and T. G. Pierce

Department of Applied Science, University of California at Davis/Livermore,

and Lawrence Livermore National Laboratory, Livermore, California

Post Office Box 808, L-794, 94551-808, United States of America.

MANUSCRIPT COMPLETED 8 JUNE 1993

Abstract:

Atomistic Molecular Dynamics and Lagrangian Continuum Mechanics can be very similarly adapted to massively-parallel computers. *Millions* of degrees of freedom can be treated. The two complementary approaches, microscopic and macroscopic, are being applied to increasingly realistic flows of fluids and solids. The two approaches can also be combined in a *hybrid* simulation scheme. Hybrids combine the fundamental constitutive advantage of atoms with the size advantage of the continuum picture.

1. Introduction

The computer revolution is rapidly progressing from millions of degrees of freedom to billions, and from gigaflops to teraflops. The impact of this ever-faster ever-cheaper computational power on physics and materials science is both exciting and unpredictable. Certainly we will have access to more realism and understanding, and to more detail in simulation. The consequences strain the imagination.

These gains are being achieved through *parallelism* in computation, the subject of this Conference. Parallel computers do best with problems which can be partitioned into weakly-interacting parts. Nodal descriptions of these parts are then assigned to individual processors. With more programming effort, the assignment of parts to processors can be made dynamically, redistributing coordinates, velocities, and energies as the nodes move. Again, with more effort, "Load Balancing" can be achieved by transferring work from busy processors to their less-busy neighbors. Even in the simplest case it is necessary to communicate at least some positions and velocities between neighboring processors, so as to calculate the accelerations. The time involved in such "Message-Passing" needs to be small compared to the simulation time steps. At the moment, the hardware limits imposed on this parallel simulation approach are changing much more rapidly than the software can follow. As a result, it is a frustrating task to remain at the state of the art. It is much simpler to use the best readily-available commercial equipment.

With the help of Tony De Groot, who is in the process of building yet another massively-parallel machine, this one with 256 transputers, and my wife, Carol Hoover, who has been working on the 512-node CM5 Connection Machine at Minnesota for a year, I am in the fortunate position of seeing the best in both the home-built and commercial worlds of computer hardware. Tim Pierce, a student in our Department, who is also a fulltime programmer at the National Energy Research Supercomputer Center, has provided enthusiastic help and insight in implementing and visualizing new approaches to physical problems. My talk represents the recent efforts of all these colleagues, and so it is typical, though on a small scale, of the trend away from individual efforts and toward cooperating research groups.

The headlong advances in hardware are a cliché. But caution is desirable because *more* is not necessarily *better*. Atomistic force models proliferate and undergo *ad hoc* adjustment. Continuum "Failure Models" for simulations of elastic-plastic flow and fracture are a small industry. It is difficult, in both these typical cases, to have confidence in the predictive ability of the models. They inspire confidence only when used as interpolation devices. Extrapolation to new problems is risky.

Computers need to be used wisely. Cost-effective projects are likely to be neither so grandiose nor so predictable in their outcomes as are the so-called "Grand Challenges" — the genome, weather, and proton-mass problems. Lorenz' "Butterfly-Effect" weather model, Feigenbaum's logistic map studies, and Mandelbrot's complex-plane version of that map, have all had impacts completely out of proportion to the small-scale calculations leading to their discoveries. As computing machines evolve, their enhanced capacity and speed can be used for a more comprehensive treatment of flow and failure properties in which strengths are exploited and weaknesses avoided.

2. Equations of Motion

Dynamics means motion. Newton's Second Law of motion can be applied equally well to individual atomistic masses or to the lumped continuum mass densities associated with individual nodes. In either case, the simplest way to generate approximate solutions of the equations of motion is to iterate Stoermer's "leapfrog" recipe through a series of timesteps separated by intervals of length dt:

$$\{ [q_{t+dt} - 2q_t + q_{t-dt}] = a_t(dt)^2 \} .$$

Here past, present, and future are the three times $\{t-dt, t, t+dt\}$. Future coordinate sets $\{q_{t+dt}\}$ can be calculated from the present and past ones, $\{q_{t-dt}\}$ and $\{q_t\}$, by using present accelerations $\{a_t\}$. It is straightforward to generalize Stoermer's algorithm to include the velocity-dependent driving and constraint forces required in nonequilibrium simulations.

Stoermer's algorithm has several nice features. It is patently time-reversible. Yoshida showed that there is a hidden and significant Hamiltonian basis underlying this simple reversible algorithm. The finite-difference solutions of Stoermer's equations, using forces from a Hamiltonian H, trace out a sequence of phase points $\{q,p\}$. These same phase points lie on the exact continuous trajectory generated by a slightly-different perturbed Hamiltonian, H + ΔH, where ΔH is linear in the timestep dt. This Hamiltonian basis for Stoermer's algorithm accounts for its excellent stability properties.

In addition, for *either* atomistic or continuum simulations, the Stoermer leapfrog algorithm minimizes storage requirements. In continuum mechanics the largest possible timestep is typically used, so as to minimize spurious numerical diffusion. In atomistic mechanics a smaller, more conservative, choice is typical. If more thorough, or more speculative, investigations require it, even higher accuracy can be obtained from fourth-order integrators.

In the continuum case the degrees of freedom at locations $\{r\}$ have associated with them all the variables considered by molecular dynamics: density (or mass), velocity, and energy. But in addition the pressure tensor and heat flux vector must be known in order to evaluate the time evolution of a continuum system.

3. Work, Heat, and Boundary Conditions

In the atomistic case the flows of momentum and energy are local mechanical variables. By measuring these, relative to the local stream velocity, the pressure tensor and heat flux vector can be identified. Thus, the *dynamical* aspect of the First Law of Thermo*dynamics*, usually written $dE \equiv dQ - dW$, can be made more-explicit:

$$dE/dt = dQ(\{\delta p\})/dt - dW(\{\delta q\})/dt .$$

As indicated here, the two types of power associated with (i) extracting heat Q and (ii) doing work W involve momentum and coordinate changes, respectively. About ten years ago the *thermal* part of *thermo*dynamic energy flows was introduced into the differential equations of nonequilibrium molecular dynamics in a novel way. This *thermostatted* molecular dynamics incorporated frictional constraint forces,

$$\{F_{CONSTRAINT} = - \zeta p\} ;$$

$$\zeta_{GAUSS} \equiv -d\Phi/dt/(2K) \text{ or } \zeta_{NOSÉ-HOOVER} \equiv \int[(K/K_o) - 1]dt/\tau^2 .$$

$\Phi(\{q\})$ and $K(\{p\})$ are the potential and kinetic energies. The friction coefficient(s) $\{\zeta\}$ obey one of the two feedback equations ("differential control", based on Gauss' Principle of Least Constraint, or Nosé-Hoover "integral control") and thereby *control* the temperature(s) of selected degrees of freedom. Similar feedback ideas could be used to stabilize the zero-point energies associated with individual molecular degrees of freedom, so as better to describe quantum systems.

The external heat sources or sinks represented by either of these reversible friction coefficients $\{\zeta\}$ undergo entropy changes, $dS_{EXTERNAL}/dt = d(Q/T)/dt$, where T is the temperature associated with a particular source or sink, and the sum of these changes can be proved to satisfy the Second Law of Thermodynamics. Through either the Gauss or the Nosé-Hoover feedback equations of motion, the time-averaged values of the friction coefficients $\{<\zeta>\}$ can also be directly related to the spectrum of Lyapunov exponents $\{\lambda\}$. These relationships are:

$$<dS_{EXTERNAL}/dt> \equiv <\Sigma\zeta> \equiv <-\Sigma\lambda> \geq 0,$$

where the equals sign corresponds to the case where the net heat transfer vanishes. Though the individual friction coefficients fluctuate, and can be either positive or negative, the time-reversible microscopic equations of motion containing them have stable long-time solutions only in the case that the time-averaged friction coefficient sum is non-negative and the Lyapunov-exponent sum is negative. *This inequality is the mechanical form of the Second Law of Thermodynamics.* In geometrical terms the inequality states that, over time, phase-space volumes must shrink. Long-term growth, in a stationary state, would mean illegal instability.

The signatures of nonequilibrium states, either stationary or time-periodic, are the multifractal strange attractors which they generate in phase space. **Figure 1** shows such objects for five small few-body systems.

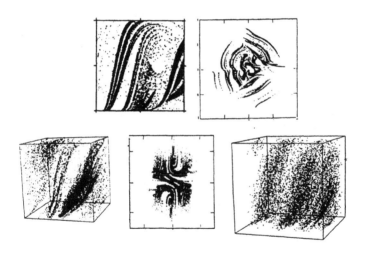

Figure 1. Two-and Three-Dimensional Poincaré sections of multifractal strange attractors with $<\Sigma\zeta> \equiv <-\Sigma\lambda> \geq 0$. These time-reversible distributions were all generated with time-reversible nonequilibrium equations of motion. For detailed references, see "Nonequilibrium Molecular Dynamics: the First 25 Years", Physica A **194**, 450 (1993).

It is still an unsolved problem how to describe the topological "lumpiness" of these objects. For larger many-body systems a geometric description of phase-space attractors is thoroughly hopeless. Instead, a simpler time-averaged description of the local rates of dissipation can be expressed in terms of the Lyapunov spectrum. The spectrum of Lyapunov exponents quantifies the *direction*-dependent stability of the underlying phase space flow. Each exponent describes the time-averaged rate of growth, or decay, of one of the principal axes of a comoving and *corotating* infinitestimal phase-space hyperellipsoid.

Because dissipation *always* corresponds to overall decay, the sum of the Lyapunov exponents is necessarily negative. Thus a comoving phase-space volume *must* shrink, and eventually vanish, as time goes on. On the other hand, the steady-state or time-periodic strange attractor, to which the motion is restricted once transients have decayed, *must* be stationary. The apparent paradox of "stationary shrinkage" can be resolved by noting that the zero-volume attractor has a *reduced dimension* [the "information dimension"]. Kaplan and Yorke suggested estimating this attractor dimension by finding the number of Lyapunov exponents in the spectrum required for their sum to vanish [corresponding to a topological object which neither grows nor shrinks]. Information dimensions have been estimated for nonequilibrium systems of up to a few hundred particles.

Today, just as in the early days of simulation following the Second World War, a 100-hour computer calculation represents a reasonable upper limit on one's attention span. In such a calculation today we can calculate only a few hundred Lyapunov exponents. A complete spectrum of N exponents requires following N additional trajectories, each described by N ordinary differential equations of motion. The work involved typically varies (at least) as the cube of the number of phase-space coordinates N. My work with Harald Posch on systems with up to a few hundred degrees of freedom established that *losses* in dimension (embedding dimension less information dimension) can be substantial. The problem of characterizing this loss is one which will become much simpler with the next generation of parallel computers.

In the continuum case the proper treatment of material boundaries is less natural than in the atomistic case. Surface energy, essential to understanding failure, is most often ignored in numerical continuum treatments. The usual finite-element or finite-difference treatments rely on spatial grids, either "Eulerian" grids, fixed in space, or comoving "Lagrangian" grids, fixed in the material and following the flow.

To simplify intercomparisons between microscopic and macroscopic simulations, and to facilitate hybrid simulations, we have chosen here to concentrate on a "smoothed" or "smeared-out" free-Lagrange form of continuum mechanics called "Smoothed-Particle Hydrodynamics". This approach, invented by Lucy and Monaghan about 20 years ago, is nearly isomorphic to molecular dynamics, and so provides a natural extension of that microscopic approach. The equations of motion in smoothed-particle hydrodynamics incorporate accelerations depending upon the particle stress tensors $\{\sigma\}$ and on the gradients of normalized weighting functions $\{w(r_{ij})\}$, which represent the mass distribution in the vicinity of each particle. We will describe this approach in more detail in Section 5.

4. Molecular Dynamics

In atomistic simulations, the goal of *realism*, quantitative agreement with experiment, remains elusive. After all, there is no practical approach to a nonequilibrium quantum many-body problem. But the still-worthy goal of understanding the mechanisms underlying classical nonequilibrium processes is now firmly within our grasp. Simulations of flows in channels with walls, of inelastic collisions between large bodies, of plastic flow with rapid deformation, and of shock deformation are becoming commonplace.

With CRAY1-speed work stations, simulations involving 10,000 atoms are routinely feasible. In the 40-hour length of what most people consider a "long calculation" such a system can be followed through several sound traversal times. By linking together 1000 fast processors there is no difficulty in treating several million atoms, for a few specimen simulations. The Los Alamos CM5 "Connection Machine" has recently been used to provide timing tests for systems of as many as 10^8 individual atoms.

Figures 2 and 3 illustrate the simulated plastic deformation of solid silicon. The workpiece was originally a perfect cube, containing 373,248 silicon atoms. It was deformed by pressing a tetrahedral indentor into the workpiece. Though the microscopic details of the deformation are complicated, the energy relationships for the deforming silicon turn out to be relatively simple, justifying both the microscopic mechanistic approach and the macroscopic thermodynamic description of the results.

Figure 2. Final configuration of 373,248 silicon atoms after indentation. The temperature, maintained by a single Nosé-Hoover thermostat, is 15% of melting. The indentation velocity is about 1/3 the sound velocity.

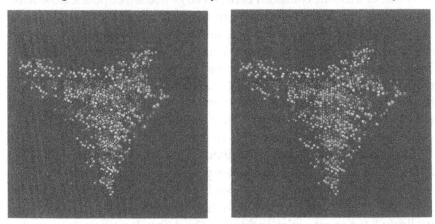

Figure 3. The *initial* positions of those atoms which interact with the indentor in Figure 2 are shown as a stereo pair. The images have been reversed, so that they need to be viewed with *crossed* eyes.

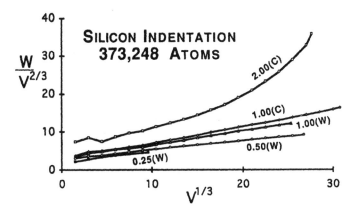

Figure 4. Variation of the work of indentation W with the tetrahedral indentation volume V for crystals of 373,248 silicon atoms. The energy, length, and mass units are 50 kilocalories/mole, 0.21 nanometers, and the mass of a silicon atom, respectively. The intercept is proportional to surface energy, while the slope is proportional to the plastic yield strength. C = Cold and W = Warm correspond to temperatures of about 15% and 45% of the melting temperature. The smooth-indentor speeds, with unity corresponding to 2.7 kilometers/second, are given.

In **Figure 4** the macroscopic work of deformation W is displayed as a function of indentation volume V, so as to separate the bulk and surface contributions to the energy. For a tetrahedral indentor of height h, the volume of indentation V is $(3^{1/2}/8)h^3$. We have separated the surface contributions ($\propto h^2$) from the bulk contributions ($\propto h^3$) by plotting $W/V^{2/3}$ as a function of $V^{1/3}$. The intercept then provides a surface energy estimate while the slope provides the yield strength. Our work on a variety of such systems shows that slowing the simulated indentation rate, to about one-tenth the sound speed, and increasing the workpiece size, to 10,000 atoms, provides very reasonable estimates of the quasistatic large-crystal yield strength, without much further sensitivity to speed or size.

Reproducing the rate- and temperature-dependence of the shapes of indentation pits is a challenging goal for continuum mechanics. To make headway on this problem with conventional continuum mechanics requires that a failure criterion be specified. The criterion allows computational nodes to divide, introducing new free surfaces within the material.

With the use of work stations it is possible to analyze such nonequilibrium atomistic flows for information required for complementary continuum simulations. Where do the new surfaces come from in indentation? This question can be answered by coloring particles in the indented crystal according to their depth, but at positions corresponding to the *undeformed* crystal. **Figure 3** shows those atoms destined to become surface atoms during the course of the indentation process. Detailed knowledge of this kind is vital to constructing faithful continuum models for failure.

5. Smoothed Particle Hydrodynamics

Smoothed particle hydrodynamics converts the *partial* differential equations of continuum mechanics into *ordinary* differential equations for particles. The resulting particle motion equations have nearly the same form as the molecular equations. The "particles" or nodes, each with mass m, can be imagined to be distributed ("smoothed") over space, with a weighting function w. The smoothed-particle equation of motion for the ith particle is a sum of pair interactions with nearby particles {j}:

$$\{ (r_{t+dt} - 2r_t + r_{t-dt})_i = m(dt)^2 \Sigma \nabla_i w_{ij} \cdot [(\sigma/\rho^2)_i + (\sigma/\rho^2)_j] \} ,$$

where σ and ρ are local values of the stress tensor and mass density, and where the pairwise-additive weighting function $w(r_{ij})$ is normalized and short-ranged. A simple choice for w, a caricature of a Gaussian weighting function, but with two vanishing derivatives at a maximum cutoff radius (here 1, for simplicity) is Lucy's:

$$w(r) \propto (1 + 3r)(1 - r)^3, \text{ for } r < 1 .$$

In validating the smoothed-particle approach it is natural to begin by checking that the linear hydrodynamic laws are satisfied. We have first to establish that shear flow and heat flow are correctly treated by the model. We did so by carrying out simple simulations of the types shown in **Figure 5**. The top and bottom boundaries are defined by constrained rows of smoothed particles, with fixed temperature and velocity. If the density of these particles is sufficiently high, the resulting barriers resemble Ashurst's

"fluid wall" boundaries. The boundaries act as sources and sinks of momentum and energy, while preventing an outflux of mass. To prevent the occasional escape of bulk particles through the boundary, a Maxwell Demon reflects the normal velocity of any particle reaching the boundary. We built our confidence in the smoothed-particle method by verifying that the viscous shear stress and linear heat flux expected between walls of different temperatures and velocities were correctly reproduced, with statistical uncertainties of no more than a few percent.

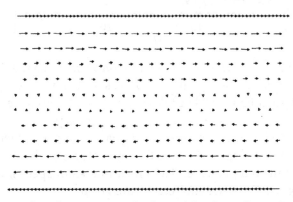

Figure 5. Snapshot from a smoothed-particle shear flow simulation. Reservoirs, with temperature and average velocity fixed, are modelled by the constant-velocity constant-temperature smoothed particles.

Most applications of smoothed-particle hydrodynamics have been astrophysical. These are hard to validate because no independent trustworthy solutions are available. Because we wish to simulate relatively simple laboratory flows of fluids and solids we have chosen to investigate a simpler fluid flow problem, the Rayleigh-Bénard instability. This problem is two-dimensional, which simplifies visualization, and has previously been studied both with molecular dynamics and with conventional continuum methods. The three-equation caricature of this problem generates Lorenz' familiar "butterfly" attractor. Note that the smoothed-particle equations of motion reduce exactly to those of molecular dynamics [with *pair potential* w(r)] in the special case that the stress tensor is replaced by a hydrostatic stress corresponding to a two-dimensional isentropic ideal gas with $\sigma \propto -\rho^2$.

The *nonlinear* Rayleigh-Bénard problem combines all three kinds of hydrodynamic flows: mass, momentum, and energy. In Rayleigh-Bénard flow a compressible fluid, in a gravitational field, is simultaneously heated from below and cooled from above. Two of the many earlier approaches to this problem, one atomistic and the other continuum, are shown in **Figures 6 and 7**. Snapshots from Rapaport's atomistic Rayleigh-Bénard simulation are shown in **Figure 6**. The system, hot on the bottom and cold on the top, transports heat with convective rolls. Rapaport's side walls are insulating. **Figure 7** is a typical snapshot from Goldhirsch, Pelz, and Orszag's continuum simulation of Rayleigh-Bénard flow, based on a different boundary condition, with the temperature of the side walls varying linearly from the top to the bottom temperature.

In preparation for hybrid simulations combining the atomistic and continuum approaches, we have simulated this unstable Rayleigh-Bénard flow too, using a variety of boundary conditions. The constitutive model illustrated here is an ideal gas (with constant heat conductivity and shear viscosity). See **Figures 8 and 9** for some or our sample results, not far from the 776-particle threshhold for convective transport. Our comparisons so far suggest that our particle description of the flow is inherently more chaotic than are the more-traditional Eulerian approaches.

In our first efforts to replicate Rayleigh-Bénard flow we again used Lucy's weight function, and noticed an unphysical tendency for the smoothed particles to clump together. The model's bland acceptance of high-density collapse occurs because the gradient of the weighting function, which contributes to the repulsive force between the particles, *vanishes* (linearly) as r approaches zero. This tendency toward collapse can be eliminated by using an even simpler form for the weighting function (with a repulsive cusp at the origin): $w(r) \propto (1 - r)^3$. Unfortunately, weighting functions such as this, with cusps at the origin, provide a less-accurate interpolation than do the flat-topped functions. The *range* of the weighting function is important too. In two dimensions our results for simulations using several hundred smoothed particles suggest that an interaction range covering about a dozen particles is optimum.

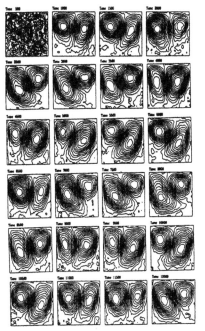

Figure 6. Rapaport's simulation of Rayleigh-Bénard flow. The time exposures [left] show vertical oscillations of the two vortices. The underlying fluid consists of 57,600 hard disks at about half the freezing density.

Figure 7. Goldhirsch, Pelz, and Orszag's simulation of Rayleigh-Bénard flow. Boundary collocation, with 32^2 points, was used. This Figure [right] shows a four roll convective structure which recurs periodically between two mirror-image structures, each of which is dominated by a single diagonal roll. Here the fluid is incompressible.

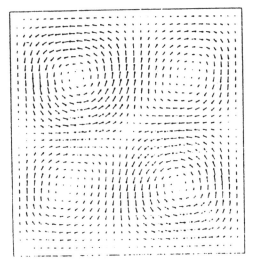

Figure 8. Smoothed-particle Hydrodynamic simulation of Rayleigh-Bénard flow for an ideal gas at unit mean density. The dimensionless analog of the Rayleigh number, $gh^3/(\nu\kappa)$, where ν and κ are the kinematic viscosity and thermal diffusivity, is 25×10^6. 200 of the 776 smoothed particles are fixed, to define the four boundaries. The smoothed velocities $\{<v>\}$ of the individual particles are shown as arrows.

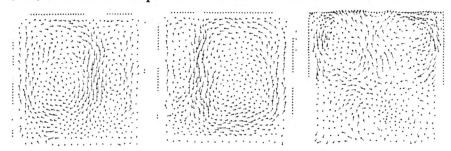

Figure 9. Smoothed-particle Hydrodynamic simulations of Rayleigh-Bénard flow. See Figure 8. Here $gh^3/(\nu\kappa)$ is near the apparent convection threshhold, 6×10^6. The snapshots are for three different simulations, with weighting function ranges of 2.0(left), 2.5(center), and 3.0(right).

6. Surfaces, Failure, and Hybrid Models

Failure, whether of a liquid or a solid, involves the energy cost of bond breaking. New surfaces form through microscopic and chaotic irreversible processes. Despite the chaos, a detailed atomistic description of such a failure process is a straightforward application of Newton's motion equations. No special boundary conditions or constitutive assumptions are required. **Figure 10** shows the breakup of a hot liquid drop.

Throughout any such failure process the forces on each atom follow from the same continuous force law. In the solid-phase deformation shown in **Figures 2 and 3**, our 373,248-atom crystal of indented silicon did not crack, even though solid silicon is normally a brittle material. The ductile behavior results because the strain energy, proportional to the solid's *volume*, does not exceed the *surface* energy necessary to nucleate a crack. Crack energy varies as *area*, so that large enough specimens *do* crack. The ductile small-scale behavior makes it possible to *machine* normally-brittle materials provided that sufficiently small tools (typically microscale single-point diamonds) are used.

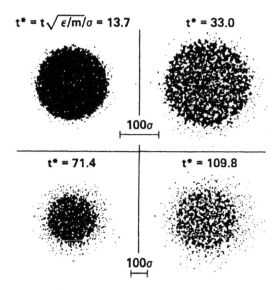

Figure 10. Fragmentation of a (two-dimensional) liquid drop of 14,491 liquid atoms, as described by Lennard-Jones' potential. From Blink's 1984 Ph. D. thesis work at the University of California at Davis/Livermore.

With a failure strain of order 1%, the elastic energy stored in a solid workpiece volume V is approximately 0.0001BV, where B is the bulk modulus. The modulus itself is an energy density, of order ε/σ^3, where ε and σ describe the strength and range of a nearest-neighbor interaction. When $0.0001V\varepsilon/\sigma^3$ exceeds the surface energy, $(\varepsilon/\sigma^2)V^{2/3}$, brittle fracture occurs. For fracture (V/σ^3) must be of order 10^{12}, a bit bigger than the biggest feasible simulations. Thus a quantitative study of the limits of ductile machining, including fracture, requires a supporting substrate for the atomistic indented region in which to store the failure energy. The continuum substrate needs to join smoothly to the atomistic region, and to transmit phonons and heat, without excessive scattering at the boundary.

, From the continuum perspective, failure is complicated by phase discontinuities and by surface tension. There is no problem in treating those parts of a solid remote from the indentor. For most of the workpiece material Hooke's Law should do. But whenever fracture occurs, an atomistic separation occurs, with a part of the stored energy of the solid localized on a fresh surface, and with the recoil of the fracture surfaces depending sensitively on unstable multiple-valued regions of the phase diagram. It is therefore logical to combine the accurate atomistic description of failure, in the region of the indentor, with the more efficient continuum model for the remote substrate. Such a description can be facilitated by spanning the junction with a "hybrid" model combining atoms with Lagrangian zones. This is a promising research area.

We have already studied, as is described in our 1992 Computers in Physics article, a cell-based approach to a hybrid model, filling some Lagrangian zones with atoms while treating others as continua. The impulses due to atomistic collisions with a zone wall (treated by constructing image particles on the other side of that wall) can then be summed up and used to accelerate those continuum nodes contiguous to that wall.

An aesthetically appealing method for joining the atomistic and continuum models is to use a particle description for them both. The enhanced continuum fluctuations in this approach resemble the thermal motion of an atomistic system. In the next Section we describe such an approach, in which the atomistic and continuum descriptions both use particles. It is to be expected that, in the absence of thermal motion, both descriptions provide exactly the same adiabatic response to accelerations.

7. Simple Hybrid Model

The simplest hybrid atomistic+smoothed-particle description has a fixed weighting function w(r), varying neither in time nor in space. Provided that the masses of the smoothed particles are the same as those of the atoms we then have a variety of *ad hoc* recipes which could be used to accelerate the atomic masses and the continuum nodes. The weighting function itself appears to be crucial to the success of the smoothed-particle approach. How should it be chosen? A choice based on reproducing the pair distribution function is a natural one. Thus the fundamental statistical mechanics of the correspondence between the atomistic and smoothed-particle distribution functions is well worth pursuing.

Even with an appropriate weight function selected, the hybrid dynamics is not entirely straightforward. In order to use the current information {r,v,e} for the atoms and the nodes to calculate the time derivatives {ṙ,v̇,ė}, stress, smoothed density and velocity, and the velocity gradient need to be estimated. In the mixed case this means estimating values for the tensors (σ/ρ^2) and ∇v for an atomistic particle. This can be done by summing the local contributions to the stress tensor and density in the neighborhood of the particle using the weight function w. Once this averaging has been completed, the pair contributions to the accelerations can be based on a coupling parameter λ:

$$a_{ij} = -(\lambda/m)\nabla\phi_{ij} + (1-\lambda)m\nabla_i w_{ij} \cdot [(\sigma/\rho^2)_i + (\sigma/\rho^2)_j] \,.$$

It is natural to choose the values {0,1/2,1} for the three possible types of ij combinations. A successful hybridization of the two approaches must reproduce not only mechanical and thermal equilibria; it must also describe the linear transport of momentum and energy consistently.

For the atomistic part of these simulations we chose a very simple pair potential, with three vanishing derivatives at the cutoff, r = 1:

$$\phi(r) = 100(1 - r^2)^4 \,.$$

In the smoothed-particle part of the simulations we use the constitutive model measured for this force law, including the transport coefficients η

and κ. For this purpose, a limited portion of the energy-density phase diagram was covered, using 100 particles. The specific heat and pressure-volume-energy constitutive equations could then be expressed as low-order polynomials in density and energy.

The smoothed particle idea has such flexibility that combinations of it with other forms of mechanics suffer from excessive richness. Nevertheless, the promise of hybrid simulations demands an exploration of this uncharted but promising territory. At the time of this writing (June, 1993) we have not completed hybrid simulations of shear flows and heat flows. I expect to describe such simulations in my talk in October.

, Much still remains to be done in extending the range of applications for smoothed particle hydrodynamics. One particularly promising application of the smoothed-particle approach is the study of mesoscopic hydrodynamic fluctuations. The method is ideal for treating fluctuations on intermediate length and time scales.

8. Summary

With massively-parallel teraflop computers on the near horizon the transition from millions to billions of degrees of freedom is quite near. This development suggests connecting the microscopic models with more macroscopic approaches, so as to combine microscopic realism with macroscopic size in dealing with real problems.

9. Acknowledgment

I thank Professor Steinhauser for the opportunity to attend and to address this conference. Larry Cloutman was a helpful guide to smoothed-particle lore. Harald Posch provided some welcome assistance with the molecular dynamics. Brad Holian alerted me to the Beazley-Lomdahl preprint listed in the references. I thank Drs. Beazley and Lomdahl for sending me an advance copy of their work. The Lawrence Livermore National Laboratory and the University of California at Davis/Livermore both provided resources necessary to the completion of this work. Work performed at the Livermore Laboratory was carried out under the auspices of the United States Department of Energy, pursuant to Contract W-7504-Eng-48.

Some General References:

Microscopic Molecular Dynamics:
    See W. G. Hoover, **Computational Statistical Mechanics** (Elsevier, Amsterdam, 1991) and **Microscopic Simulations of Complex Flows** (M. Mareschal, editor), NASI Series B, Volume 236 (Plenum, New York, 1990) and the references below for an introduction to the literature. For a sample of recent timing results see D. M. Beazley and P. S. Lomdahl, "Message-Passing Multi-Cell Molecular Dynamics on the Connection Machine 5" (Parallel Computing, to appear).

Macroscopic Smoothed-Particle Hydrodynamics:
    L. B. Lucy, "A Numerical Approach to the Testing of the Fission Hypothesis", Astronomical Journal 82, 1013 (1977).
    J. J. Monaghan, "Smoothed Particle Hydrodynamics", Annual Review of Astronomy and Astrophysics 30, 543 (1992).
    L. Hernquist, "Some Cautionary Remarks about Smoothed Particle Hydrodynamics", The Astrophysical Journal 404, 717 (1993).
    W. G. Hoover, T. G. Pierce, J. Shugart, C. Stein, C. G. Hoover, and A. L. Edwards, "Molecular Dynamics, Smoothed-Particle Hydrodynamics, and Irreversibility", Computers & Mathematics with Applications (to appear, 1994).

Microscopic and Macroscopic Simulations of Rayleigh-Bénard Instability:
    Goldhirsch, R. B. Pelz, and S. A. Orszag, "Numerical Simulation of Thermal Convection in a Two-Dimensional Finite Box", Journal of Fluid Mechanics 199, 1 (1989).
    D. C. Rapaport, "Molecular Dynamics Study of Rayleigh-Bénard Convection", Physical Review Letters 60, 2480 (1988) and "Temporal Periodicity in Microscopic Simulation of Rayleigh-Bénard Convection", in **Microscopic Simulations of Complex Hydrodynamic Phenomena** (M. Mareschal and B. L. Holian, editors), NASI Series B, Volume 292 (Plenum, New York, 1992).

Microscopic Simulations of Silicon Indentation:
    W. G. Hoover, A. J. De Groot, and C. G. Hoover, "Massively Parallel Computer Simulation of Plane-Strain Elastic-Plastic Flow *via* Nonequilibrium Molecular Dynamics and Lagrangian Continuum Mechanics", Computers in Physics 6, 155 & cover (1992).
    J. S. Kallman, W. G. Hoover, C. G. Hoover, A. G. DeGroot, S. M. Lee, and F. Wooten, "Molecular Dynamics of Silicon Indentation", Physical Review B 47, 7705 (1993).

Further Results of the Relaxed Timing Model for Distributed Simulation

Álvaro Garcia Neto

alvaro@uspfsc.ifqsc.usp.br
Grupo de Instrumentação e Informática
Departamento de Física e Ciência dos Materiais
Universidade de São Paulo
Caixa Postal 369
13.560-980 São Carlos, SP, Brazil

Abstract. A novel model for distributed event-driven simulation, *Relaxed Timing*, was proposed in an earlier article. In this paper, a simulator using this model is used to study the behaviour of the accuracy of relaxed simulations, comparing the results of a real-life test case with those obtained from a conventional simulator. The results of the Time Granularity Experiment show that the Relaxed Timing model is stable and yields results comparable to those of a conventional simulator. A spectrum of accuracy, ranging from strictly accurate to fully relaxed is obtained, and the distribution of these spectral lines is compatible with the known clock skews introduced by the relaxed model. The quantification of these clock skews is an important step in confirming the suitability of the model for distributed simulations.

1   Introduction

Simulation is a essential tool in computer architecture research. The complexity of today's proposed architectures make it difficult for a designer to proceed based only on the mathematical properties or on the qualities of the model under investigation. It is unwise to elaborate on designs only to find, latter, that they harbour basic flaws. Hence, the importance of fully studying a new design using simulation.

Conventional event-driven simulations running on single processors are too slow to adequately study today's parallel computer designs — the imbalance between the processing capacity of the simulating and of the simulated processor are so big that only unrealistically simple experiments can be done. One way to lessen the imbalance is to host the simulation on a high-performance computer. Unfortunately, neither of the two classes of high-performance machines is suited for this task. One class, the vector processors, exploits parallelism on data regularity, absent in simulations. The other class, broadly composed by the MIMD machines, does not handle efficiently the centralized event-list which is the basis of conventional event-driven simulation.

There are models for distributed event-driven simulation, such as Time Warp [13, 14, 15], Sequence of Parallel Computations [2, 3, 4, 5], Moving Time Window [18], Phase Transition [17] and Probing [12, 16]. Most of them tend to be either difficult to implement or wasteful of resources. To overcome some of these drawbacks we proposed a novel simulation model called *Relaxed Timing* [8] which is simpler to implement, runs faster and can produce comparable results, thus enabling larger (and more realistic) simulations.

The Relaxed Timing Model has been described elsewhere [7, 9]. This article reports a second battery of tests and an experiment in investigating the behaviour of accuracy of the simulation when the degree of freedom in a relaxed simulation changes.

2 The Relaxed Timing Model

2.1 Principles

The Relaxed Timing Model for distributed event-driven simulation [8] yields higher simulation speed by consuming data in the fashion of Chandy and Misra's model, but by *not blocking when it cannot guarantee correct consumption*. In practice, this means that any data in the input buffers of a merge process can trigger the execution of this process. A Relaxed Timing simulator trades timing accuracy for speed by not remembering any previous processing (as in Virtual Time) and by not delaying the consumption of available data for the sake of maintaining proper timing order (as in the Sequence of Parallel Computations model.)

Common sense says that this approach would quickly and increasingly loose any temporal resemblance to the system being modeled. Relaxed Timing clearly causes preemptions, but we have demonstrated that the magnitude of errors introduced by this approach can be tolerated [7, 8]. This article does not aim to prove the correctness of the model, but section 2.2 will briefly show that, for simulating the Manchester Multi-ring Dataflow Machine [10, 11, 19], this model produces results of acceptable accuracy with better performance.

Relaxed Timing works because:

• Many of the simulated systems are self-ordering, *i.e.*, they do not need timing as a sequencer for their actions. The Manchester Dataflow Machine is one such system, as the implementation of a timeless simulator shows [1, 6]. In these systems, the sole function of timing is of a *quantifier* — the events that compose the system behaviour will occur even if time is skewed.

• In many detailed simulations of computer architectures, the fine-grain and high diffusivity of events ensures that most processes have a pool of events from which to choose the next event to be interpreted. By correctly choosing the next event, the processes can minimize the effects of earlier preemptions. In this approach, *preemptions are neither avoided nor corrected: their effects are attenuated.*

- In large simulations, where timing is only a quantifier and where the effects of preemptions are minimized, a small percentage of preemptions will not affect the overall picture, and can, thus, be tolerated.

2.2 Validation

In a real-life test case, a Relaxed Timing simulator has been able to predict the behaviour of the internal units of a complex machine. Figure 1 is a typical example of the behaviour predicted by the simulator. Two different simulators were used in this work: a conventional event-driven simulator (MR) and a relaxed simulator (DF). Many characteristics where studied (token queue length, matching store occupancy, processor utilization, matching faults and token replication) for many different benchmarks (binary integration, Laplace relaxation, matrix multiplication, vector smoothing and calculus of Ackermann's function), and, in all cases, the results from the relaxed simulator always matched those of the conventional simulator.

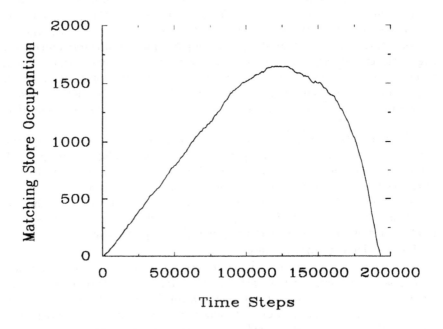

Fig. 1. Matching Store Occupancy, Binary integration, MR

Each event is time-stamped (E_{ts}). Because the local clock of each process (LC) is always updated to $\mathbf{max}(LC,E_{ts}) + \delta_{delay}$, where δ_{delay} is the simulated time required by this event, a preemption will make the local clock advance

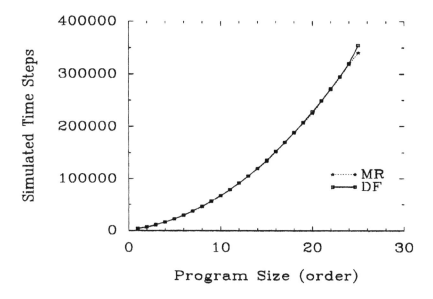

Fig. 2. Time stamp drift for the Ackermann's Function benchmark

improperly. The drift of the simulation clock, compared to the progress of the clock in a convention simulator is, therefore, a good measure of the imprecision introduced by the relaxed model. Figure 2 shows that the measured time drifts do not diverge strongly. Figure 3 plots the ratio of clock skew between the DF and MR simulators, showing that the difference between the final time stamp in both simulations, as the size os simulation increases, tends to be constant. In this figure, 100% means "no clock skew". Note that the worst case benchmark peaks under 400%, falling sharply as the size of simulation increases.

Another way to assess the imprecision of the relaxed model is to count the number of preemptions. Figure 4 shows that, for the matrix multiplication algorithm, these preemptions are somewhat frequent but of small magnitude. In each interval of 1,000 time steps, the error counts range from 0 to 7. The peak error magnitude accumulated in a slice of 1,000 time steps is 18 time steps; the average accumulated error magnitude is 8 time steps. The other benchmarks yield similar data, justifying the conclusion that *Relaxed Timing introduces timing skews of low magnitude and of medium frequency*.

Figure 5 shows the performance gain of the Relaxed Timing Model for one experiment. The absolute values should be disregarded, since the simulations were executed in machines of different performances. Importance should, instead, be placed on the fact that the time of processing for the conventional simulator in-

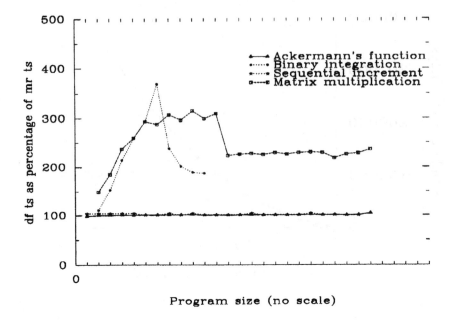

Fig. 3. Time stamp drift compared

creases exponentially, while the time for the Relaxed simulator increases linearly. This behaviour was observed in all experiments.

3 The Time Granularity Experiment

3.1 Experiment Aims

The previous results show that there is no simple choice between performance and accuracy for time modelling in distributed simulations — precision comes at the expense of performance and vice-versa. Therefore, by enforcing full accuracy, the current paradigms for distributed simulation may be incurring in heavy performance penalties.

The Time Granularity Experiment, now described, in an investigation on the correlation between accuracy and performance. The relaxed model suits such experiment well: it is possible to build a tool capable of controlling the extend to which the processes may get out of synchronization. Such tool can execute either as a conventional event-driven or as a relaxed simulator.

This experiment also allows insights into determining the circumstances where loss of precision becomes unacceptable. This threshold from acceptability to un-acceptability probably differs for individual simulations, and therefore, experi-

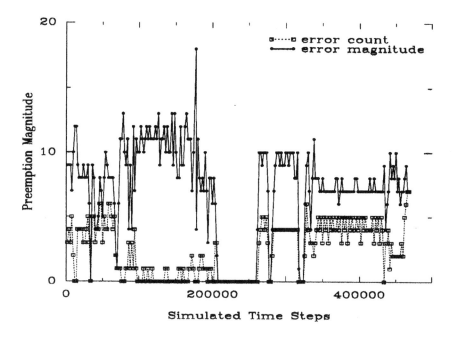

Fig. 4. Error count and magnitude of preemptions per interval

mentation is the best way to determine how relaxed can a simulation be, while still yielding results within the required accuracy.

3.2 Implementation

The Time Granularity Experiment was implemented by modifying the relaxed simulator whose results were reported in section 2.2, enabling the experimenter to specify by how much each process can advance its local clock out of step with its peers. The technique used is to force periodic global synchronizations via a *conductor* process, which broadcasts permission for the processes to advance until a certain local clock value. Each individual process proceeds independently, consuming all tokens of smaller time stamp in a relaxed fashion. The conductor issues the next permission when all processes have finished, a condition detected by either scoreboarding or deadlock detection. Each interval between conductor broadcasts is called a *time slice*. This self-blocking mechanism is reminiscent of Schneider's Phase Transition scheme [17], and, although not practical due to the high starvation levels, it allows interesting experimentation.

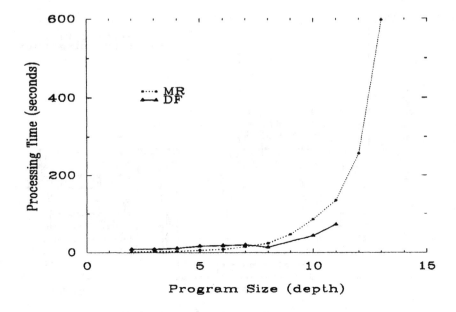

Fig. 5. Performance gain for the Binary Integration benchmark

3.3 Results and Interpretation

The behaviour of the Matching Store of the Manchester Multi-ring Dataflow
Machine for the benchmark programs of Binary Integration and Matrix Multiply are reported in Figs. 6 and 7. For comparison, the results generated by a
conventional simulator are also plotted, indicated by a diamond.

The asymptotic behaviour of the separation of these time slice curves is coherent with the preemption count and preemption magnitude measurements earlier
reported: Since we know that preemptions tend to be somewhat frequent and
of low magnitude, it is expected that, once the few large bursts are eliminated,
further restrictions in time slices only yield small improvements in precision.
This is mirrored in the concentration of lines with simulated time step around
ts = 130,000 (for **slice_size** between 40 and 1,000) in Fig. 6. When small time
slice sizes are reached (*e.g.* under 5), precision begins to improve significantly
again, because most preemptions are in this range.

A desirable result would be to have the line for **slice_size = 1** close to the
curve generated by the conventional simulator. This would indicate that we can
achieve the same level of precision with a relaxed simulation in constrained
mode as with a conventional time-driven simulator. A tentative explanation
for the 30% offset in this curve is that the modified relaxed simulator used in
this experiment remains idle most of the time when time slice values are small,

confusing the starvation detection algorithm. This could cause the terminator process to advance the time slice boundary before all event from the last time slice were fully consumed, thus causing preemptions. Another possibility is that ·the time steps in this modified simulator are not as finely tuned to the model of the machine under simulation as those of the simulator whose results were reported in section 2.2. Since this tunig is a labour-intensive exercise, it was not carried out extensively in this modified simulator version as in the original relaxed simulator, where precise determination of the model's inaccuracy was at stake.

4   The "Engineering" and the "Mathematical" approach

The Relaxed Timing model is a deep change in the philosophy to the distributed event-driven problem. The most common approaches to this problem are "mathematically oriented", *i.e.*, they attempt to provide a solution that correctly models time in all circumstances. The fact that the behaviour curves maintain their shape even with distorted time suggests that, perhaps, an "engineering approach" to the problem is possible.

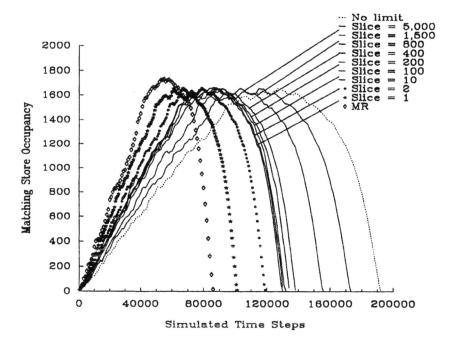

Fig. 6. Timing precision variation, Binary Integration

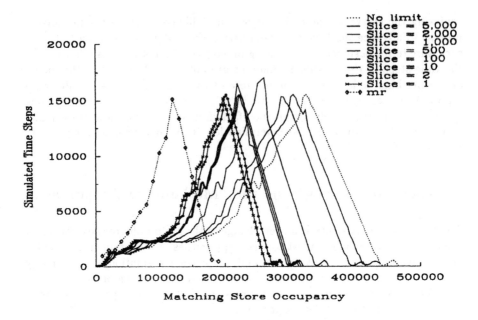

Fig. 7. Timing precision variation, Matrix Multiplication

Figure 8 shows a striking similarity between the preemption count profile in a relaxed simulation and some noise profiles common in tele-communications. The "engineering approach" for noise in tele-communications is not to attempt to eliminate it. Instead, noise is accepted as inevitable, and techniques to minimize its effects are used. The philosophy of accepting time modelling errors as inevitable in a distributed environment and the search for techniques to minimize the clock skew may yield interesting results of practical significance.

5   Conclusions

The results of the Time Granularity Experiment lend credence to the model of Relaxed Simulation. Previously published results show that, even at the most relaxed, the model can produce acceptable results. The experiment now reported show the existence of a spectrum of accuracy, ranging from strictly accurate to fully relaxed. This opens new avenues of research, where a simulating tool can be constructed in such a way as to produce results as accurate as required, charging, for each increase in accuracy, a correspondent toll in simulation speed.

The stablily of the model, with the general curves for all time slices retaining the same general shape, shows that the considerations in section 2.1 are correct.

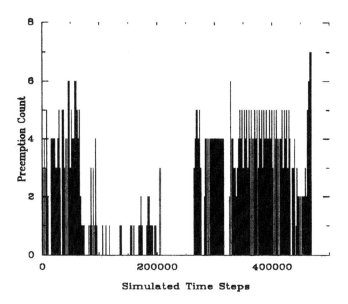

Fig. 8. Preemption count profile, Matrix Multiplication

Acknowledgements

Part of this work was financed by CAPES (Coordenação de Aperfeiçoamento de Pessoal de Nível Superior. Current work is partially financed by FAPESP (Fundação de Amparo à Pesquisa do Estado de São Paulo) and CNPq (Conselho Nacional de Pesquisas), foment agencies of the Brazilian Federal and State Government. The earlier part of this work was done at the Dataflow Research Group in the University of Manchester, UK, in collaboration with Prof. J. R. Gurd and Dr. W. Böhm. Most data were obtained using the T-Rack, a transputer-based experimental processor built as part of the ParSiFal project, a research consortium of British Universities and Industries.

References

1. P. M. C. C. Barahona. Performance Evaluation of a Multi-Ring Dataflow Machine. Technical Report, Dept. Computer Science, Univ. Manchester, UK, Oct. 1984.
2. K. M. Chandy and L. Lamport. Distributed Snapshots: Determining Global States of Distributed Systems. *ACM Trans. Comp. Systems*, 3(1):63–75, Feb. 1985.
3. K. M. Chandy and J. Misra. Deadlock Absence Proofs for Networks of Communicating Processes. *Information Processing Lett.*, 9(4):185–189, Nov. 1979.

4. K. M. Chandy and J. Misra. Distributed Simulation: A Case Study in Design and Verification of Distributed Programs. *IEEE Trans. Software Engineering*, SE-5(5):440–452, Sep. 1979.

5. R. C. de Vries. Reducing Null Messages in Misra's Distributed Discrete Event Simulation Method. *IEEE Trans. Software Engineering*, 16(1):82–91, Jan. 1990.

6. J. F. Foley. A Hardware Simulator for a Multi-ring Dataflow Machine. Technical Report Series UMCS–86–1–3, Dept. Computer Science, Univ. Manchester, UK, May 1986.

7. A. Garcia Neto. *Distributed Parallel Simulation Using "Relaxed Timing"*. PhD thesis, Dept. of Computer Science, Univ. of Manchester, Manchester, UK, Jan. 1991.

8. A. Garcia Neto. Relaxed Distributed Simulation Using the ParSiFal Processor. In T. S. Durrani *et alli* (Ed.), Applications of Transputers 3, IOS Press, Amsterdam, pp. 780–785, 1991.

9. A. Garcia Neto, A. P. W. Böhm, and M. C. Kallstrom. Um Simulador Dataflow Implementado em uma Rede de Transputers. In *Anais do II Simpósio Brasileiro de Arquitetura de Computadores*, pp 5.A.5.1 – 5.A.5.6, Águas de Lindóia, SP, Brasil, Sep. 1988. Soc. Bras. Computação e Instituto Nacional de Pesquisas Espaciais.

10. J. R. Gurd, C. C. Kirkham, and W. Böhm. *The Manchester Dataflow Computing System, Special Topics in Supercomputing*, vol. 1. North-Holland, Jan. 1987.

11. J. R. Gurd and I. Watson. Data Driven System for High Speed Parallel Computing — Part 2: Hardware Design. *Computer Design*, 9(7), July 1980.

12. V. Holmes. *Parallel Algorithms for Multiple Processor Architectures*. PhD thesis, Computer Science Dept., Univ. of Texas, USA, 1978.

13. D. R. Jefferson. Fast Concurrent Simulation Using the Time Warp Mechanism. In *Proc. Conf. on Distributed Simulation*, Soc. Computer Simulation. San Diego, USA, Jan. 1985.

14. D. R. Jefferson. Virtual Time. *ACM Trans. Programming Languages and Systems*, 7(3):404–425, July 1985.

15. D. R. Jefferson and B. Beckman. Distributed Simulation and the Time Warp Operating System. Technical Report, Jet Propulsion Laboratory, Pasadena, USA, Aug. 1987.

16. J. K. Peacock, J. W. Wong, and E. G. Manning. Distributed Simulation Using a Network of Processors. *Computer Networks*, 3:44–56, 1979.

17. F. B. Schneider. Synchronization in Distributed Programs. *ACM Trans. Programming Languages and Systems*, 4(2):179–195, Apr. 1982.

18. L. M. Sokol, B. K. Stucky, and V. S. Hwang. MTW: A Control Mechanism for Parallel Discrete Simulation. In Plachy and Kogge (Ed.), *Proc. 1989 Internl. Conf. Parallel Processing*, pp 250–254. Pennsylvania State Univ. Press, Aug. 1989.

19. I. Watson and J. R. Gurd. A Practical Dataflow Computer. *IEEE Computer*, 15(2), Feb. 1982.

Pipelining Computations on Processor Arrays with Reconfigurable Bus Systems

Hossam ElGindy *

Dept of Computer Science, The University of Newcastle,
New South Wales 2308, Australia

Abstract. The *k-selection* problem asks for the k-th smallest element in a set S of n unordered items to be identified. We present two k-selection randomized SIMD algorithms for *two*-dimensional processor arrays with reconfigurable bus systems, **RM** for short. First we use an efficient *prefix sums* computation to develop $O(\log \log n \log n)$ time implementations on a $\sqrt{n} \times \sqrt{n}$ **RM**. We then show that *pipelining* the operation of counting n binary numbers can be efficiently implemented on the **RM** to achieve a running time of $O(\log \log n \frac{\log n}{\log \log \log n})$.

1 Introduction

The *k-selection* problem asks for the *k-th* smallest element in a set S of n unordered items to be identified. Solutions for the selection problem are used in enhancing speech and image data by smoothing the signal and removing noise [13], and as a building block in many algorithms that utilise the divide-and-conquer paradigm. Many $O(n)$ time, both expected and worst-case, sequential algorithms for the selection problem are known [7]. However the desire to further reduce the running time, beyond that which can be achieved by sequential computation, has generated great interest in parallel algorithms which can be executed on multi-processor architectures.

Two models of parallel computation are usually considered when designing parallel algorithms: shared memory (**PRAM**) models and computing network models. For the shared memory model, an algorithm which achieves optimal efficiency was developed by Cole [3]. The algorithm has a running time of $O(\log^* n \log n)$ on the EREW-**PRAM** model, and of $O(\log^* n \frac{\log n}{\log \log n})$ on the CRCW-**PRAM** model. Algorithms for a variety of computing network models have been developed. A listing of k-selection algorithms for architectures based on a mesh of processors is shown in Table 1.

Węgrowicz [16] introduced the first algorithm to run in polylogarithmic time on an architecture based on a mesh of processors. The algorithm is based on a sequential technique due to Munro et al [10] and runs in $O(\log^3 n)$ time on a

* This research is supported by a grant from the Research Management Committee, The University of Newcastle.

Computing Model	Complexity	Remarks
Mesh-Connected-Computers	$O(\sqrt{n})$	sorting on a $n^{1/2} \times n^{1/2}$ mesh
Mesh with a single bus [15]	$O((n \log n)^{1/3})$	
Mesh with multiple buses [12]	$O(n^{1/6} \log^{2/3} n)$	mesh of size $n^{1/2} \times n^{1/2}$
Mesh with multiple buses [2]	$O(n^{1/8} \log n)$	mesh of size $n^{3/8} \times n^{5/8}$
Reconfigurable Mesh [4]	$O(\log^2 n)$	mesh of size $n^{1/2} \times n^{1/2}$
Reconfigurable Mesh [6]	$O(1)$	sorting on a mesh of size $n \times n$

Table 1. k-Selection Algorithms for Computing Networks

$n^{1/2} \times n^{1/2}$ **RM**. Using intricate data movement operations, an improved implementation with an $O(\log^2 n)$ running time was presented in [4]. In this paper, we continue our study of basic operations for the reconfigurable mesh architectures by developing two randomized selection algorithms. The first solution is based on a recursive application of an efficient *prefix sums* computation for integer numbers [11] to develop $O(\log \log n \log n)$ time algorithms on a $\sqrt{n} \times \sqrt{n}$ **RM**. We then utilise the *pipelining* technique to achieve the running time of $O(\log \log n \frac{\log n}{\log \log \log n})$ on a $\sqrt{n} \times \sqrt{n}$ **RM**.

After describing the reconfigurable mesh model of computation in the following section, we give an outline of the randomized selection algorithm in **section** 3. Two implementations are then presented in **sections** 4 & 5. We then summarize our contributions and discuss future research in **section** 6.

2 Definitions and Notation

A *two*-dimensional processor array with a reconfigurable bus, *reconfigurable mesh* for short, of size n consists of n processors arranged in an $n^{1/2} \times n^{1/2}$ grid, and a grid reconfigurable bus. Each processor has $O(1)$ storage units of size $O(\log n)$ bits each, and is connected to its four neighbours for local communication and to the broadcasting bus through four locally controlled switches (refer to [8] for a complete description of this model). Each processor stores its row and column indices.

Operations on a reconfigurable mesh proceed in synchronous cycles. During a cycle, each processor can perform the following tasks:

1. select a connection pattern for its four switches,
2. send/receive $O(\log n)$ bits of data from the bus and/or from its neighbours, and
3. perform a constant number of operations manipulating its local storage units (e.g., addition, logic, and mask operations).

Since buses are capable of carrying $O(\log n)$ bit data only, algorithms designed for a reconfigurable mesh must ensure that no two processors attempt broadcasting to the same connected subbus during the same cycle.

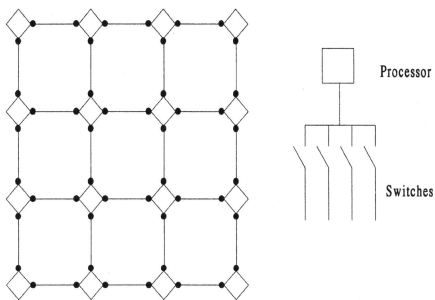

Fig. 1. The Reconfigurable Mesh Organization & a Simple Switch Model

3 Randomized Selection Algorithms: Outline

A straightforward randomized algorithm [1] for the k-th smallest element in a set S of n elements drawn from a set with linear order $\leq$, proceeds as follows:

Procedure SELECT-1(k, S)
if $|S| = 1$ **then**
  return the single element in S.
else
   choose a *splitter* "a" uniformly at random from S;
   let S_1, S_2, and S_3 be the sequences of elements in S
     less than, equal to, and greater than a, respectively;
  if $|S_1| \geq k$ **then**
    return SELECT-1(k, S_1)
  else
    if $|S_1| + |S_2| \geq k$ **then**
      return a
    else
      return SELECT-1$(k$ - $|S_1|$ - $|S_2|, S_3)$

With high probability, each recursive call reduces the size of the set under consideration by at least a constant fraction. Thus an $O(T \cdot \log n)$ expected running time is achieved, where T is the time to perform non-recursive tasks of the procedure; namely – identifying and counting each of the sets S_1, S_2, and S_3, and choosing an element uniformly at random. A method for performing the first task which runs in $O(\log \log n)$ time on a $n^{1/2} \times n^{1/2}$ **RM** is given in [9]. An implementation of the latter task within the same time bound, through the recursive use of a prefix sums computation for integer numbers [11], is detailed in **section** 4. Hence the complexity of our first algorithm can be stated as follows:

Theorem 1. *Procedure SELECT-1 can be implemented with an $O(\log \log n \log n)$ expected running time on a reconfigurable mesh of size $n^{1/2} \times n^{1/2}$.*

Greenberg et al [5] proposed the use of multiple, say p, splitters at each stage to reduce the number of recursive calls. Such an algorithm may be described as follows:

Procedure SELECT-2(p, k, S)
if $|S| = 1$ **then**
    return the single element in S.
else
    choose p *splitters* $a_1, a_2, \ldots, a_p$ uniformly at random with replacement from S;
    let $S_0, S_1, \ldots, S_p$ be the sequences of elements in S separated by the p splitters;
    identify the sequence S_i which contains the k-th element;
    return SELECT-2$(p, k - \sum_{j=0}^{i-1}(|S_j|), S_i)$

With high probability the number of recursive calls is reduced to $O(\log n / \log p)$ [5]. However the time required to process a sufficiently large number of splitters, in a sequential fashion, will offset the reduction in the number of recursive calls. In **section** 5, we show that the task of counting the number of n binary digits, stored one digit per processor can be *pipelined* efficiently. It then follows that "$\log \log n$" splitters can be processed in a *pipelined* fashion within $O(\log \log n)$ cycles on a $n^{1/2} \times n^{1/2}$ **RM**. Therefore complexity of implementing **procedure** SELECT-2, which is detailed in **section** 5, can be stated as follows:

Theorem 2. *Procedure SELECT-2 can be implemented with an $O(\log \log n \frac{\log n}{\log \log \log n})$ expected running time, for $p = \log \log n$, on a reconfigurable mesh of size $n^{1/2} \times n^{1/2}$.*

4 An $O(\log \log n \log n)$ Implementation for SELECT-1

A straightforward approach for choosing and processing a splitter uniformly at random from a set of m numbers stored in a $n^{1/2} \times n^{1/2}$ **RM**, proceeds as follows:

Procedure SPLITTER

1. apply **procedure** UNIQUE-LABELS to assign unique labels to each of the m numbers.

2. an appointed processor chooses an integer $I \in [1..m]$ uniformly at random, and broadcasts the integer "I" on the bus.
3. the processor storing the number with the label i then announces the splitter's value on the bus.
4. processors of the RM cooperate in computing the rank of the announced splitter.

An $O(1)$ time is clearly sufficient to perform steps 2 & 3, and step 4 can be computed in $O(\log \log n)$ time [9]. For step 1, a processor storing one of the m numbers is marked with "1", and "0" otherwise. We then use the following divide-and-conquer procedure, which uses the prefix sums of an integer sequence [11, Theorem 4][2], to assign unique labels to them:

Procedure UNIQUE-LABELS

1. Partition the mesh into $\sqrt{n}$ square sub-meshes.
2. In parallel, each sub-mesh assigns locally unique labels to its marked processors and computes their *count*, in a recursive fashion.
3. Move the $\sqrt{n}$ counts to the first row of the mesh.
4. Apply the procedure of [11, Theorem 4] to perform prefix sums of the $\sqrt{n}$ counts.
5. Move the $\sqrt{n}$ prefix sums to the appropriate sub-meshes, where they are *added* to the previously assigned labels to generate globally unique labels of the marked processors.

Lemma 3. *Procedure UNIQUE-LABELS requires $O(\log \log n)$ cycles on a $n^{1/2} \times n^{1/2}$ reconfigurable mesh.*

This completes the proof of Theorem 1.

5 An $O(\log \log n \frac{\log n}{\log \log \log n})$ Implementation for SELECT-2

Counting the number of "1's", stored one digit per processor in an RM, is the operation used for ranking a splitter in step 4 of **procedure** SPLITTER. Miller et al [9] described an $O(\log \log n)$ time recursive algorithm for performing such an operation. The method used has the drawback of using all processors in the RM at each level of the recursion (i.e., processors of the RM need to be dedicated to the execution of a specific counting process for the duration of $O(\log \log n)$ cycles). A different method, **procedure** COUNTING below, can perform counting within the same time bound while using an asymptotically smaller number of processors to perform the tasks at each recursive level. Since an asymptotically large number of square sub-meshes are not used during each

---

[2] The prefix sums of an integer sequence $a_0, a_1, \ldots, a_{n-1}$ with $0 \le a_i \le n-1$ can be computed in $O(1)$ time on a reconfigurable mesh of size $n \times n$.

recursive call, independent executions of the procedure may be pipelined through the **RM**. A top-down description of such a procedure proceeds as follows:

Procedure td-COUNTING

1. Partition the mesh into $\sqrt{n}$ square sub-meshes, of size $n^{1/4} \times n^{1/4}$ each, and count the number of "1's" in each sub-mesh independently.
2. Each sub-mesh assigns $n^{1/8}$ rows and columns, of the $n^{1/2} \times n^{1/2}$ **RM**, to add the $n^{1/2}$ counts.
3. compute the total sum of the $\sqrt{n}$ counts using the procedure for computing prefix sums of an integer sequence [11, Theorem 5][3].

Lemma 4. Procedure *td-COUNTING requires* $O(\log \log n)$ *recursive calls on a* $n^{1/2} \times n^{1/2}$ **RM** *to count the numbers of binary digits stored one digit per processor. In addition,* $n^{\frac{3}{2^{l+1}}}$ *square sub-meshes each of size* $Z - 1 \times Z - 1$, *where* $Z = n^{\frac{1}{2^{l+2}}}$, *are not used during the l-th recursive call,* $l = 1, 2, \ldots, \log \log n - 2$.

Proof: The non-recursive task, at the l-th level of recursion, is to add $n^{\frac{1}{2^l}}$ integers whose values are bounded by $n^{\frac{1}{2^l}}$ using $n^{\frac{1}{2^{l+2}}}$ rows and columns of an $n^{\frac{1}{2^{l+1}}} \times n^{\frac{1}{2^{l+1}}}$ **RM**. Therefore, a constant number of calls to the procedure of [11, Theorem 5] is sufficient to compute the total count with the above described **RM**. □

A bottom-up implementation for the counting procedure bu-COUNTING, which we use to implement **procedure** SELECT-2, proceeds as follows:

Procedure bu-COUNTING

1. Partition the mesh into square sub-meshes, of size $B \times B$ each $(B = 9)$, and count the number of "1's" in each sub-mesh independently.
2. stay *idle* for a number of cycles equal to those required to perform the above step[4].
3. **for** $i = 1 \ldots \log \log n - 1$ **do**
   (a) form non-overlapping square sub-meshes of size $B^{2^i} \times B^{2^i}$.
   (b) compute the total sum of the $B^{2^{i+1}}$ counts using the procedure for computing prefix sums of an integer sequence [11, Theorem 5].
   (c) stay *idle* for a number of cycles equal to those required to perform the above two steps.

It is easy to see that bu-COUNTING has the same complexity bounds as those stated in **Lemma** 4 for **procedure** td-COUNTING. The procedure for

---

[3] The prefix sums of an integer sequence $a_0, a_1, \ldots, a_{n-1}$ with $0 \leq a_i \leq n^c - 1$ can be computed in $O(c)$ time on a reconfigurable mesh of size $n \times n$.

[4] This idle period is essential to stagger independent executions of this procedure on the same **RM**.

choosing and processing p splitters, uniformly at random with replacement, from a set of m numbers can be described as follows:

Procedure p-SPLITTERs

1. apply **procedure** UNIQUE-LABELS to assign unique labels to each of the m numbers.
2. **for** $i = 1 \ldots p$ **do**
   (a) an appointed processor chooses an integer $I_i \in [1..m]$ uniformly at random, and broadcasts the integer "I_i" on the bus.
   (b) the processor storing the number with the label I_i then announces the splitter's value on the bus.
   (c) processors of the **RM** initiate a new execution of **procedure** bu-COUNTING to compute the rank of the announced splitter.
3. choose the two splitters which form the minimal interval that contains the k-th smallest number, and mark the appropriate processors.

Lemma 5. *Procedure p-SPLITTERs requires $O(p + \log \log n)$ cycles on a $n^{1/2} \times n^{1/2}$ reconfigurable mesh.*

By selecting a value of $\log \log n$ for the parameter p, we complete the proof of Theorem 2.

6 Epilogue

The main result of this paper is a randomized procedure for the k-selection problem with a running time of $O(\log \log n \frac{\log n}{\log \log \log n})$ on a reconfigurable mesh of size $n^{1/2} \times n^{1/2}$. An optimal, and preferably less complex, randomized algorithm remains our objective. Another unresolved question is the feasibility of a $o(\log^2 n)$ deterministic selection algorithm for the reconfigurable mesh architecture[5].

However the main contribution of this paper is to demonstrate that *pipelining* multiple executions of $\sqrt{n}$-way divide-and-conquer procedures on reconfigurable mesh architectures is feasible, and can lead to an improved running time of certain algorithms. Future research will investigate the use of pipelining to improve the running time of other problems, and to simulate architectures that are hierarchical in nature (e.g., fat tree, hypertree/Banyan network, hypercube, ... , etc) efficiently.

References

1. A.V. Aho, J.E. Hopcroft and J.D. Ullman, *The Design and Analysis of Computer Algorithms*. Addison-Wesley Publishing Company, 1975.

---

[5] $O(\log^2 n)$ running time [4] is the best known result to date for $n^{1/2} \times n^{1/2}$ **RM**.

2. Y.C. Chen, W.T. Chen, and G.H. Chen, "Two-variable linear programming on mesh connected computers with multiple broadcasting," *Proc. of 1990 International Conference on Parallel Processing*, August 1990.

3. R. Cole, "An optimally efficient selection algorithm," *Information Processing Letters*, **26**, 295–299 (1987/88)

4. H. ElGindy and P. Węgrowicz, "Selection on the reconfigurable mesh," *Proc. of 1991 International Conference on Parallel Processing*, August 1991, pp. III-26 – 33.

5. A.G. Greenberg and U. Manber, "A probabilistic pipeline algorithm for k-selection on the tree machine," *Proc. of 1985 International Conference on Parallel Processing*, 1985, pp. 1 – 5.

6. Ju-Wook Jang and Viktor K. Prasanna, "An optimal sorting algorithm on reconfigurable mesh," *Proc. of 6*th *International Parallel Processing Symposium*, pp. 130 – 137.

7. D.E. Knuth, *The Art of Computer Programming: Sorting and Searching*. Addison-Wesley, 1973.

8. R. Miller, V.K. Prasanna-Kumar, D.I. Reisis and Q.F. Stout, "Meshes with reconfigurable buses," *MIT Conference on Advanced Research in VLSI*, 1988, pp. 163 – 178.

9. R. Miller, V.K. Prasanna-Kumar, D.I. Reisis and Q.F. Stout, "Parallel computations on reconfigurable meshes," manuscript.

10. J.I. Munro and M.S. Paterson, "Selection and sorting with limited storage," *Theoretical Computer Science*, **12**, 315–323 (1980).

11. A. Olariu, J.L. Schwing, and J. Zhang, "Fast computer vision algorithms for reconfigurable meshes," *Proc. of 6*th *International Parallel Processing Symposium*, 1992, pp. 258 – 261.

12. V.K. Prasanna Kumar and C.S. Raghavendra, "Array processors with multiple broadcasting," *Journal of Parallel and Distributed Computing*, **4**, 173–190 (1987).

13. D.S. Richards, "VLSI median filters," *IEEE Trans. on ASSP*, vol. 38, January 1990, pp. 145 – 153.

14. L. Shrira, N. Francez and M. Rodeh, "Distributed k-selection: From a sequential toa distributed algorithm," *Proc. ACM Symposium on Principles of Distributed Computing*, August 1983, pp. 143 – 153.

15. Q.F. Stout, "Mesh-connected computers with broadcasting" *IEEE Transactions on Computers*, **9**, 826–830 (1983).

16. P. Węgrowicz, "Linear programming on the reconfigurable mesh and the CREW PRAM," Masters Thesis, McGill University (1991).

An Effective Algorithm for Computation of Two-Dimensional Fourier Transform for NxM Matrices*

Maria Lucka**

Institute of Control Theory and Robotics, Slovak Academy of Sciences,
Dubravska cesta 9, 842 37 Bratislava, Slovak Republic

Abstract. The paper presents a recursive method for computation of 2DFT for rectangular matrices that decreases the number of complex multiplications and leads to very effective implementation on computers with SIMD architecture.The matrix is in every step divided into four submatrices that are processed in parallel.Rapid reduction of multiplications makes this method attractive also for sequential computation.The algorithm was implemented on MasPar MP-1 computer and the time measurements are involved.

1 Introduction

The Fourier transform is one of the most widely used and studied numerical algorithms.Among its many uses in science,engineering, and applied mathematics are signal and image processing,time series and spectral analysis,image restauration and solution of partial differential equations [4]. Fastest methods for solving discrete form of Poisson's equation in simple geometries are based on Fourier transform.Fourier transform techniques are applicable to radar and medical analysis as well as for signal-to-noise enhancement and filtering images.

The most of the practical applications require time-expensive multiple computation of Fourier transform of large matrices.The usual algorithm for calculation of two-dimensional Fourier transform is succesive application of one-dimensional Fast Fourier Transform (FFT).FFT is first applied on each row of given matrix,then the result matrix is transposed and one-dimensional transform is applied again on each of its rows.The number of complex multiplications used by this method is $MN(\log_2 M + \log_2 N)/2$.

The compact symmetric algorithms that use certain symmetric properties of data represent another trend [8] in the speed-up of FFT's.These algorithms have also straightforward extensions to shared memory parallel computers and cause significant computational savings.The computation of Fourier transform

---

* This work has been done in frame of the common project "Parallel Algorithms for SIMD Architectures" of the Institute for Statistics and Informatics,University of Vienna and Control Theory and Robotics,Bratislava,Slovak Republic

** Present adress of the author:Institute for Statistics and Informatics,University of Vienna,Bruennerstr.72, 1210 Vienna

can be essentially speeded-up by using SIMD parallel computers such as STA-RAN,ILLIAC IV and MasPar MP-1.The super parallel algorithm which simultaneously solve any combination of different spatial dimensionalities has been theoretically developed and also implemented on MasPar MP-1 by Munthe-Kaas [3].This algorithm is composed of two main parts: symbolic preprocessing and actual transform.Most of the computational time is taken by the former part.

In our paper we present theoretical base as well as time performance results of an recursive algorithm for computation of two-dimensional Fourier transform for rectangular matrices NxM.The matrix is in every step divided into four submatrices of equal size that can be calculated in parallel.In the last step submatrices of the size 4x4 are processed without multiplication. Described algorithm was implemented on parallel SIMD computer MasPar MP-1 and its time performance has been compared with algorithm published in [3].

2   Theoretical Background

Two-dimensional direct discrete Fourier transform (2DFT) of matrix $H_{N \times M} = (h_{pq})$ is defined [1] as

$$\tilde{h}_{nm} = \sum_{q=0}^{M-1} \sum_{p=0}^{N-1} h_{pq} w_N^{np} w_M^{mq} \tag{1}$$

for n,p=0,1,...N-1 and m,q=0,1,...M-1, where $w_N = \exp(-j2\pi/N)$ and $w_M = \exp(-j2\pi/M)$, $j = \sqrt{-1}$.

The inverse transform maps one-to-one $\tilde{H}_{N \times M}$ to the matrix $H_{N \times M}$ according to the relationship

$$h_{pq} = \frac{1}{M} \sum_{m=0}^{M-1} \frac{1}{N} [\sum_{n=0}^{N-1} \tilde{h}_{nm} w_N^{-np}] w_M^{-mq} \tag{2}$$

for n,p=0,1,...N-1 and q,m=0,1,...M-1.

Let $N = 2^a, M = 2^b$,a,b $\geq$ 2 are integers and n=2r , m=2s.
Then the relationship (1) can be [2] rewritten as

$$\tilde{h}_{2r,2s} = \sum_{p=0}^{N-1} \sum_{q=0}^{M-1} h_{pq} w_M^{2sq} w_N^{2rp} \tag{3}$$

for r=0,1,...N1-1 and s=0,1,...M1-1, where $N1 = N/2$ and $M1 = M/2$.
Exploiting the equalities

$$w_N^{2r(i+N1)} = w_N^{2ri} \quad \text{and} \quad w_N^{(2r+1)(i+N1)} = -w_N^{(2r+1)i}$$

$$w_M^{2s(k+M1)} = w_M^{2sk} \quad \text{and} \quad w_M^{(2s+1)(i+M1)} = -w_M^{(2s+1)k}$$

for i=0,1,...N1-1 and k=0,1,...M1-1,

we get from (3) the following set of equations

$$\tilde{h}_{2r,2s} = \sum_{i=0}^{N1-1} \sum_{k=0}^{M1-1} [h_{ik} + h_{i+N1,k} + h_{i,k+M1} + h_{i+N1,k+M1}](w_M^2)^{ks}(w_N^2)^{ir}$$

$$\tilde{h}_{2r,2s+1} = \sum_{i=0}^{N1-1} \sum_{k=0}^{M1-1} [(h_{ik} + h_{i+N1,k} - h_{i,k+M1} - h_{i+N1,k+M1})w_M^k](w_M^2)^{ks}(w_N^2)^{ir}$$

$$\tilde{h}_{2r+1,2s} = \sum_{i=0}^{N1-1} \sum_{k=0}^{M1-1} [(h_{ik} - h_{i+N1,k} + h_{i,k+M1} - h_{i+N1,k+M1})w_N^i](w_M^2)^{ks}(w_N^2)^{ir}$$

$$\tilde{h}_{2r+1,2s+1} = \sum_{i=0}^{N1-1} \sum_{k=0}^{M1-1} [(h_{ik} - h_{i+N1,k} - h_{i,k+M1} + h_{i+N1,k+M1})w_M^k w_N^i](w_M^2)^{ks}(w_N^2)^{ir}$$

for r=0,1,...N1-1 and s=0,1,...M1-1 .
According to the above equations with regard to the fact that all expressions involving N-th resp.M-th root of unity can be expressed by means of N/2-th resp.M/2-th root of unity,the calculation of 2DFT of the matrix $H_{N \times M}$ can be reduced to the application of 2DFT to four matrices of the size $N/2 \times M/2$.
So we get

$$f_{00}(r, s) = (h_{rs} + h_{r+N1,s} + h_{r,s+M1} + h_{r+N1,s+M1}) \qquad (4)$$

for r=0,1,...N1-1 and s=0,1,...M1-1

$$f_{01}(r, s) = (h_{r,s-M1} + h_{r+N1,s-M1} - h_{r,s} - h_{r+N1,s})w_M^{s-M1} \qquad (5)$$

for r=0,1,..N1-1 and s=0,1,..M1-1

$$f_{10}(r, s) = (h_{r-N1,s} - h_{r,s} + h_{r-N1,s+M1} - h_{r,s+M1})w_N^{r-N1} \qquad (6)$$

for r=N1,...N-1 and s=0,1,...M1-1

$$f_{11}(r, s) = (h_{r-N1,s-M1} - h_{r,s-M1} - h_{r-M1,s} + h_{rs})w_N^{r-N1} w_M^{s-M1} \qquad (7)$$

for r=N1,...N-1 and s=M1,...M-1 .

ALGORITHM I

Recursive computation of 2DFT for $M, N > 4$

Let $H = (h_{pq})$, for p=0,1,...N-1 and q=0,1,...M-1 and M,N are powers of two. Then the algorithm for computing 2DFT of matrix H is the following:

begin

1)$N1 := N/2, M1 := M/2$;
2)if $(N1 \geq 4)$ and $(M1 \geq 4)$ go to CASE A ;
3)if $(N1 = 2)$ and $(M1 \geq 4)$ go to CASE B ;
4)if $(N1 \geq 4)$ and $(M1 = 2)$ go to CASE C ;
5)if $(N1 = 2)$ and $(M1 = 2)$ go to CASE D ;

CASE A

A1)compute matrices $f_{00}, f_{01}, f_{10}, f_{11}$ according to the relationships (4)-(7) for all submatrices of the matrix H of the size$(2N1) \times (2M1)$
A2)$h_{pq} := f_{pq}$; p=0,1,...N-1 , q=0,1,...M-1
A3)$N1 := N1/2$; $M1 := M1/2$;
A4)w:=w^2 ;
A5) go to 2)

CASE B

B1) compute matrices f_{00}, f_{01} for all submatrices of the matrix H of the size$N \times (2M1)$ by means of (4),(5)
B2)$M1 := M1/2$;
B3)$h_{pq} := f_{pq}$; p=0,1,...N-1 , q=0,1,...M-1
B4)w:=w^2 ;
B5)go to 3)

CASE C

C1)compute matrices f_{00}, f_{10} according to (4),(6) for all submatrices of the matrix H of the size $(2N1) \times M$
C2)N1:=N1/2;
C3)$h_{pq} = f_{pq}$; p=0,1,...N-1 , q=0,1,...M-1
C4)w:=w^2;
C5) go to 4)

CASE D

D1)compute the Fourier for all submatrices of the size 4×4 according to the**AL-GORITHM II**

6)unscramble the elements of matrix h into the bitreversed order

end

ALGORITHM II

Computation of 2DFT for matrices of the size 4×4

Let H=(h_{ik}),i,k=0,1,2,3 and $j = \sqrt{-1}$ is the imaginary unit.Then the Fourier transform of H can be computed according to the following relationships for i=0,1,2,3 :

$$
\begin{aligned}
c_{0i} &= h_{0i} + h_{2i} & d_{0i} &= c_{0i} + c_{1i} \\
c_{1i} &= h_{1i} + h_{3i} & d_{1i} &= c_{0i} - c_{1i} \\
c_{2i} &= h_{0i} - h_{2i} & d_{2i} &= c_{2i} + c_{3i} \\
c_{3i} &= (h_{1i} - h_{3i})(-j) & d_{3i} &= c_{2i} - c_{3i}
\end{aligned}
$$

$$
\begin{aligned}
e_{i0} &= d_{i0} + d_{i2} & \tilde{h}_{i0} &= e_{i0} + e_{i1} \\
e_{i1} &= d_{i1} + d_{i3} & \tilde{h}_{i0} &= e_{i0} - e_{i1} \\
e_{i2} &= d_{i0} - d_{i2} & \tilde{h}_{i2} &= e_{i2} + e_{i3} \\
e_{i3} &= (d_{i1} - d_{i3})(-j) & \tilde{h}_{i3} &= e_{i2} - e_{i3}
\end{aligned}
$$

It can be easy seen that the **ALGORITHM II** need no multiplication (elements c_{3i} and d_{3i} can be computed by exchange of their corresponding real and imaginary parts).We remark,that the elements $\tilde{h}_{ik}$ of the matrix $\tilde{H}$ are ordered in bitreversed order.

The number of complex multiplication for overall method is at most $3/4MN$ [min$(a, b) - 2$]+$1/2MN$[max$(a, b) -$ min(a, b)] for a matrix of size MxN, where $N = 2^a$ and $M = 2^b$,against $MN(a + b)/2$ of complex multiplications that are used by succesive application of FFT.

So the number of complex multiplications can be reduced for example for a matrix of the size 256x1024 from 2 359 296 to 1 441 792 .Implementation of this algorithm on sequential computer has already shown three-times speed-up [5].

3 Parallel Implementation

The proposed algorithm was implemented on MasPar MP-1 computer system. The MasPar System [6, 7] is a massively parallel computer system that enables SIMD processing at least 1024 data elements. Its Data Parallel Unit (DPU) contains a two-dimensional matrix of Processor Elements (PE) that does all the parallel processing and is controlled by Array Control Unit (ACU). Each PE in PE-array has its own memory and high performance registers.It receives an instruction from the ACU and then executes it but on different data. There are two possibilities of communications between PEs: on a straight line or by means of the global router.The former are called X-net communications and enable direct to send (or receive) the data any distance in one of the following eight directions:north,northwest,... They are significantly faster than global router communications,but the latter are more general and have no built-in direction of communication.

When the real and imaginary data are stored into the PE array such that every processor contains (NxM)/(nxproc x nyproc) complex elements,nxproc resp.nyproc is the number of PEs in x resp.y direction,then until the sizes of submatrices are greater than nxproc and nyproc,the sums in (4)-(7) can be calculated in parallel for all PEs in array without shifting of elements. If we denote the complex matrix containing the values of w in relationship (5) to W_M (its real part contains the values of cos and its imaginary part the values of sin) and W_N will be the matrix of w in (6) then it holds $W_M^T = W_N$ .Moreover the arguments for calculation of sin and cos functions for the matrix W_{MN} in(7) are equal the dot sum of corresponding elements of W_M and W_N.Besides of that all elements in every column of W_M have the same value as well as all row elements in W_N and so all these matrices can be generated in parallel for the whole PEs array.The multiplication in (4)-(7)is dot multiplication and so can be also done in one step for all processor elements. For evaluation of the sums in **ALGORITHM II** X-net communications were used. For the unscrambling of elements in our implementation the method described in [3] and [9] was used.

	N=64	N=128	N=256
Overall time	50	175	730

Table 1:Time in milliseconds for the proposed algorithm

Table 1 shows the elapsed time needed for calculation of 2DFT for various sizes of input square matrices.The algorithm was implemented on MasPar MP-1 parallel computer system at the University of Vienna. The size of its PEs array is 32×32 and the measured time is in milliseconds.Proposed algorithm was written in the language MPL (extension of the language C).

In Table 2 figures the elapsed time of the programm for calculation of 2DFT that was proposed and implemented by H.Munthe-Kaas from the University of Bergen [3]. This algorithm has two main parts:symbolic preprocessing and actual transform. The algorithm is general and can be used for arbitrary sizes (powers of two) and arbitrary dimensionalities (up to three).The time for preprocessing of data takes approximately 10 times more than the time for actual transform,but it has to be calculated only once for a given size of the transform.

	N=64	N=128	N=256
Preprocessing of data	126	347	1457
Transform	14	40	147
Overall time	140	387	1604

Table 2:Time in milliseconds for the H.Munthe-Kaas algorithm

Remark. Both programms have been tested on the same computer.

4 Conclusion

Fast algorithm for computation of two-dimensional Fourier transform for rectangular matrices NxM was theoretical developed and also implemented on MasPar MP-1 SIMD parallel system.This algorithm decreases the number of complex multiplications and leads to effective sequential and parallel implementation. All steps of this algorithm can be realised in parallel and many of them need no interprocessor communication.The algorithm can create the base for fast calculation of partial differential equations (Fast Poisson Solver).

5 Acknowledgements

The author would like to thank Prof.H.Zima for the possibility to work with parallel computer system MasPar MP-1 and to Prof.H.Munthe-Kaas for his articles and parallel programs.

References

1. E.Oran Brigham:The Fast Fourier Transform and Its Applications,Prentice-Hall,1988, pp.240-254
2. A.Huebner,R.Klette:Zur Parallelen Ausfuehrung der Schnellen Fourier Transformation fuer NxN Matrizen, Wiss.Zeitschr.,F.Schiller-Univ.Jena,1980,H.2,pp.251-261
3. Hans Munthe-Kaas:Super Parallel FFT's,Report No.52,May 1991,Department of Informatics, University of Bergen,Hoyteknologisenteret,N-5020 Bergen
4. M.Vajtersic:Modern Algorithms for Solving Some Elliptic Problems,Veda Bratislava,1988(in Slovak)
5. M.Lucka:Two-dimensional Fourier Transform,Proceedings Library of Algorithms VI., Algorithms'81,High Tatras(in Slovak)
6. MasPar Programming Language User Guide,Software Version 3.0,Revision:A2,July 1992, MasPar Computer Corporation
7. MasPar Fortran Reference Manual,Software Version 2.0,MasPar Computer Corporation Sunnyvale,California,July 1992
8. J.Dongarra at all:Vector and Parallel Computing,Issues in Applied Research and Development,Elis Horwood Series in Computers and Their Applications,1989,pp.153-161,V.E.Henson: Parallel Compact Symmetric FFT's
9. Hans Munthe-Kaas:Practical Parallel Permutation Procedure,Dep.of Informatics,University of Bergen,N-5020 Norway,Support for the Lectures in Course "Parallel Algorithms",1992

Rational Number Arithmetic by Parallel P-adic Algorithms

Carla Limongelli

Hans Wolfgang Loidl

Dipartimento di Informatica
e Sistemistica
Universitá "La Sapienza"
Roma, Italy
limongel@disco1.ing.uniroma1.it

Research Institute for
Symbolic Computation (RISC-Linz)
Johannes Kepler University
Linz, Austria
hwloidl@risc.uni-linz.ac.at

Abstract. In this paper we analyze the possibility of speeding up rational number arithmetic by using a parallel p-adic approach.

Approximated p-adic arithmetic has received much attention in the last years and several contributions made this arithmetic more efficient. Moreover, p-adic arithmetic is very appropriate for parallel computations over rational numbers as it is based on the multiple homomorphic images technique and the computations are performed independently in each image.

However, to reconstruct the unique result a very time consuming algorithm (the Chinese Remainder Algorithm) has to be used. In order to improve the performance of the recovery step, we propose a specific parallel algorithm and we show that this new algorithm is faster with respect to an already existing algorithm.

To compare these algorithms we have implemented the parallel p-adic arithmetic with both of them. The analysis of the dynamic behaviour of the algorithms shows that the proposed algorithm needs a smaller amount of synchronization, yielding an efficient parallel algorithm.

1 Introduction

Big rational numbers appear in many computer algebra algorithms such as the Gröbner Basis algorithm ([1]), Cylindrical Algebraic Decomposition ([7]) and in algebraic number computations. Furthermore, in [14] an example for the application of a Gröbner Basis algorithm is given, where the final result is larger than 10^{900}. In these algorithms the operations on big rational numbers dominate the overall computation time. Therefore, it is important to speed up this rational number arithmetic.

Several approaches for reaching a more efficient rational number arithmetic have been studied in [10]. Among these approaches the p-adic approach has recently received much attention as it shows a good asymptotic behaviour. Furthermore, it is very appropriate for parallelism as it uses the multiple homomorphic images technique.

The idea of the parallel p-adic approach is to represent each rational number by a truncated power series (Hensel code) with base p and truncation order r

(code length). This is done for several different values of p, each representing one homomorphic image. The computations are then performed independently in each image. The unique result has to be constructed out of the results in the images in a recovery step by using the Chinese Remainder Algorithm (CRA). Finally, a backward mapping has to be performed that retrieves a rational number from the Hensel code.

The most time consuming part of this process is the recovery step. A parallel algorithm that computes the recovery step, using a stepwise CRA, is described in [15].

In this paper we propose an algorithm that improves the practical computing time of the recovery step by applying the CRA only once (pure CRA). In order to show the better behaviour of the proposed algorithm, both algorithms have been implemented on a shared memory machine and their dynamic behaviour has been analyzed. It turns out that the version using the pure CRA is more efficient in practice.

However, the analysis of both algorithms also shows a serious problem of p-adic algorithms concerning their efficiency: the backward mapping in a p-adic algorithm is very hard to parallelize as it requires the application of an inherently sequential algorithm (the Extended Euclidean Algorithm) and it is not yet parallelized.

The structure of the paper is as follows. In Section 2 we present some basics about p-adic arithmetic and the schema of its parallelization. In Section 3 we discuss the parallelization of the recovery step by discussing the two algorithms mentioned above. In Section 4 we present the implementation of the parallel arithmetic, comparing the two different algorithms proposed for the reconstruction step. Further remarks about the implementation and open problems conclude the paper.

2 Parallel p-adic Approach

2.1 Basics about p-adic Arithmetic

The reason of our interest in p-adic arithmetic, shown in [11] derives from the fact that p-adic arithmetic is an error-free arithmetic based on the application of the method of a single homomorphic image and of Hensel construction [8]. In this arithmetic any rational number is represented by a fixed number of base p digits, as stated in the following definition.

Definition 1 (Hensel Codes). Given a prime number p, a Hensel code of length r of any rational number $\alpha = (c/d) \cdot p^e$ is a pair

$$(mant_\alpha, exp_\alpha) = (.\, a_0 a_1 \cdots a_{r-1}, e),$$

where the r leftmost digits and the value e of the related p-adic expansion are called the mantissa and the exponent, respectively. Moreover the r digits of the code mantissa are the coefficients of the truncated power series given by the following computation:

$$|c \cdot d^{-1}|_{p^r} = \sum_{i=0}^{r-1} a_i \cdot p^i \in \mathbb{Z}_{p^r}. \quad \square$$

Let $\mathbb{H}(p, r)$ indicate the Hensel's codes set w.r.t. the prime p and the approximation r and let $H(p, r, \alpha)$ indicate the Hensel code representation of the rational number $\alpha = (a/b) \cdot p^e$ w.r.t. the prime p and the approximation r.

The forward and the backward mappings between rational numbers and Hensel codes can then be defined on the basis of the following theorems.

Theorem 2 (Forward Mapping). *Given a prime p, an integer r and a rational number $\alpha = (c/d) \cdot p^n$, such that $GCD(c, p) = GCD(d, p) = 1$, the mantissa $mant_\alpha$ of the code related to the rational number α, is computed by the Extended Euclidean Algorithm (EEA) applied to p^r and d as:*

$$mant_\alpha \equiv c \cdot y \quad (\text{mod } p^r)$$

where y is the second output of the EEA.

Proof. See [17]. $\square$

Definition 3 (Farey Fraction Set). The Farey fraction set $\mathbb{F}_{p,r}$ is the subset of rational numbers a/b such that:

$$a, b \in \mathbb{N}, \quad 0 \le a \le N, \quad 0 < b \le N, \quad N = \left\lfloor \sqrt{\frac{p^r - 1}{2}} \right\rfloor,$$

where $\mathbb{N}$ indicates the set of natural numbers. $\square$

$\mathbb{F}_{p,r}$ will be also called the Farey fraction set of order N, being $N = N(p, r)$.

Theorem 4 (Backward Mapping). *Given a prime p, an integer r, a positive integer $m \le p^r$ and a rational number $c/d \in \mathbb{F}_{p,r} \subset \mathbb{Q}$, and m is the value in $\mathbb{Z}_{p^r}$ of the Hensel code mantissa related to c/d, then the EEA applied to p^r and m computes a finite sequence of pairs (x_i, y_i) such that there exists an index i for which $x_i/y_i = c/d$.*

Proof. See [17]. $\square$

Arithmetic operations on Hensel codes are carried out, digit by digit, starting from the leftmost digit, as in usual base p arithmetic operations [6].

The possibility of performing an exact arithmetic sequence of operations on $\mathbb{H}(p, r)$ is ensured by the following theorem.

Theorem 5. *Given p and r, given an arithmetic operator Φ and given, for every $\alpha_1, \alpha_2 \in \mathbb{Q}$, the related $H(p,r,\alpha_1)$, $H(p,r,\alpha_2) \in \mathbb{H}(p,r)$, if*

$$\alpha_1 \Phi \alpha_2 = \alpha_3, \quad \alpha_3 \in \mathbb{F}_{p,r},$$

there exists only one $H(p,r,\alpha_3)$ such that

$$H(p,r,\alpha_3) = H(p,r,\alpha_1)\Phi' H(p,r,\alpha_2)$$

where Φ' is the operator in $\mathbb{H}(p,r)$ which corresponds to Φ in $\mathbb{Q}$.

Proof. See Theorem 2, Theorem 4 and [8]. □

On the basis of this last theorem, every computation over $\mathbb{H}(p,r)$ gives a code which is exactly the image of the rational number given by the corresponding computation over $\mathbb{Q}$. So, a schema of a general computation consists of mapping the rational input numbers on $\mathbb{H}(p,r)$ and then performing the computations over $\mathbb{H}(p,r)$. However, by Theorem 4, the inverse mapping can be performed only when the expected result belongs to $\mathbb{F}_{p,r}$.

Example 1. We want to compute the following addition:

$$1/4 + 2/3, \text{ in } \mathbb{Z}_{5^4}$$

so we choose $p = 5$, $r = 4$, and $\mathbb{F}_{5,4} = 17$. The Hensel codes related to $1/4$ and $2/3$ are respectively:

$$H(4,5,4) = (.4\,3\,3\,3\,,\,0) \text{ and } H(4,5,12) = (.4\,1\,3\,1\,,\,0)$$

These codes are obtained by applying Theorem 2. In fact, in order to obtain the Hensel code related to $1/4$ we have to compute:

$$|1 \cdot |4^{-1}|_{5^4}|_{5^4} = 469 = 4 \cdot 5^0 + 3 \cdot 5^1 + 3 \cdot 5^2 + 3 \cdot 5^3.$$

The same procedure applied to $2/3$ gives:

$$|2 \cdot |3^{-1}|_{5^4}|_{5^4} = 209 = 4 \cdot 5^0 + 1 \cdot 5^1 + 3 \cdot 5^2 + 1 \cdot 5^3.$$

The addition is shown below:

$$
\begin{array}{r}
.4\,3\,3\,3\,,\,0 \\
+\,.4\,1\,3\,1\,,\,0 \\
\hline
=\,.3\,0\,2\,0\,,\,0
\end{array}
$$

The code result represents the integer number $11/12$. This is the exact result since $11/12$ belongs to $\mathbb{F}_{5,4} = 17$. □

Let us note that the truncation order r and the base p are chosen according to a previous estimate of the problem solution. An apt Farey fraction set $\mathbb{F}_{p,r} \subset \mathbb{Q}$, to which the rational solution will belong, must be identified and the appropriate choice for p and r is made accordingly.

Once a given algorithm is stated for the solution of the problem, the related estimate of the solution can be evaluated. This can come out to be a not simple problem, but such an estimate can be computed on the basis of the number of operations that must be performed in order to reach the rational solution. For example it is well known that the determinant $D(A)$ of a given n-dimensional square matrix A is bounded by $n! \cdot a^n$, where $a = max\{| a_{i,j} |\}$, $1 \leq i, j \leq n$. It is also trivial to estimate the maximum coefficient which raises by polynomial multiplication: Given the polynomials $\sum_{i=0}^{n} a_i \cdot x^i$ and $\sum_{j=0}^{m} b_j \cdot x^j$, if $a = max\{| a_i |\}_{1 \leq i \leq n}$, $b = max\{| b_j |\}_{1 \leq j \leq m}$ and $c = max\{a, b\}$, then the larger coefficient of the resulting polynomial is bounded by $max\{n, m\} \cdot c^2$. Also the problem of rational exponentiation is immediately estimated: If we have to compute a/b^c the size of the result will be given by $c \cdot log_2(max\{a, b\})$.

2.2 The Parallelization of p-adic Arithmetic

The parallelization of p-adic arithmetic is based on the multiple homomorphic images technique which offers the following advantages:

- the forward mapping preserves the operations as stated by the Theorem 4;
- the image domains are simpler than the original domain so as to solve the problem more efficiently;
- the transformation leads to several independent homomorphic image problems each of which can be solved exactly, independently and in parallel as Figure 1 shows.

Let us suppose to compute an arithmetic expression over n rational numbers $q_1, \ldots, q_n$. By "arithmetic expression" we mean any kind of expression involving the four basic arithmetic operators $+, \cdot, -, /$, over the rational numbers. Our goal is to evaluate it, obtaining a rational result q. We proceed in three main steps (see also Figure 1):

- Each rational number q_h ($h = 1 \ldots n$) is mapped via a prime bases p_i to its related Hensel codes $\bar{q}_h^{(i)}$ ($i = 1 \ldots k$), with a certain truncation order r. All the mappings are computed in parallel.
- The arithmetic expression is evaluated over the $\bar{q}_h^{(i)} \in \mathbb{H}(p_i, r)$ (sets of Hensel codes).
  The image problem is solved in parallel over k finite fields $\mathbb{H}(p_i, r)$ whose elements are the coefficients of the truncated power series with base p_i and approximation r.
- The unique solution $\bar{q} \in \mathbb{H}(p_1 \cdot \ldots \cdot p_k, r)$ is recovered from the k code results $\bar{q}^{(1)} \in \mathbb{H}(p_1, r), \ldots, \bar{q}^{(k)} \in \mathbb{H}(p_k, r)$, by applying the CRA. The CRA is parallelized.

- The rational output $q \in \mathbb{F}_{p,r}$ is obtained via the backward mapping algorithm.

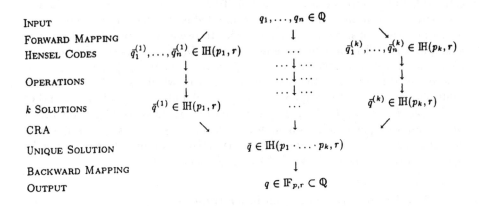

INPUT $\quad\quad\quad\quad\quad\quad\quad\quad\quad q_1, \ldots, q_n \in \mathbb{Q}$

FORWARD MAPPING

HENSEL CODES $\quad \bar{q}_1^{(1)}, \ldots, \bar{q}_n^{(1)} \in \mathbb{H}(p_1, r) \quad \cdots \quad \bar{q}_1^{(k)}, \ldots, \bar{q}_n^{(k)} \in \mathbb{H}(p_k, r)$

OPERATIONS

k SOLUTIONS $\quad\quad \bar{q}^{(1)} \in \mathbb{H}(p_1, r) \quad\quad \cdots \quad\quad \bar{q}^{(k)} \in \mathbb{H}(p_k, r)$

CRA

UNIQUE SOLUTION $\quad\quad\quad\quad \bar{q} \in \mathbb{H}(p_1 \cdot \ldots \cdot p_k, r)$

BACKWARD MAPPING

OUTPUT $\quad\quad\quad\quad\quad\quad q \in \mathbb{F}_{p,r} \subset \mathbb{Q}$

Fig. 1. General schema of parallel p-adic computations.

Let us note that the correspondence between $\mathbb{F}_{p,r}$ and $\mathbb{H}(p, r)$ is injective, hence if the solution does exist in $\mathbb{F}_{p,r}$, then it is unique.

The multiple homomorphic images technique requires the application of the CRA, to obtain the unique code result. This algorithm combines the results from several domains, to obtain the solution in the original domain. Then the modified version of the EEA can be applied to recover the rational result. Actually the crucial step of this approach is the detection of the unique solution via the CRA. Therefore, special attention will be payed to the efficient implementation of the CRA in Section 4.

3   A Parallel Recovery Step

As it has been mentioned in the previous section, the CRA is a very important part in getting an efficient algorithm for p-adic computation, as it is very time consuming and hard to parallelize. Therefore, this section focusses on getting an efficient parallel CRA to compute the recovery step.

It is very hard to parallelize the sequential CRA as it is optimized for the sequential case by iterating over the input lists, where in each iteration only a quite cheap computation is necessary (the intermediate result has to be extended by only one β-digit[1]). For a more detailed discussion of the problems in

---

[1] β is the internal base representation for large integers. In most implementations where a word has n bits the setting is $\beta = 2^{n-3}$.

parallelizing this algorithm see [16].

Therefore, it would be better to base the implementation of the parallel CRA on an idea that contains more inherent parallelism. The following theorem, which is taken from [12], is a good basis for a parallel implementation:

Theorem 6 (Chinese Remainder Theorem). *Let $m_1, \ldots, m_k$ be k relatively prime integers > 1. Then for any $s_1, \ldots, s_k (s_i < m_i)$ there is a unique integer s satisfying*

$$s < \prod_{i=1}^{k} m_i =: M$$

and $s_i \equiv s \mod m_i$; the integer s can be computed using

$$s = \sum_{i=1}^{k} (\frac{M}{m_i}) s_i T_i \mod M, \tag{1}$$

where T_i is the solution of

$$(\frac{M}{m_i}) T_i \equiv 1 \mod m_i. \quad \square$$

In [15] an efficient algorithm is proposed to compute the recovery step which makes use of this theorem. In the following we will briefly describe the main steps of this algorithm and of a new algorithm that applies the CRA in a more natural way. Furthermore, we will compare the complexities of these two algorithms.

RECOVERY STEP

INPUT: $p_1, p_2, \ldots, p_k$: k prime modules;
              $g = p_1 \cdot p_2 \cdot \ldots \cdot p_k$;
              r: code length;
              $(mant_{\gamma_i}, exp_{\gamma_i}) = (\gamma_{0,i} \ldots \gamma_{j,i} \ldots \gamma_{r-1,i}, exp_{\gamma_i})$, $i = 1, \ldots, k$:
              k Hensel code results;
OUTPUT: $d = \sum_{j=0}^{r-1} \delta_j \cdot g^j$: the unique code result.

Let us note that we have arbitrarily many virtual processors available that will be automatically mapped on the real processors.

The first method is based on a "Hensel like" lifting approach. Essentially it uses the first $j - 1$ digits of each Hensel code γ_i to obtain the j-th digit δ_j of the g-adic expansion of the result:

$$d = \delta_0 + \delta_1 g + \cdots + \delta_{r-1} g^{r-1} \tag{2}$$

according to the following steps.

STEPWISE CRA ALGORITHM (SCA)

SCA.1: Apply CRA to the Hensel codes' digit $\gamma_{0,i}$ and moduli p_i, for $i = 1, \ldots, k$, to obtain δ_0;

SCA.2: For all j from 1 to $r - 1$ do the following:

SCA.2.1: Apply the lifting algorithm as described in [5] to δ_{j-1}, $\gamma_{j,i}$ and moduli p_i to obtain the values $\overline{\gamma}_{j,i}$, for $i = 1, \ldots, k$;

SCA.2.2: Apply the CRA as it is given in Theorem 6, to the images $\overline{\gamma}_{j,i}$ and to the moduli p_i to obtain δ_j. In this case we put $s = \delta_j$, $s_i = \gamma_{j,i}$, $m_i = p_i$, $M = g = p_1 \cdot p_2 \cdot \ldots \cdot p_k$, so we have $(M/m_i) = g_i$ and $T_i = |g_i^{-1}|_{p_i}$. Hence the summation (1) becomes:

$$\delta_j = \sum_{i=1}^{k} g_i \cdot \gamma_{j,i} \cdot \overline{g}_i \ mod \ g \tag{3}$$

SCA.3: Transform the digits of the p-adic expansion already obtained, according to the relation (2);

Pure CRA Algorithm (PCA)

PCA.1: From each Hensel code $(\gamma_i, exp_{\gamma_i})$ compute in $\mathbf{Z}_{p_i^r}$

$$d_i = \sum_{j=0}^{r-1} \gamma_{j,i} p_i^j = \gamma_{0,i} + \gamma_{1,i} p_i + \ldots + \gamma_{r-1,i} p_i^{r-1}$$

PCA.2: Compute the moduli p_i^r;

PCA.3: Apply the CRA as it is given in Theorem 6 to the values $d_i = s_i$ and to the moduli g_i^r to obtain the unique $d \in \mathbf{Z}_{g^r} = s$. Then the summation (1) becomes:

$$d = \sum_{i=1}^{k} (g_i)^r \cdot d_i \cdot |((g_i)^r)^{-1}|_{g^r} \ mod \ g^r \tag{4}$$

where $g_i^r = (M/m_i)$, $d_i = s_i$ and $|((g_i)^r)^{-1}|_{g^r} = T_i$.

By a rough analysis of the algorithms described above we note that in the algorithm SCA the CRA is applied r times and each application requires multiplications between numbers of size at most $log \ p^k$, where $p = max(p_1, \ldots, p_k)$ and where $size(p) = size(p_i)$, $i = 1, \ldots, k$.

In the algorithm PCA the CRA is applied only one time to numbers of size $(p^k)^r = g^r$.

A rough computational complexity of the parallelized CRA used in the algorithm SCA takes $O_B(r \ (k \ log \ p)^{log_2 \ 3})$ time. The computational complexity of the CRA applied to the algorithm PCA takes $O_B((r \ k \ log \ p)^{log_2 \ 3})$ and it seems to be heavy with respect to the previous one.

Our purpose in the following sections is to compare from a practical point of view, the behaviour of the two algorithms.

4   Implementation of the Parallel Algorithms

The description of the algorithms in the previous section was general enough to allow an implementation in various different systems. However, such a system has to provide the following features:

- *Creation of parallelism* by forking parallel processes. This operation should be as cheap as possible in order to allow fine-grain parallelism.
- *Synchronization of parallelism* by the availability of the results. Hence, there is no further communication between the processes necessary.
- *Automatic Garbage Collection*. As both algorithms make heavy use of dynamic data structures, the memory occupied by data structures that are not used any more should be automatically made available to the system.

One system that provides these facilities is PACLIB (see [9]), which has been designed at the RISC-institute especially for the implementation of computer algebra algorithms. This system combines the features of the SACLIB library (see [2]), which is based on a heap management kernel with automatic garbage collection and which contains a large number of computer algebra algorithms written in C, with the features of the μSystem (see [3]), which is a package supporting light-weight processes under UNIX[2] on shared memory multiprocessors and on workstations. However, it should be emphasized that any system supporting the above facilities, like PARSAC-2 ([13]) or ||MAPLE|| ([18]), can be used for an implementation of these algorithms[3].

In Section 3 two algorithms for computing the recovery step in a p-adic algorithm have been described. The first of these two algorithms was based on a stepwise CRA and the second was based on a CRA that is applied only once. In this section we will discuss details of this recovery step in an implementation of an exponentiation algorithm in PACLIB based on the p-adic approach. For these algorithms both variants have been implemented and their dynamic behaviour has been evaluated.

In the discussion of the dynamic behaviour we will concentrate on the case of integer exponentiation and all timings will refer to this case. The reason for choosing this special case is the fact that almost all the implicit parallelism of the p-adic approach lies in the parts that suffice to perform an integer exponentiation (see Figure 1). Furthermore, it can be easily extended to the general rational case by just adding a final backward mapping step.

4.1   The Stepwise CRA

As one can see from the description of Algorithm SCA most of the time is spent inside the for loop in the lifting step obtaining $\overline{\gamma}_{j,i}$ out of the values $\delta_{j-1}, \gamma_{j,i}$ and the moduli p_i and then in applying the CRA on these $\overline{\gamma}_{j,i}$ and moduli p_i,

---

[2] UNIX is a trademark of AT&T.

[3] As the Linda-Maple system ([4]) contains an automatic garbage collection only in the sequential parts, it is less usable for our algorithms than the other two systems.

yielding δ_j. Since the result of the lifting step $(\overline{\gamma}_{j,i})$ is needed for the *CRA* and the result of the *CRA* (δ_j) is needed for the lifting in the next loop iteration, it is not possible to perform these steps in parallel. However, the *CRA* algorithm, which is the most time consuming part, is parallelized.

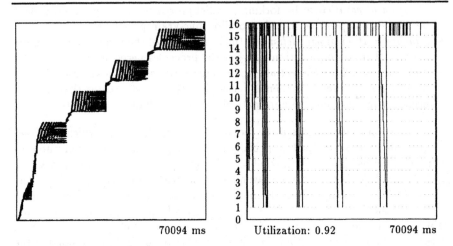

70094 ms   Utilization: 0.92   70094 ms

Fig. 2. Dynamic Behaviour of the Algorithm SCA

Figure 2 shows the dynamic behaviour and the utilization of Algorithm SCA. In the first graph the horizontal axis represents time and the vertical axis represents the different tasks. In the second graph again the horizontal axis represents time but the vertical axis represents the number of active processes.

In this figure the applications of the *CRA* can be seen as blocks of parallel processes. In the above example 87654^{500} was computed with $k = 120$. This delivered a Hensel code length of $r = 6$, yielding 5 blocks of parallel processes. As for all timings mentioned in this paper, 16 processors have been used. Since k is bigger than the number of processors, many short processes have to be executed. This can be seen from the presence of short lines, instead of long straight lines, inside the blocks. The overhead for starting many parallel processes means an additional loss of efficiency. However, if one uses a smaller k the value for r becomes larger, which means that there are more sequential steps necessary. The dependence between k, r and the runtime of the program will be discussed further in Section 4.4.

It can be also seen from this figure that the later blocks are longer i.e. more time consuming than the first blocks. In the above example the first iteration of the main loop in Algorithm SCA required 1396 ms whereas the last but one iteration required 16524 ms. When one examines the different steps within one loop iteration more carefully one sees that this is mainly due to the time needed for the *CRA*, which requires in the last but one iteration 13934 ms. Such a behaviour is easily explained when one regards that for the j-th iteration the size of δ_j can only be bounded by g^j.

4.2 The Pure CRA

Contrary to the previous algorithm, Algorithm PCA is based on the idea of applying the *CRA* only once on the list of recovered Hensel codes d_i and the moduli m_i. All d_i and m_i can be computed in parallel as their values do not depend on each other. However, the efficiency of this part can be improved by computing blocks of d_i and m_i in each parallel process.

However, the evaluation of d_i and m_i is rather cheap. Timings have shown that these computations require only about 3% of the time needed for the *CRA*. Therefore, the efficiency of this approach mainly depends on the efficiency of the parallel *CRA*. Therefore, we will discuss in this section the implementation of the parallel *CRA* that is based on Theorem 6.

The big advantage of an algorithm based on this theorem is the fact that it is inherently parallel as all summands in the definition of s (see Equation (1)) can be evaluated in parallel. Furthermore, the combination of the intermediate results to the final result is rather cheap as only $n - 1$ additions mod M have to be performed.

Although it would be possible to compute all summands of Equation (1) in parallel this would be quite inefficient as one would get a too fine-grain algorithm. Therefore, the input lists are decomposed into as many blocks as there are processors available. Inside these blocks the summands are computed sequentially. The results of the blocks are then added mod M. This can also be done in a parallel way by for example using a tree structure. Note that the additions and the computations in the summands can be overlapped.

As in the computation of each summand M is needed, this product of all moduli has to be computed before the summands. Therefore, the algorithm is naturally split into four parts, where the third part is the most time consuming one:

PARALLEL CHINESE REMAINDER ALGORITHM

CRA.1: *Decompose* the input lists m and s into blocks $mL_1, \ldots, mL_{proc}$ and $sL_1, \ldots, sL_{proc}$ i.e. into as many blocks as there are processors.

CRA.2: *Multiply* all moduli in m_i in parallel yielding M.

CRA.3: For all blocks mL_i and sL_i compute in parallel

$$s_i = \sum_{m \in mL_i, s \in sL_i} (\frac{M}{m}) sT \mod M$$

where $T = (\frac{M}{m})^{-1} \mod m$.

CRA.4: *Add* all s_i mod M in parallel yielding the final result s.

The main part of the algorithm is step CRA.3, which takes about 90% of the computation time. This step is essentially a parallel loop, where in each loop iteration one block of numbers sL_i with the corresponding moduli mL_i is evaluated. Note that the evaluation inside one summand can be performed sequentially as there are as many blocks as processors, which guarantees an evenly spread load among all processors.

The additions in the final step can be overlapped with the computation of the summands in step CRA.3. Furthermore, as all these additions can be done independently they can also be evaluated in parallel. For a more detailed discussion of the parallel *CRA* and its implementation see [16].

4.3 The Dynamic Behaviour of the Algorithm

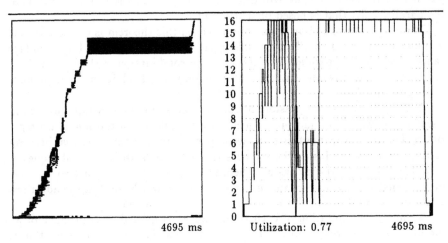

4695 ms   Utilization: 0.77   4695 ms

Fig. 3. Dynamic Behaviour of the Algorithm PCA

Figure 3 shows the dynamic behaviour and the utilization of Algorithm PCA in the evaluation of 87654^{222} with $k = 80$, delivering a Hensel code length of $r = 5$. That input values are different to those for Algorithm SCA in order to see the parallel parts in the execution better. For a comparison of the runtimes of the two algorithms see Section 4.4.

Contrary to Algorithm SCA, there are only twice as much processes as processors necessary in the main step of the algorithm (CRA.3). This minimizes the overhead for creating parallel processes. Furthermore, as these processes are completely independent there is no synchronization necessary. This can be seen in Figure 3 where now the main block consists of straight lines instead of interrupted lines as in Figure 2.

From these graphs it can be seen that there are three major parts determining the time consumption of Algorithm PCA:

1. The *forward mapping* of each input number and the *computation of the solution in the homomorphic image*. This is done in parallel for each prime number p_i ($i = 1, \ldots, k$). In the example of Figure 3 this part forms the first block of k parallel tasks and takes 1203 ms (26% of the overall computation time).

2. The *exponent normalization and code recovering* of all Hensel codes and the computation of $m_i = p_i^r$ ($i = 1, \ldots, k$). This corresponds to the steps PCA.1 and PCA.2 of Algorithm PCA. In the above example this takes 87 ms (2% of the overall computation time).

3. The application of the parallel *CRA* to the d_i and the moduli m_i ($i = 1, \ldots, k$). This part, which corresponds to step PCA.3 of Algorithm PCA, forms the most time consuming block of parallel processes and takes 3384 ms (72% of the overall computation time).

Note that in the implementation of the integer exponentiation a backward mapping of the result is not necessary as it is guaranteed that the resulting number is an integer number. However, other timings have shown that the backward mapping that is required for the rational case needs about half the time of the overall computation. Therefore, after having parallelized the main steps of the p-adic approach the sequential backward mapping step becomes the dominant part. As for this backward mapping the application of an *EEA* is necessary, which is inherently sequential, it is very difficult to parallelize this part.

4.4 Comparison of the Two Algorithms

Earlier timings with sequential versions of both algorithms have already shown that Algorithm PCA is significantly faster than Algorithm SCA. From the parallelism point of view the comparison of Figures 2 and 3 shows that Algorithm PCA contains a smaller amount of synchronization than Algorithm SCA, where a synchronization is necessary after each iteration of the loop in step SCA.2. This small amount of synchronization guarantees a high utilization during the most time consuming part of the computation. Therefore, Algorithm PCA is also in the parallel case much faster than Algorithm SCA.

k	r	SCA	PCA	k	r	SCA	PCA
20	31	37511	15579	80	9	62226	12894
40	16	39690	12401	100	7	61205	13407
60	11	45425	11809	120	6	68525	14507

Table 1. Execution times of the Algorithms SCA and PCA (in ms)

Table 1 shows the execution times for the two algorithms for computing 87654^{500}. The algorithms have been executed with different numbers of primes

(k) yielding different Hensel code lengths (r). From this table one can see that in average Algorithm PCA is about 3 – 5 times faster than Algorithm SCA.

It has to be emphasized that this behaviour of these algorithms is quite independent of the underlying exponentiation routines. This can be seen from the fact that e.g. in Algorithm PCA the computation in the homomorphic images takes, together with the forward mapping, only 26% of the overall computation time.

5 Conclusion

When using the parallel p-adic approach to parallelize rational number arithmetic, the recovery of a unique result from the results in the homomorphic images is the most time consuming part. Therefore, we have compared two algorithms that use two different ways of performing this recovery.

This comparison shows that in practice the new Algorithm PCA, which applies the *CRA* only once on big numbers, is more efficient than the previously known Algorithm SCA, which uses a stepwise *CRA* but operates on smaller numbers.

The analysis of the dynamic behaviour of both algorithms revealed that Algorithm PCA requires a lower amount of synchronization and therefore is better suited for a parallel execution than Algorithm SCA. This fact is not captured in the rough complexity analysis of Section 3 as details like the overhead for the creation of parallel processes are omitted there.

Although only algorithms for rational number exponentiation have been implemented and analyzed, these results hold for general p-adic algorithms as the recovery step is independent of the computation that is performed on the rational numbers.

However, this paper also shows that the p-adic approach has two major problems concerning its efficiency:

– *It requires a big number of operations over huge numbers to be efficient.* For the very small values that were used for analyzing the dynamic behaviour of the algorithms the sequential exponentiation algorithm is even faster than the parallel p-adic algorithm on 16 processors. However, as it is shown in [14] there are applications that require computations on numbers that are larger than 10^{900}, where this approach will surely pay off.
– *The backward mapping step is hard to parallelize,* as it consists essentially only of an *EEA*. Further research in this field will be necessary to improve the efficiency of the backward mapping, via its parallelization.

References

1. Bruno Buchberger. *Ein Algorithmus zum Auffinden der Basiselemente des Restklassenringes nach einem nulldimensionalen Polynomideal (An Algorithm for Finding a Basis for the Residue Class Ring of a Zero-dimensional Polynomial Ideal)*

(In German). PhD thesis, University of Innsbruck, Department of Mathematics, Austria, 1965.

2. Bruno Buchberger, George Collins, Mark Encarnation, Hoon Hong, Jeremy Johnson, Werner Krandick, Rüdiger Loos, Ana Mandache, Andreas Neubacher, and Herbert Vielhaber. A SACLIB Primer. Technical Report 92-34, RISC-Linz, Johannes Kepler University, Linz, Austria, 1992.

3. Peter A. Buhr and Richard A. Stroobosscher. The μSystem: Providing Lightweight Concurrency on Shared-Memory Multiprocessor Computers Running UNIX. *Software — Practice and Experience*, 20(9):929–964, September 1990.

4. Bruce W. Char. Progress Report on a System for General-Purpose Parallel Symbolic Algebraic Computation. In *Proceedings of the ISSAC'90, Tokyo, Japan, August 20–24*, pages 96–103, Department of Computer Science, University of Tennessee, Knoxville, TN 37996-1301, 1990. ACM Press, New York.

5. A. Colagrossi and C. Limongelli. Big numbers p-adic arithmetic: a parallel approach. In *Proc. AAECC-6*, LNCS Series n. 357. Springer, 1988.

6. A. Colagrossi, C. Limongelli, and A. Miola. Scientific computation by error-free arithmetics. *Journal of information Science and Technology*, July-October 1993. To appear.

7. George E. Collins. Quantifier Elimination for Real Closed Fields by Cylindrical Algebraic Decomposition. In *Proceedings of the 2nd GI Conference*, volume 33 of *Lecture Notes in Computer Science*, pages 134–183, Kaiserslautern, 1975. Springer.

8. R.T. Gregory and E.V. Krishnamurthy. *Methods and Applications of Error-Free Computation*. Springer, 1984.

9. Hoon Hong, Wolfgang Schreiner, Andreas Neubacher, Kurt Siegl, Hans-Wolfgang Loidl, Tudor Jebelean, and Peter Zettler. PACLIB User Manual. Technical Report 92-32, RISC-Linz, Johannes Kepler University, Linz, Austria, May 1992.

10. D. Knuth. *Seminumerical Algorithms*, volume 2. Addison Wesley Publishing Company, 1981.

11. N. Koblitz. *p-adic Numbers, p-adic Analysis and Zeta Functions*. Springer, 1977.

12. E. V. Krishnamurthy. *Error-Free Polynomial Matrix Computation*. Texts and Monographs in Computer Science. Springer, 1985.

13. Wolfgang Kuechlin. A Parallel SAC-2 Based on Threads. Technical report, Computer and Information Sciences, Ohio State University, Columbus, Ohio, April 1990.

14. D. Lazard. Stewart platform and Gröbner basis. In Parenti-Castelli and Lenarcic, editors, *Proc. 3rd Int. Workshop on Robot Kinematics*, Ferrara, Sept., 1992.

15. C. Limongelli. On an Efficient Algorithm for Big Rational Number Computations by Parallel p-adics. *Journal of Symbolic Computation*, 15(2):181 – 197, February 1993.

16. Hans Wolfgang Loidl. A Parallel Chinese Remainder Algorithm on a Shared Memory Multiprocessor. Technical report, RISC-Linz, Johannes Kepler University, Linz, Austria, 1993. To appear.

17. A. Miola. Algebraic approach to p-adic conversion of rational numbers. *Information Processing Letters*, 18:167–171, 1984.

18. Kurt Siegl. ∥MAPLE∥ — A System for Parallel Symbolic Computation. In Hussein M. Alnuweiri, editor, *Parallel Systems Fair at the Seventh International Parallel Processing Symposium*, pages 62–67, Newport Beach, CA, April 14, 1993.

Shortest Non-Synchronized Motions
–
Parallel Versions for Shared Memory CREW Models *

Sabine Stifter

RISC-Linz
(Research Institute for Symbolic Computation)
Johannes Kepler University
A-4040 Linz, Austria

Abstract: This papers treats parallel versions of the path finding problem for robots whose joints cannot be controlled in such a way that the endeffector follows a prespecified trajectory. This means, if two or more joints are moving at the same time, the relative positions at each time moment for the joints, i.e. the exact positions of the endeffector, are not known. This may be due to the low level control of the robot (for example, with heavy load robots), or due to a complicated kinematics structure. For such mechanisms a motion is specified by certain intermediate positions (values for all joints) along a desired path. These intermediate positions ("synchronization points") and the requirement that the motions in the single joints are monotonous between consecutive synchronization points guarantee a certain structure of a path. There are several possibilities for parallelizing such algorithms: one may apply known parallel graph search techniques or develop a new concept. We discuss known approaches and argue why they are not really appropriate for our algorithm. New concepts for parallelizing the algorithm are discussed.

---

* Supported by the Austrian Ministery for Science and Research.

1 Introduction

Consider a robot that has to perform a certain task under the following assumptions:

- Each joint has a certain maximal velocity.
- A joint can move with maximal velocity in certain regions, but has, possibly, to reduce it in certain other regions. For example, it may have to reduce the speed if the endeffector is close to some obstacle.
- Two or more joints may move at the same time. However, the movements of different joints are not synchronized. This means that during a movement one does not know the relative positions of the respective joints.
- So it is not possible to follow a prespecified trajectory for the endeffector.

Paths for such robots are characterized by the following items:

- The motion of the robot is described by synchronization points, i.e. by positions in which the motions are synchronized. One waits till each joint has reached a certain prespecified position and only then the motion is continued.
- Between two synchronization points each joint performs a monotonous motion (if it moves at all).
- If two or more joints move at the same time it has to be guaranteed that no collision with the environment takes place, no matter which trajectory is followed between the synchronization points.
- The time needed for a motion depends on the number of synchronization points as well as on the path (i.e. the positions of the synchronization points).

How to compute a shortest collision free path for such a robot? Solutions to shortest path problems in weighted regions (which can handle different speeds) always assume that the joints of the robot can be synchronized, see e.g. [Gewali, Meng, Mitchell, Ntafos 1988]. Minimal rectilinear distance paths, see e.g. [de Rezende, Lee, Wu 1989], [Ke 1989], [Mitchell, Rote, Woeginger 1990], have a relation to non-synchronized motions (although this has not yet been studied in detail, [Stifter 1992]), but are not suited for considering weighted regions. The other algorithms for computing shortest collision free paths do neither consider non-synchronized motions nor do they allow weighted regions, like regions with different speeds for the joints.

In [Stifter 1992, 1992a] we investigate a new approach for determining shortest collision free paths for robots of the above type. Our algorithm is based on a partition of free space into cells, representing the structure of the partition by a connectivity graph with weights assigned to the edges, and computing all shortest paths in this graph. Since not only during the motion itself but also at the synchronization points time is spent, a shortest path with respect to time has to keep the number of synchronization points small. This is achieved by assigning additional weights to the edges in the connectivity graph dynamically during the algorithm. These weights are used to keep the information when a next synchronization point is needed. Different optimality criteria can be handled by considering different types of weights for motions and synchronization points.

This algorithm is especially well suited for parallelization. On the one hand, the underlying algorithmic technique is a graph search; parallelization of graph search techniques have already been studied in the literature, e.g. [Lakhani, Dorairaj 1987], [Quinn, Yoo 1984], [Paige, Kruskal 1985], [Takaoka, Umehara, 1982]. On the other hand, the data structures are open for applying parallel algorithms to them.

The paper is organized as follows: In Sections 2 and 3 we present the basic concepts and the sequential algorithm, respectively. Section 4 presents different parallelizations of the algorithm and discusses there relevance and their effects.

2   Basic Concepts

We treat the problem in configuration space. For a robot with d joints, the *configuration space* is the d-dimensional space with coordinates representing the joint values of the different joints. The subset of the configuration space that contains those joint values for which the robot does not collide with any obstacle in the environment nor with itself is called *free space*. In this representation, collision free paths for the robot are (connected) curves in the free space. Figure 1 shows a simple example of a robot work cell. The robot has three joints: a translatorial joint along the "axis", a rotatorial joint around the axis, and a translatorial joint for extending the arm. The task of the robot is to grip the elements on the block to the left and put them to the block at the bottom. The free space of the environment is the interior of the polyhedron shown in Figure 2.

We assume that we are already given a representation of free space $F(\subseteq \mathbf{R}^d)$ and two positions, s and t, the start and goal positions of the desired path. The goal is to compute a sequence $\Phi = (s = \phi_0, \ldots, \phi_k = t)$ of points in F, the sequence of synchronization points, such that all componentwise monotonous curves between ϕ_i and ϕ_{i+1} are contained in F, i.e. all possible paths meeting the ϕ_i's are collision free. One usually requires that the synchronization points are contained in the interior of F. This is motivated by the fact that at the beginning and at the end of a motion there are vibrations. These vibrations should not result in collisions.

In the sequel, we concentrate on 3-dimensional space. The algorithm works also in higher dimensions. However, the goal of this paper is to illustrate the principle and the structure of the algorithm. The emphasis of this paper is on parallelizing the algorithm.

Definition: A sequence $\Phi = (\phi_0, \ldots, \phi_k)$ *specifies a safe path* iff for all pairs of consecutive points ϕ_{i-1}, ϕ_i, all componentwise monotonous curves[2] from ϕ_{i-1} to

---

[2] A curve in $\mathbf{R}^d$ is componentwise monotonous iff it is monotonous with respect to each coordinate axis. In terms of the robot this means that each joint is moving monotonously.

ϕ_i are contained in the free space.

The elements ϕ_i of a sequence specifying a safe path are called *synchronization points*.

For each pair of synchronization points ϕ_{i-1}, ϕ_i, we define $B_i(\Phi)$ to be the isothetic rectilinear box[3] with ϕ_{i-1} and ϕ_i as diametral vertices. Note that in case some of the coordinates of the synchronization points are equal, this box may degenerate to a rectangle or even a line segment. In these degenerate cases, we take some box $B_i(\Phi)$ containing the synchronization points as vertices and being contained in free space.

It is easy to see that for safe paths all cells $B_i(\Phi)$ are contained in the free space.

In the sequel, isothetic rectilinear boxes are called *cells*. We use the terms *facet* (or *face*) and *edge* in the usual sense. In d-dimensional space a facet is a $(d-1)$-dimensional face and an edge is a $(d-2)$-dimensional face of a box.

Specification of the Problem of Optimal Safe Paths: .

Given: F a closed and bounded subset of $\mathbf{R}^d$,
                                being the closure of its interior, and
                                with the interior of it being connected;
                                the free space,
         $s, t \in F$,   start and goal position of the desired path.
Find: $\Phi = (s = \phi_0, \phi_1, \ldots, \phi_{k-1}, \phi_k = t)$,
                                (with $\phi_i \in F$), such that Φ specifies a safe path,
                                and Φ is optimal.

(The last two conditions of F guarantee that F is not "degenerated". We discuss several criteria for optimality in this paper. In the rest of the paper we assume that F, s, t are given as in the problem specification.)

As stated above, a sequence Φ specifying a safe path defines (not necessarily uniquely) a sequence of cells $(B_i(\Phi))$ with $B_{i-1}(\Phi) \cap B_i(\Phi) \neq \emptyset$ (for example, ϕ_{i-1} is contained in both) and $B_i(\Phi) \subseteq F$. However, this works also the other way round. Consider a sequence of cells $(C_0, \ldots, C_{k-1})$ that are contained in free space such that $C_{i-1} \cap C_i \neq \emptyset$. Let ϕ_i be a point in the intersection of C_{i-1} and C_i, for $1 \leq i < k$, $\phi_0 \in C_0$, $\phi_k \in C_{k-1}$. Then $\Phi = (\phi_0, \ldots, \phi_k)$ specifies a safe path.

    This entails that the problem of constructing safe paths can be reduced to the problem of constructing sequences of cells $(C_0, \ldots, C_{k-1})$ with $C_i \subseteq F$ and $C_{i-1} \cap C_i \neq \emptyset$. In the sense of the lemma above, such a sequence of cells specifies also a safe path, although the synchronization points are not defined uniquely.

---

[3] An isothetic rectilinear box is a box with faces normal to the coordinate axes.

We assume in this paper that the free space F for an environment is given as (a set of) polygonal regions, with all facets in the contour[4] being normal to one of the coordinate axis. So F is a union of cells. So we can restrict the facets in the contour of F to facets of cells, i.e. rectangles, and the edges in the contour of F to edges between such rectangular facets. We use the terms facets (faces) and edges in connection with the contour of F in this sense. Let $B(F)$ denote the set of edges in the contour of F. Even if the free space is not a union of cells, it is necessary to approximate it by a union of cells, since safe paths require that the sequence of cells is contained in free space. How good the approximation of the free space as a union of cells has to be depends on the application.

As a preparatory step to the algorithm for computing shortest paths, the free space has to be represented as a graph $G(F)$ in the following way:

1. The free space is partitioned into cells: Each facet in the contour of F is extended till it hits another facet in the contour of F. Denote the resulting set of cells by $C(F)$.
2. The graph $G(F) := (C(F), E(F))$ has as set of vertices, $C(F)$, the cells in the partition of the free space F. Two vertices are connected by an edge in $E(F)$ iff the respective cells have a facet in common.

It suffices to connect only cells by an edge that have a common facet. One could also connect cells by an edge that have at least a point in common. However, this would increase the number of edges per node. Since we require synchronization points to be in the interior of F, connecting only cells with a common facet by an edge does not change the minimal number of synchronization points.

Figure 3 shows the partition of the free space from Figure 2 into cells. Figure 4 shows the respective connectivity graph $G(F)$. In Figure 3 only those edges of the cells in $C(F)$ are drawn that are visible or are edges of F. It should become clear from this simplified representation what the partition looks like.

Definition: Let C be a cell in the partition $C(F)$. Each facet f_C of the cell C has been obtained by extending one or more facets in the contour of F. We say that the facet f_C *is obtained from* these facets in F.

(Note that each facet of a cell is obtained from at least one facet in the contour of F. If several facets of F are contained in the same plane, there may also be more than one.)

A facet f_C of a cell in $C(F)$ *corresponds to* a facet f_F in the contour of F iff the two facets are parallel and by translating f_C along the coordinate axis to which it is normal, the first part of the contour of F that is reached is the facet f_F.

(Note that for each facet of a cell in $C(F)$ there are exactly two facets in the contour of F that correspond to it (one in positive, one in negative direction of the respective coordinate axis). On the other hand, for each facet in the contour of F, there can be several facets (on different cells) to which it corresponds.)

---

[4] The contour of F is defined as $F -$ (interior of F).

Consider a facet f_C of a cell C. Consider all the edges in the contour of F that belong

- to a facet corresponding to some facet f'_C of the cell C, where f_C and f'_C form an edge, and
- to a facet from which f_C is obtained.

Denote this set of edges by $e(C, f_C)$.

Consider Figure 5. There are two cells, one behind the other, in the lower left part of the free space F. Call the one in the front C, the one at the back D. f is the common facet of C and D. f is obtained from the haceted facet in the Figure. The two facets to which f corresponds are the front facet of C and the back facet of D. $e(C, f)$ consists of the four edges of f.

Definition: Let $e = (u, v) \in E(F)$. Let f_C be the common facet of u and v (regarded as cells). Then $b(e) := e(u, f_C) \cup e(v, f_C)$; $b(e)$ is the *set of critical edges for u and v*.

$b(e)$ is stored together with the edges $E(F)$ of the graph.

For constructing optimal safe paths, it suffices to decide locally whether two cells should be joined together. Cells can be joined together whenever this is possible and meaningful in the local situation. It is not necessary to refrain from joining cells together in order to globally get a "better" maximal partition, i.e. one that yields a shorter sequence of maximal cells. More precisely, during the computation of (all shortest) paths in the graph $G(F)$ cells *along the path* are joined together whenever this is possible, i.e. whenever the resulting cell is contained in the free space F. Roughly, the different "meaningful" possibilities of joining cells together are covered by considering the different paths in the graph. The information, which cells have been joined together is stored in $J(v)$ together with each cell v. $J(v)$ are organized as dictionaries.

3   The Algorithm

We next present the algorithm. For more explanations and for the correctness proof we refer to [Stifter 1992, 1992a].

Algorithm: .

Optimal-Safe-Path($\downarrow G(F)$, $\downarrow s$, $\downarrow t$, $\uparrow \Phi$)
    $v_s :=$ an element in $V(F)$ with $s \in v_s$
    $v_t :=$ an element in $V(F)$ with $t \in v_t$
    cost(v_s):= 0
    path(v_s):= ()
    weight(v_s):= ()
    $U := \{v_s\}$
    for all $v \in V(F) - \{v_s\}$ **do**

```
                cost(v) := ∞
                J(v):= "empty"
    endfor
    while U ≠ ∅ do
                select u ∈ U with cost(u) minimal
                delete u from U
                for all (u, v) ∈ E(F) do
                        e := (u, v)
                        c(u, v) := 0
                        for all f in b(e) do
                                if f ∈ J(u)
                                then    c(u, v) := 1
                                endif
                        endfor
                        if cost(u) + c(u, v)S + w(u, v) < cost(v)
                        then    cost(v) := cost(u) + c(u, v)S + w(u, v)
                                path(v) := path(u) ∘ v
                                weight(v) := weight(u) ∘ c(u, v)
                                if c(u, v) = 0
                                then    J(v) := J(u) ∪ b(e)
                                else    J(v) := "empty"
                                endif
                        endif
                        U := U ∪ {v}
                endfor
    endwhile
    C := ()
    D:= first element in path(vₜ)
    delete D in path(vₜ)
    while path(vₜ) ≠ ∅ do
                E:= first element in path(vₜ)
                w:= first element in weight(vₜ)
                delete E in path(vₜ)
                delete w in weight(vₜ)
                if w = 1
                then    C := C ∘ D
                        D := E
                else    D:= join(D, E)
                endif
    endwhile
    k:= length of C
    for all i = 1, ..., k − 1 do
                φᵢ:= a point in Cᵢ ∩ Cᵢ₊₁ in the interior of F
    endfor
    k := k + 1
```

$$\phi_0 := s$$
$$\phi_k := t$$
$$\Phi := (\phi_0, \ldots, \phi_k)$$

Theorem The algorithm Optimal-Safe-Path called for $G(F)$, s and t, $S = 1$ and $w(e) = 0$ for all $e \in E(F)$ computes a sequence Φ that specifies a safe path with a minimal number of synchronization points. (For a proof see [Stifter 1992].)

The complexity of the algorithm Optimal-Safe-Path is $O(d^2 n^d \log n)$. (For the proof we again refer to [Stifter 1992].)

Different Optimality Criteria

As already mentioned above, the algorithm works for different optimality criteria. We list a few of them here.

1. Shortest paths with respect to minimal number of synchronization points.
2. Shortest paths with respect to time for different velocities in different regions.
3. Shortest paths with respect to time for different velocities in joints.
4. Partition into regions is not fine enough.
5. Shortest paths with respect to the length.
6. Paths keeping the energy minimal.
7. Avoiding critical joint values.

Figures 6 and 7 show two examples for different optimality criteria. In Figure 6, we are looking for a safe path with a minimal number of synchronization points. In Figure 7, a safe path that is shortest with respect to time is constructed. We assume that the time needed by a joint for crossing a cell is the same for all cells, but different for the single joints.

4 Parallelizations of Optimal-Safe-Path

There exist several sequential algorithms for computing all shortest paths for single source nodes in graphs. Some of the best known ones are Dijkstra's method, Ford's method and the matrix-product-algorithms; see e.g. [Paige, Kruskal 1985]. These methods have also been parallelized for different parallel computation models. An overview is also contained in [Paige, Kruskal 1985].

Our algorithm for computing shortest paths is based on Dijkstra's method. Dijkstra's method is only applicable to graphs with non-negative weights. This restriction is, however, satisfied for our applications. For making the notion of this section quite clear, we start with a formal description of Dijkstra's method. Let $G = (V, E)$ be a graph with set of vertices V and set of edges E and with weights $w(e) \geq 0$ assigned to each $e \in E$.

Dijkstra($\downarrow G, \downarrow s$)
    cost(s):= 0

```
path(s):= ()
U := {s}
for all v ∈ V(F) − {s} do
        cost(v) := ∞
endfor
while U ≠ ∅ do
        select u ∈ U with cost(u) minimal
        delete u from U
        for all (u, v) ∈ E do
                e := (u, v)
                if cost(u) + w(u, v) < cost(v)
                then    cost(v) := cost(u) + w(u, v)
                        path(v) := path(u) ∘ v
                endif
                U := U ∪ {v}
        endfor
endwhile
```

When the algorithm terminates, path(v) contains a sequence of nodes in V that represent a shortest path from s to v. cost(v) contains the "costs" or "length" of this path.

For selecting a $u \in U$ with cost(u) minimal, there are basically two possibilities: Either keep U sorted (then the first element is one with minimal costs) or keep U unsorted and apply a search whenever a new u is needed. It mainly depends on the outdegree of the graph which way of organizing U is better, see e.g. [Mehlhorn 1984].

In [Paige, Kruskal 1985] parallel versions of Dijkstra's method are given for shared memory CRCW and EREW machines for unbounded parallelism and also for limited numbers of processors. They could achieve the following results (m is the number of vertices in the graph, e is the maximum number of edges per vertex, p is the number of processors): With m processors the complexity of the algorithm is $O(m \log m)$. They use an unsorted list U and search for the minimal cost element. This is the complexity one could immediately achieve with e processors and keeping U sorted by taking one processor for each edge (u, v) in the while-loop.

We consider this in more details in the next subsection. In the sequel, we only consider the first part of the algorithm Optimal-Shortest-Path, i.e. the algorithm without the extraction of the synchronization points from path(v_t). We assume a shared memory CREW computation model.

4.1 Parallelizing the while-loop

The above considerations suggest to parallelize the inner part of the while-loop, i.e. to consider all the "neighbours" of a node u in parallel.

The outdegree e is relatively small in our case, namely $2d$. $2d$ processors are preferable to m processors (which is $O(n^d)$ here), since $2d$ is usually much smaller than $O(n^d)$. Furthermore, we get a dependency on the dimension only, not on the concrete input data. (Note that the dimension d is fixed once the robot or mechanism for which a collision free path is constructed is specified.)

However, we must not forget that in the algorithm Optimal-Safe-Path we have to update (or create) $J(v)$. Inserting one element into $J(u)$ needs $O(\log n)$, since $J(u)$ can contain up to $O(n)$ elements. All elements of $b(e)$ have to be inserted, these are up to $O(d)$ elements, so updating one neighbour needs $O(d \log n)$ on one processor or $O(\log n)$ on d processors. Hence, we get an overall complexity of $O(dn^d \log n)$ with $o(d)$ processors and of $O(n^d \log n)$ with $o(d^2)$ processors.

We discuss other parallelizations below. As it will turn out, parallelizing the while-loop with $o(d)$ or $o(d^2)$ processors is the most efficient one (when speaking about worst-case complexity) in the sense that the best results can be achieved relative to the number of processors, i.e. the ratio of complexity to number of processors is the best one for this version.

4.2 Choice of the Graph Search Technique

It is especially important that the graph search technique applied in the algorithm is Dijkstra like. The reason is that for the computation of $J(v)$ and, hence, weight(v) it is essential that a path is built up in a sequential order from node to node (in the sequence of the final path). The algorithm will not work correctly if different parts of the solution path are computed in an unordered sequence. Although, in general, other graph search techniques might be more efficient on parallel machines or might be better suited for parallelizations, there is no possibility to change the basic concept of the underlying graph search technique.

4.3 $o(n^d)$ Processors

As an extreme situation, in the sense of unlimited parallelism, we could assume that there are $o(n^d)$ processors, or as many processors as there are vertices in the graph, respectively. Note that this number is input dependent and can (and usually will) be quite large.

There are mainly two possibilities which task each processor performs. They can be shortly characterized as

− distribution per node, and
− update per node.

We consider these two possibilities in more details in the next two subsections.

Distribution per Node The processor of node u, in one iteration step, considers the $O(d)$ neighbours of u (i.e. the nodes for which an edge to u exits in E) and *computes the costs of path$(u) \circ v$*, compares it to the current costs of

v and possibly updates the data of v. One need not take care here in which sequence the processors try to update the information for the same vertex, since the smallest value among all the possibilities in one iteration step will be kept for the next iteration step. One of course has to take care that the whole data of a node is updated by the same processor in order not to mix up data of different paths.

So in each iteration step each processor executes the inner part of the while-loop once, i.e. needs $O(d^2 \log n)$. In the worst case the algorithm needs n^d iteration steps, so we get an overall complexity of $O(d^2 n^d \log n)$, i.e. the same as for the sequential version. However, if path(v_t) contains k elements, the complexity of finding the shortest path from v_s to v_t is $O(d^2 k \log n)$ since there are only k iteration steps necessary. Note that this is not true for the sequential algorithm! The parallel algorithm can be stopped as soon as v_t has the jth smallest value for costs, where j is the number of iterations already performed (and one is only interested in a shortest path to v_t). However, one does not know when this happens unless one protocols a list of nodes sorted with repect to their costs after each iteration step.

There are also relations between certain vertices that could especially be exploited by this parallel version of the algorithm. We explain the situation for 2D; similar relations hold in higher dimensions too. Assume a vertex u with four edges to it in E. The following picture shows the situation in configuration space:

Let e_i be the edge (u, v_i). (Index arithmetic is done modulo 4. We identify $w_{i,j}$ with $w_{j,i}$.) If $J(u) \cap b(e_i) = \emptyset$ and $J(u) \cap b(e_{i+1}) = \emptyset$ then $J(v_i) \cap b((v_i, w_{i,i+1})) = \emptyset$ and $J(v_{i+1}) \cap b((v_{i+1}, w_{i,i+1})) = \emptyset$. This especially means that $J(w_{i,i+1})$ can be set to $J(v_i)$ in the respective iteration steps for the respective nodes. If $J(u) \cap b(e_i) \neq \emptyset$ and $J(u) \cap b(e_{i+1}) = \emptyset$ then $J(v_{i+1}) \cap b((v_i, w_{i,i+1})) = \emptyset$, i.e. $J(w_{i,i+1}) = J(v_{i+1})$ by the processor for v_{i+1}, and $J(w_{i,i+1})$ by the processor for v_i. So by a kind of pipelining the information certain nodes can be updated in constant time instead of $O(d^2 \log n)$.

However, these are not so many nodes that the overall worst-case complexity is decreased. Nevertheless, for practical purposes, this incorporation of the additional knowledge can improve the running time of the algorithm by a relatively large factor since it can be applied iteratively, i.e. the information from one iteration step can be processed from processor to processor during several iteration steps and can be used for many nodes.

Update per Node The processor of node u, in one iteration step, considers the $O(d)$ neighbour nodes v_i of u and *computes the costs of path(v_i)$\circ u$, compares the results with the current costs of u, and takes the one that yields the minimum for updating the data at u. This computations should be done only for neighbours of which the costs are smaller than the current costs of u. Since costs can only be increased with the length of the path but never be decreased. So for any pair $(u, v) \in E$, either for node u node v is considered as a neighbour of u that could decrease the costs of u, or vice versa, for node v node u is considered as a neighbour of v that could decrease the costs of v, but never both. If costs(u) = costs(v) then none of the two possibilities can decrease any of the costs of u or v. So in each iteration step of the while-loop at least one node less than in the previous iteration has to be considered: the node with minimal costs that is chosen as next element from U in the sequential algorithm. So more and more processors solve their task in $O(d)$, i.e. by only comparing the values of the costs of u with the costs of its $O(d)$ neighbours. However, there is always at least one node for which a real computation has to take place. So the worst-case complexity is still $O(d^2 n^d \log n)$. If one would like to express it outputsensitve, one gets a complexity of $O(d^2 k \log n)$, where k is the number of elements in path(v_t) (and one is only interested in a path to v_t).

The considerations for computing new values $J(v)$ for certain neighbour nodes in constant time can be applied here too. This kind of pipelining additional information is even more worthwile here since it corresponds quite well to the way of treating neighbouring nodes, i.e. to the tasks of the single processors.

4.4 Treating Nodes with the Same Costs in Parallel

In the sequential algorithm, an element $u \in U$ with minimal costs is taken as the next one to be considered in the while-loop. Taking an element with minimal costs is necessary to ensure that each node is put only once into U. However, there is no criteria which node among all nodes with equal minimal costs to consider next. So considering all these nodes in parallel seems very reasonable. Of course, there may be always a unique minimal element in U. In an extreme case all elements in U might have the same costs, although this is not very likely. It mainly depends on the optimality criteria, how often it will happen that elements in U have the same costs and how many elements these will be. For example, taking the number of synchronization points as optimality criterion makes it very likely that there are several elements with minimal costs in U. (We discuss this in more details in the next subsection.)

Of course, this way of parallelizing the algorithm does not improve the worst case complexity, it is more a heuristics that can improve the actual running time of the algorithm.

4.5 Optimality Criteria "Number of Synchronization Points"

If one takes the number of synchronization points as optimality criteria, then it is very likely that there are several elements with equal minimal costs in U. Namely all nodes that belong to the same "box" as u have the same costs as u. So it is especially meaningful in this situation of costs computation to treat all elements of U with minimal costs in parallel.

If one knows that each "box" has at least a certain number of elements (i.e. a lower bound for the number of elements per box is known) then the overall complexity of the algorithm can be improved by a factor of one over this lower bound.

4.6 Parallelizing the Determination of the Synchronization Points

So far we only considered the first part of the algorithm, but not the part in which the synchronization points are computed from path(v_t). We will discuss their parallel computation in this subsection.

For this part of the algorithm there are much fewer possibilities for a parallelization. Actually, there are only two "loops" in the algorithm, which are straightforward to parallelize: the while-loop over all elements in path(v_t), and the for-loop over all "boxes" C_i.

The while-loop over the elements in path(v_t) is iterated as many times as there are elements in path(v_t). These may be up to $O(nd)$ elements. However, it is not meaningful to treat all elements in path(v_t) in parallel, since these elements have to be put together to boxes. weight(v_t) indicates which elements of path(v_t) should belong to the same box.

Let E_i be the elements in path(v_t), w_i be the elements of weight(v_t). Assume $w_j = w_k = 0$, and $w_i \neq 0$ for $j < i < k$. The all E_i for $j \leq i \leq k$ will be joined together to the same box. so one may either treat all elements that will be joined together to the same box in parallel, or, just to the contrary, build up the boxes in parallel (i.e. treats elements that will be joined together to the same box sequentially). The organization of the algorithm for building up the boxes in parallel is more complicated than for building one box after the other but treating its elements in parallel. Treating the elements in parallel means that one can find the bounding coordinates along the coordinated axis in parallel. $o(d)$ processors would be fine here. Then each processor can do the comparisons of all the respective bounding coordinates along one coordinate axis. Finding the bounding coordinates for a box from its elements can be done in $O(f)$ if there are f elements in the box.

Parallelizing the for-loop is more straightforward: each synchronization point ϕ_i is independent from the other ones and, hence, all synchronization points can be computed in parallel.

5 References

de Rezende, P.J., Lee, D.T., Wu, Y.F., 1989: Rectilinear shortest paths with rectangular barriers; Discrete and Computational Geometry, vol. 4, no. 1, pp. 41–53.

Gewali, L., Meng, A., Mitchell, J.S.B., Ntafos, S., 1988: Path planning in $0/1/\infty$ Weighted Regions with Applications; Proceedings of the International Symposium on Computational Geometry, June 4–8, 1988, Urbana-Champaign, Illinois, pp. 266–278.

Ke, Y., 1989: On efficient algorithm for link distance problems; 5th ACM Symposium on Computational Geometry, pp. 69–78, ACM, June 1989.

Lakhani, G. Dorairaj, R.A., 1987: A VLSI implementation of all-pair shortest path problem; Proc. 1987 Int. Conf. on Parallel Processing, IEEE Computer Society, pp. 207–209.

Mehlhorn, K., 1984: Data structures and algorithms 2: graph algorithms and NP-completeness; EATCS Monographs on Theoretical Computer Science, Springer.

Mitchell, J.S.B., Rote, G., Woeginger, G., 1990: Minimum link paths among obstacles in the plane; 6th ACM Symposium on Computational Geometry, pp. 63–72, ACM, June 1990.

Paige, R.C., Kruskal, C.P., 1985: Parallel algorithms for shortest path problems; IEEE, 1985, pp. 14–20.

Quinn, M.J., Yoo, Y.B., 1984: Data structures for the efficient solution of graph theoretic problems on tightly-coupled MIMD computers; IEEE, 1984, pp. 431–438.

Stifter, S., 1992: Path planning for non-synchronized motions; Technical Report 92-41, RISC-Linz, Johannes Kepler University, A-4040 Linz, Austria.

Stifter, S., 1992a: Optimal collision free path planning for non-synchronized motions; Technical Report, RISC-Linz, Johannes Kepler University, A-4040 Linz, Austria.

Takaoka, T., Umehara, K., 1992: An efficient VLSI algorithm for the all pairs shortest path problem; Journal of Parallel and Distributed Computing, vol. 16, pp. 265–270.

Figure 1: A Robot Workcell.

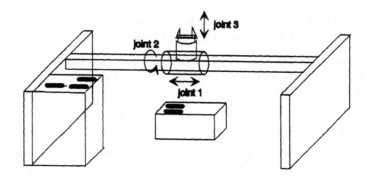

Figure 2: The Free Space for the Environment in Figure 1.

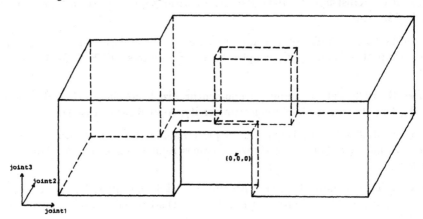

Figure 3: Partition of Free Space into Cells.

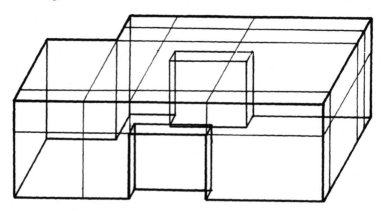

Figure 4: The Connectivity Graph $G(F)$.

Cells are labeled from left to right, from bottom to top, and from front to back. Horizontal, vertical, and diagonal edges in the graph correspond to motions of joint 1, joint 3, and joint 2, respectively.

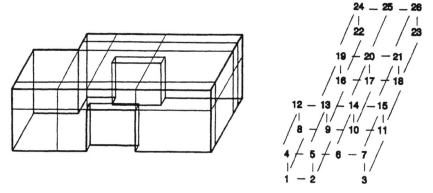

Figure 5: Illustration of Definitions.

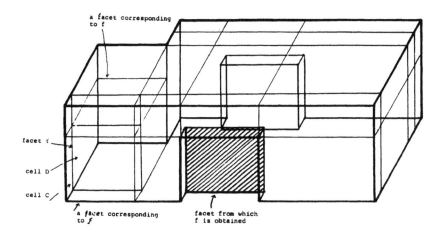

Figure 6: A Safe Path with a Minimal Number of Synchronization Points.

Let s, t be as in the picture. C_0 is the cell in the lower left corner in the front, i.e. cell 1, C_k is the cell in the upper right part, the second one counted from the front, i.e. cell 15.
The output of the algorithm Optimal-Safe-Path is
    path$(t) = (1, 8, 12, 13, 14, 15)$,
    weight$(t) = (0, 0, 0, 1, 0)$,
    cost$(t) = 1$.
So there is one synchronization point necessary at the common face of cell 13 and cell 14. (Only cells needed for the path are drawn in the picture.)

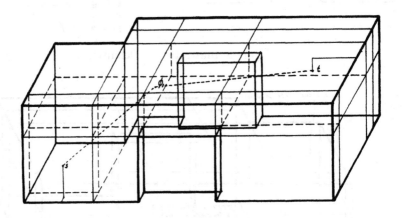

Figure 7: A Safe Path which is Shortest with Respect to Time.

Let s, t be as in the picture. C_0 is the cell in the lower left corner in the front, i.e. cell 1, C_k is the cell in the upper right corner in the front, i.e. cell 3.

Horizontal edges: weight $w(e) = 2$,
vertical edges: weight $w(e) = 3$,
diagonal edges: weight $w(e) = 5$,
time for synchronization points: $S = 4$.

The output of the algorithm Optimal-Safe-Path is

path$(t) = (1, 2, 5, 6, 7, 3)$,
weight$(t) = (0, 0, 1, 0, 1)$,
cost$(t) = 20$.

So there are two synchronization points necessary, namely at the common facet of cell 5 and cell 6, and at the common facet of cell 7 and cell 3. (Only cells needed for the path are drawn in the picture.)

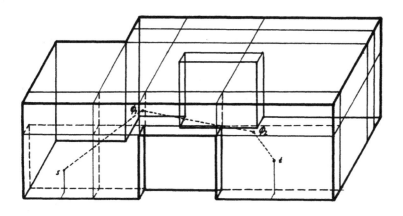

A Pipeline Algorithm for Interactive Volume Visualization

Alfred Spalt

Department for Computer Graphics and Parallel Processing
University of Linz, A-4040, Austria/Europe

Abstract. A parallel algorithm for volume visualization is presented which supports viewing of volume data from arbitrary directions. The parallelization is done by a multiple macro pipeline, because interactivity of the visualization process is the driving goal. An implementation on a distributed memory processor (nCUBE) with 64 nodes is shown, where the volume data set is cut into slices and distributed to the node processors. The processing power of this multiprocessor allows near interactive frame update rates for volumes of moderate size (128x128x128 voxels). Results of this implementation with special respect to speedup and scalability are discussed and further enhancements are proposed.

1 Introduction

Volume visualization methods [1, 2] have been gaining ever more appreciation in various fields of natural sciences, but also in medical sciences. They provide a powerful means of investigating the "inside" of volumetric data sets, which was difficult with other visualization methods known so far. However, the methods are very computationally intensive, so many scientists are being engaged in finding efficient algorithms to cope with the computational load.

Many approaches for mastering the computational challenge have been undertaken until now. One is to use the power of todays workstations, but computation times beyond 1 minute per frame are still the best one can get for volumes of reasonable size. Another approach is to build specialized hardware capable of performing only some of the volume visualization methods either on very large data sets or at interactive rates or both [3]. Here the disadvantage is the same as in most hardware solutions: less flexibility is the price for the win in performance.

The third, and probably most promising approach is to implement the algorithms on parallel architectures with general purpose node processors. They provide the greatest flexibility for applying many different volume visualization methods [4,5]. Basically, there are two possible architectures, typical for the parallel computing community as a whole: shared and distributed memory multiprocessors. The main problems with shared memory computers are memory access conflicts as soon as more than just a few processors are involved in a parallel computation task. In [6] an implementation on a BBN TC2000 is shown, where rendering times were decreased by a factor of 45 with 100 processors.

These problems are clearly solved by distributed memory systems, although developers of algorithms for this class of computers are faced with a significant increase of the implementation's complexity and with communication overhead. However, once a parallel algorithm is successfully implemented, dramatical improvements in computation times can be expected.

In the following section we will briefly describe one variant of the volume visualization methods and explain the need for interactive rendering. Then we will present a parallel pipeline algorithm which will be shown to transfer given volume data sets to the same resulting images as its sequential counterpart. In the successing sections we will show how this algorithm can be implemented on a distributed memory multiprocessor. Finally, timing results and speedup values are given which document the efficiency of our implementation.

2 Parallel Volume Visualization

2.1 Volume Visualization Methods

Volume visualization methods as such are not the topic of this paper. However, we think a basic presentation of the whole process is necessary to motivate several of the algorithm design issues described later. The starting point is a *discretized uniform* (regular) volumetric data set, described by a mapping V: NxNxN -> N.

Data sets of this kind can originate from various sources: in medicine, CT and NMR methods produce this type, but also in computational fluid dynamics, parts of the solution (e.g. temperature distributions) can be 3 dimensional scalar fields. They represent discretizations of unknown underlying continuous scalar functions or projections of higher dimensional ones.In scientific visualisation, one elementary cube of this volume is usually termed voxel or cell.

The task now is to generate *expressive* images which must not necessarily be realistic, but should reveal as much as possible of the volumes' inner structure. For this purpose, two transfer functions, O: R -> R and C: R -> R^3, can *arbitrarily* be defined, which map the scalar voxel values to opacity and color (RGB) values. One problem area in volume visualization is to find transfer functions which create the most expressive images, but we do not want to treat this subject further here.

Coloured images can now be generated in different ways. In any case, one has to define a virtual screen with a given resolution in x and y directions and in some way project the volume data onto it. One method projects voxels onto the virtual screen and computes the contributions of each voxel in the order of increasing distance from the screen. Contributions are added, until the accumulated opacity reaches unity [8].A parallel version of this algorithm is currently being developed at our department.

Other methods shoot rays from each pixel position through the volume data. The algorithm described in this paper is a variant of this technique which is nowadays usually called *ray casting* [9,10,11,12]. We can generate an image with intensities $I(x,y)_\lambda$, $0 <= x < xResolution$, $0 <= y < yResolution$, in the following way:

$$I(x, y)_\lambda = \sum_{z=0}^{Z-1} [f(z) \times C(V(x, y, z))_\lambda \times O(V(x, y, z)) \times P(x, y, z)] \qquad (1)$$

where

$$P(x, y, z) = \prod_{k=0}^{z-2} (1 - O(V(x, y, k))) \qquad (2)$$

	remaining fraction of incoming light
V	volume
C	colour transfer function
O	opacity transfer function
Z	number of voxels in direction of ray
λ	one of red, green or blue
$f(z)$	depth cueing factor

The main interest of the *user* of volume visualization systems is to get a good understanding of the (inner) structure of a given data set under investigation. Therefore providing as much visual information as possible is essential. As we are speaking of 3 dimensional data and display media are usually restricted to 2 dimensions, some visual cues have to be supplied to maintain an impression of the third dimension. Perspective projection and depth cueing are standard computer graphics techniques.

Experiments have shown however that interactive viewing (e.g. rotating around an object) is probably the best method of enhancing the perception of 3 dimensional shapes on 2D output devices. Real-time display of thousands of shaded triangles is state of the art in todays graphics workstations. So if an implementation can achieve interactive frame update rates for volume data sets, the same benefits can be exploited for volume visualization.

2.2 Parallel Algorithm

Our algorithm parallelizes at the pixel level. As individual pixel values are completely independent from one another, they can be computed in parallel, provided that each process has access to all of the voxels it needs along the ray paths it has to evaluate.

As we want to support interactive volume investigations, we were inspired by the great success of the pipelining methods in "traditional" computer graphics. So we make use of a macro-pipeline, where in addition many processes are working in parallel *within* each pipeline stage. Let L be the number of stages in the pipeline (length) and B the number of concurrent processes per stage (breadth).

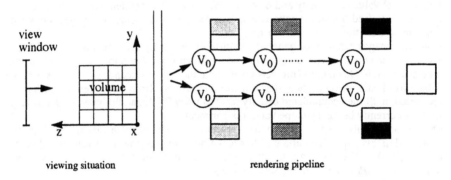

view window
y
volume
z   x

viewing situation

rendering pipeline

Fig. 1. Pipeline with 2 processes per stage

Each process in stage 0 takes as input an empty image and a set of parameters which is sufficient to define a view of the scene. Extensions of the view window, image resolution in x and y directions and viewing direction are the most important ones. We assume that the whole volume is partitioned into L slices perpendicular to the viewing direction and that all processes in stage 0 have full access to all voxels belonging to the slice which is closest to the view window.

Now each process $P_{0,k}$, $0 <= k < B$, is in charge of ($yResolution /B$) scanlines of the resulting image starting at scanline $k \times (yResolution/B)$. Each $P_{0,k}$ computes colour intensity values according to formula (1) in the previous section. However, the volume is treated as if it ended immediately after the first slice. Thus, stage 0 evaluates

$$\sum_{z=0}^{(Z/L)-1} (...) \text{ instead of } \sum_{z=0}^{Z-1} (...).$$

This produces intermediate intensities $I_0(x,y)_\lambda$ and an intermediate value for the accumulated rest of incoming light (according to formula (2))

$$P_0(x,y) = P(x,y,(Z/L)-1) = \prod_{k=0}^{(Z/L)-2} (1 - O(V(x,y,k))).$$

These two informations together with the unchanged viewing parameters form the input of stage 1. Here processes $P_{1,k}$ process the next volume slice, computing

$$I_1(x,y)_\lambda = I_0(x,y)_\lambda + \sum_{z=Z/L}^{2(Z/L)-1} (...) \text{ and}$$

$$P_1(x,y) = P_0(x,y) \times \prod_{k=Z/L}^{2(Z/L)-2} (1 - O(V(x,y,k))).$$

In the same manner, the following processes $P_{i,k}$ get intermediate results from their predecessors and compute their contributions by traversing slice i of the volume. From the above description follows immediately that the final image is just the same as if computed sequentially, applying formula (1) directly to each pixel (x,y). Figure 1 illustrates the whole process.

Rendering starts with an initial view (V_0) where the whole volume is visible and centered in the view window. In an initialization step, all stages of the pipeline have to be filled with the initial viewing parameters and compute their contribution to the final image. Let us consider a pipe of breadth 2. Here each row computes one half of the resulting image, i.e. $(yResolution / 2)$ scanlines (Fig. 1).

From now on, every incremental change in the viewing parameters causes an immediate display of the frame according to the view settings which were valid L time intervals before. If the user, for instance, initiates a rotation (V_1), the next time instance might look as follows:

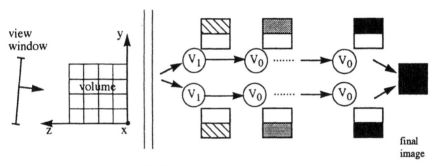

Fig. 2. Pipeline after incremental change of view

So we get a new frame every time *one* stage of the pipeline has finished, and this time is further divided by the number of processes per pipe stage. Some care has to be taken when the structure (length or breadth) of the pipeline is determined. More about this issue will be said in the next section, because these decicions depend mainly on the underlying parallel hardware achitecture.

3   Implementation

We present an implementation on a distributed memory multiprocessor with message passing programming style. The nCUBE [13,14] has a peak performance of about 2.4 MFLOPS double precicion per node, a hand-optimized version of the BLAS routines runs at an average of 1 MFLOPS sustained. The system at the University of Linz has 64 node processors, yielding about 64 MFLOPS effective accumulated performance. This processing power enables us to investigate data sets of moderate sizes (128x128x128 voxels) at near interactive rates. However, the nCUBE multiprocessor can be upgraded to 8K nodes, and as our implementation scales very well with the number of nodes, we could also cope with much larger volumes, if we had more nodes available.

We applied a host-node programming scheme, where the user interacts with the nCUBE front end processor (host), and the computation part is handled by the node processors on the nCUBE itself.

In the rendering pipeline, special viewing situations and settings of transfer functions often cause variations in the computational load of the node processors. As a consequence, the input message buffer of some stages would frequently overflow. As the nCUBE node operating system VERTEX [13] does not provide features for handling this situation, additional synchronisation messages had to be explicitly added to both the host and node programs.

These messages guarantee that at any given time, at most *two* data packets are in any of the nodes' message buffers. By this, neither the host can swamp the input buffers of the first stage with too many requests for new image updates, nor can intermediate nodes overflow their successors when they have relatively little computational load due to a particular opacity transfer function or viewing situation.

3.1 Data Distribution

For interactive rendering, it is not permissible to communicate volume data during the rendering process, at least not greater portions of them. As we want to view the data from arbitrary directions, we have to find a data distribution which saves us from the need for dynamic redistribution. We chose a slicing of the volume along the z axis, according to the pipeline stages of the processing nodes. If we have s stages and Z voxels along the z axis, each stage gets Z/L voxel planes (one slice) and these planes are accessible to all processors of that stage.

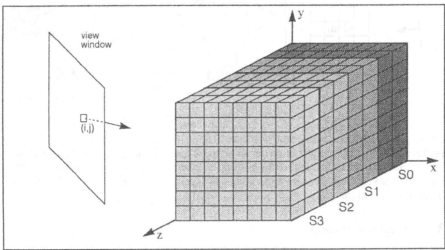

Fig.3. Data partitioning with 4 stages

With a data distribution as shown in Fig. 3 we can compute the resulting image in the order S0-S1-S2-S3 or S3-S2-S1-S0, depending on whether the view window is more on the right or the left, i.e. whether the z coordinate of the view plane normal (ray direction) is positive or negative. Thus, if we tolerate a short reconfiguration of the pipeline when we change sides, we will not have to redistribute volume data and can keep the pipeline running most of the time.

Our algorithm assumes full access to the whole slice for each processor in the same pipeline stage. Thus the ideal machine architecture for the presented algorithm would consist of a mixture of shared and distributed memory. In order to avoid duplication of the same data on more nodes, all nodes of one stage should have access to a common memory, whereas different stages can communicate via message passing. Our implementation has to duplicate the data of one stage to each node in this stage, to provide a simulation of a shared memory, limiting the maximum size of the volume data which can be processed. As our goal is interactivity, we put up with this disadvantage.

The other option would be to equally distribute the volume data among all nodes and send (parts of) them to the appropriate nodes during rendering time. This approach allows rendering of larger datasets (>100MB) but interactivity is lost [5].

3.2   Load Balance

Load balance varies, primarily depending on the setting of the opacity transfer function. In our test cases (see "Results" chapter) this function was set so that computation times reached the maximum values. In terms of load balance, however, this is the *best* case because all stages of the pipeline have the same amount of work.

If the opacity transfer function is set in this way, viewing parameters have little influence on the computational load of the processors as long as the whole volume is projected within the view window boundaries. This is evident if rays are parallel or almost parallel to the z-axis. But also in the extreme cases shown in Fig. 4 the work is almost equally distributed among the stages.

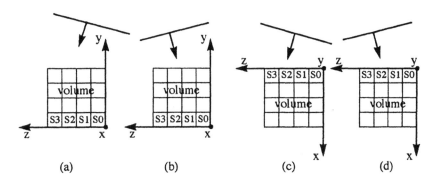

Fig. 4. Some critical viewing situations

Consider Fig. 4(a): Here processors of stage S_0 have to render just a portion of the resulting image. Only rays which hit voxels belonging to their slice have to be evaluated. However, if we look at stage S_1, we have the very same amount of rays because the parallel projection of this slice onto the view plane produces just as many pixels to compute as that of S_0. And the same is true for the two successing stages.

The only two situations when we get into load balance problems are if just small parts of the volume data are observed by the user or if the opacity transfer function is set so that many rays are stopped in early stages of the rendering process due to accumulated opacities. In the first case, only processors which have access to these parts can do useful work, while in the second case, successing stages have nothing more to contribute to the final image.

However, the key issues are that frame update rates are relatively constant and as high as possible even in *computationally* worst case situations. In our case, achieving a good load balance would mean that if the computational load is high frame update rates are low and vice versa. But as we are interested in continuous viewing, changes in frame update rates are rather confusing the user than desirable. What is important is that the pipeline keeps running no matter how disadvantageous either opacity transfer function or viewing situations may be.

3.3   Scalability

Our algorithm can be mapped to any rectangular grid of processors, but some considerations have to be taken into account. The length of the rendering pipe determines the frame update rate. If we want more frames per second, we can simply expand the pipe length. But if we want to maintain interactivity this length is constrained to a certain limit. The reason is that more stages increase the overhead introduced by the pipelining technique where the key issue is to distribute the work load equally among the stages. The *overall* time to produce an image corresponding to a specified view can only be reduced if the breadth of our rendering pipe is expanded.

The breadth however is constrained by the number of processes which can successfully work concurrently on a shared memory. As we mentioned earlier, the benefits of shared memory architectures vanish as soon as too many processors are involved. Within the Austrian ACPC network we have access to a shared memory machine and there is ongoing work to find out the upper limit of processors for our application.

In this paper we present an implementation on a distributed memory machine, and here there are only two choices: either duplicate the data on all nodes of the same stage or apply some kind of dynamic redistribution strategy.

4   Results

In this chapter we give some characteristic figures about our implementation. As mentioned earlier, we experimented on a distributed memory multiprocessor with 64 nodes, each 4 MB main memory and about 1 MFLOPS sustained performance. This multiprocessor is connected to a front end computer (a SUN 4/330 Workstation), from where executables are downloaded and all user interaction takes place. During our experiments, only standard processes such as network deamons were active on the front end workstation, no other users were logged in.

The nCUBE operating system provides the possibility of using just a portion of its computing nodes, so hypercube topologies of different dimensions can be simulated. In this fashion we experimented with four different pipeline configurations, 1x1, 1x4, 4x4 and 8x8, thus using 1, 16, 32 and all 64 nodes, respectively. Our test data set was a 128x128x128 volume with 4 Bytes (αRGB) per voxel. The values for Opacity (α) where set so that the volume rendering always had to traverse the whole data set, i.e. the worst case concerning computation time. The resulting image was sampled at a resolution of 128x128 4-Byte pixels (αRGB).

This 8 MB volume was distributed to the nodes, according to their pipeline stages, yielding 8 MB, 2 MB, 2 MB and 1 MB per node for the three cases mentioned above. As our node processors have just 4 MB of real memory, which is further shared by node operating system, communication buffer, user program and user data, we had to estimate the times for the 1x1 "pipeline" by extrapolating values obtained for 1, 2 and 3 MB test volumes.

Rendering times in the following table were obtained by the standard UNIX time command, using the real time as the result value. As every pipeline needs a startup time proportional to its length, we subtracted the time needed for displaying zero images in every case. This time corresponds to the initial filling and final emptying of the pipe stages. So the results are comparable between the different pipeline structures. Also, we did not take into account the time for initial loading of the volume data.

pipeline structure	frames	seconds total	seconds normalized	seconds per frame	speedup	efficiency
1x1 (*)	0	(**)-	0.0	-	-	-
(1 node)	100	(**)-	12000.0	120.00	1.00	1.00
1x4	0	230.1	0.0	-	-	-
(4 nodes)	100	3366.5	3136.4	31.36	3.83	0.96
4x4	0	58.9	0.0	-	-	-
(16 nodes)	100	835.7	776.8	7.8	15.38	0.96
8x8	0	37.2	0.0	-	-	-
(64 nodes)	100	239.5	202.3	2.02	59.4	0.93

Table 1: Timing results for 128^3 voxels

(*)   extrapolated, from volumes of 1, 2 and 3 MB
(**)   could not be extrapolated

The timing results in Table 1 show the good scalability of our implementation. As we used a uniform setting of opacity and color transfer functions for our test volume, the extrapolated values for the single node case give a very close approximation of what can be expected with 8 MB of available local memory.
Speedup is almost linear, and efficiency values are always close to 1.0. The slight decrease of efficiency from 0.96 to 0.93 for 64 nodes is due to the communication overhead introduced by the distributed memory implementation, combined with the small size of the data set in relation to the large number of computing nodes.

5   Conclusion

Our approach of applying a multiple pipeline for volume rendering proved to yield satisfactory results in a distributed memory implementation. We showed that the speedups we could obtain with our parallelization strategy are almost linear, with efficiency values close to 1.0 even for the case of 64 processors. Frame update rates were still greater than 1 second, but the sequential part of the algorithm has some potential for improvements. One issue is the way how ray paths throughout the volume are calculated. Currently we calculate the exact path (floating point) of each ray throughout the volume, but experiments have shown, that an integer-only digital differential analyzer approach also gives satisfactory results in many cases. This would allow a dramatic improvement in rendering times.
Another improvement can be achieved, if the depth cueing part of the summation is dropped (see section 2.1). The neglection of this factor can be motivated by the possibility of producing enough frames per second to achieve the impression of continuous motion. Depth cueing is an essential visual cue for 3D objects in still pictures, but animated scenes can most probably do without it. This is especially true for visualization tasks, where insight into unknown data sets is the most important issue. Generation of realistic images is of less importance.
A second ongoing effort at our department is the implementation of a parallel splatting algorithm [8]. Here individual voxels can be equally distributed among the available proces-

sors, probably avoiding the problems of uneven load distribution. Comparisons of this approach with the presented pipeline implementation will bring interesting results.

Acknowledgement

This work is partially sponsored by the Austrian "Ministry for Science and Research" (BMWF), project ACPC, subproject PARAGRAPH.

References

1. R. Drebin, L. Carpenter, P. Hanrahan: Volume Rendering. Computer Graphics, Vol. 22, No. 4, 1988, pp.65-74

2. C. Upson: The V-Buffer: Visible Volume Rendering. Computer Graphics, Vol. 22, No. 4, 1990, pp.59-64

3. R. Bakalash, A. Kaufman, R. Pacheco, H. Pfister: An Extended Volume Visualization System for Arbitrary Parallel Projection. Seventh Workshop on Graphics Hardware, Eurographics Technical Report Series, EG92 HW, 1992, pp.64-69

4. L. Westover: Interactive Volume Rendering. In: Proceedings of the Chapel Hill Workshop on Volume Visualization, Chapel Hill, NC, May 1989, pp.9-16

5. B. Corrie, P. Mackerras: Parallel Volume Rendering and Data Coherence on the Fujitsu AP1000. Technical Report TR-CS-92-11, Australian National University, August 1992 (available via ftp)

6. J. Challinger: Parallel Volume Rendering on a Shared Memory Multiprocessor. Technical Report UCSC-CRL-91-23, Board of Studies in Computer and Information Sciences, University of California at Santa Cruz, March 1992

7. K.H. Höhne, R. Bernstein: Shading 3D-Images from CT Using Gray-Level Gradients. IEEE Transactions on Medical Imaging, Vol. MI-5, No. 1, March 1986

8. L. Westover: Footprint Evaluation for Volume Rendering. Computer Graphics, Vol.24, No.4, 1990, pp.367-376

9. M. Levoy: Display of Surfaces from Volume Data. IEEE Computer Graphics and Applications, Vol. 8, No. 3, 1988, pp. 29-37

10. K.H. Höhne, M. Bomans, A. Pommert, M. Riemer, U. Tiede, G. Wiebecke: Rendering Tomographic Voluma Data: Adequacy of Methods for Different Modalities and Organs. In: K.H. Höhne, H. Fuchs, S.M. Pizer (eds.): 3D Imaging in Medicine, Algorithms, Systems, Applications. Springer Verlag Press, 1990

11. M. P. Garrity: Raytracing Irregular Volume Data. Comuter Graphics, ACM, Vol.24, No.5, 1990, pp.35-40

12. T.S. Yoo, U. Neumann, H. Fuchs, St.M. Pizer, T. Cullip, J. Rhoades, R. Whitaker: Direct Visualization of Volume Data. IEEE Computer Graphics and Applications, IEEE, 1992, pp.63-71

13. nCUBE 2 Programmer's Guide. nCUBE Corp., California

14. nCUBE 2 Programmer's Reference Manual. nCUBE Corp, California

Data Parallel Programming: The Promises and Limitations of High Performance Fortran

Piyush Mehrotra

ICASE, Nasa Langley Research Center, Hampton, USA

Abstract. Exploiting the full potential of parallel architectures requires a cooperative effort between the user and thelanguage system. There is a clear a trade-off between the amount of information the user has to provide and the amount of effort the compiler has to expend to generate optimal code. At one end of the spectrum are message passing languages where the user has full control and has to provide all the details while the compiler effort is minimal. At the other end of the spectrum is sequential languages where the compiler has the full responsibility for extracting the parallelism. For the past few years, we have been exploring median solutions, such as Kali and Vienna Fortran, which provide a fairly high level environment for distributed memory machines while giving the user some control over the placement of data and computation. These efforts have been very influential in the design of High Performance Fortran (HPF), an international effort to build a set of standard extensions for exploiting a wide variety of parallel architectures.

The common approach in these languages is to provide language constructs or directives which allow the user to carefully control the distribution of data across the memories of the target machine. However, the computation code is written using a global name space with no explicit message passing statements. It is then the compiler's responsibility to analyze the a distribution annotations and generate parallel code inserting communication statements where required by the computation. Thus, the user can focus on high-level algorithmic issues while allowing the software to deal with the complex low-level details.

Initial experience with HPF (and related languages) has shown that it provides excellent support for simple data parallel algorithms. However, it is clear that there are a number of scientific codes for which HPF may not be adequate. In particular, HPF may not have enough expressive power to provide all the information needed by the compiler to generate the most optimal code. Examples include, codes using block-structured and unstructured grids, adaptive computations and multi-disciplinary applications which exhibit multiple types of parallelism.

In this talk, we will provide a short overview of HPF and its capabilities. We will then discuss its limitations giving examples of codes for which HPF may not be adequate. We will also explore some extensions of HPF which provide support for such codes.

Foundations of Practical Parallel Programming Languages

Lawrence Snyder

University of Washington, Seattle WA 98195, USA

Abstract. A practical formulation of parallel programming languages is presented based on an analogy with sequential programming languages. The essential components are a machine model, a programming model and a programming language. For the parallel case, the CTA is used as the machine model, Phase Abstractions are used as the programming model, and the Orca family of languages are used to illustrate language design.

1 Introduction

In an effort to produce parallel programming facilities in which one can write efficient, portable and scalable parallel programs, it is reasonable to proceed by analogy with sequential computing. The idea is not to follow some Procrustean process of forcing sequential languages into service, but rather to identify the principles underlying its success and then to develop parallel analogues. This paper gives an overview of the approach, emphasizing the underlying principles and their analogues in sequential computing.

Scientific computing in the *sequential* context relies on three components:

> von Neumann machine model
> imperative-procedural programming model
> languages such as Fortran, C, Pascal, etc.

These components were not originally created to explain sequential scientific computing. Rather, they are recognizable in important roles when one "reverse engineers" sequential scientific computing. Consider each component in turn.

The role played by the machine model, or type architecture [16], is critical. From the programmer's viewpoint, the machine model provides an accurate enough description of the object machine's behavior to estimate how a program will function. Such estimates are essential to evaluating the performance of different programming alternatives. For example, is sequential or binary search preferred when probing n sorted items? The unit-cost memory of the von Neumann model, which is not literally achieved in contemporary machines [5], of course, but which is usually an accurate approximation, implies binary search. And indeed, except for tiny values of n, binary search performs better when the data is physically present in the computer's memory. The machine model, therefore, abstracts away the irrelevant details of physical machines while retaining the approximate truth. As a result, the specific object architecture need not be of concern and it can change.

The imperative-procedural programming model modestly extends the von Neumann machine model, providing symbolic naming, scoping, procedures with recursion, parameter evaluation, and other useful programming features. The essential benefit of the model is that it transparently enhances the raw machine model with facilities that can be efficiently compiled, and so can provide convenience without substantial overhead. The "transparency" allows programmers still to "see" the von Neumann machine beneath, and to estimate reliably how expensive the compiled facilities are to use. For example, knowing how by-reference parameters are implemented allows the programmer to know that parameter references are only trivially more expensive than local variable references. Efficient compilation and transparency are essential if the programmer is to benefit from programming abstractions without having the machine model "covered up."

Fortran, C or Pascal, are languages that directly implement the imperative-procedural programming model. The transparency and simplicity of the programming model and the modest programming facilities provided make them easy for programmers to learn. Moreover, because they are independent of most machine specifics, they can be made widely available. This means not only that the programming skills acquired by users continue to be useful for a long time, but more importantly, good compilers are potentially available for virtually all sequential machines. Programs are widely portable as a result.

To close the loop, the near universal knowledge of Fortran, C, etc. by scientists, and the portability of these programs justifies a large and continuing investment by users in more programs. This enlarges an installed software base that is already enormous. Machine designers are reluctant to ignore this code when developing their next machine. This encourages machine designs that preserve the essential assumptions of the von Neumann model, and thus the programming model, and thus the language. The feedback assures the success of the approach.

By analogy to sequential computing, then, parallel scientific computing requires a machine model, a programming model founded on it, and a language implementing the programming model, all targeted to parallel computers. The machine model to be presented here will be the CTA type architecture, the programming model will be the Phase Abstractions programming model and the language will be Orca C.

	Sequential	Parallel
machine model	von Neumann	CTA
programming model	imperative procedural	phase abstractions
language	Fortran, C	Orca Fortran, Orca C

The material on the models has been presented before in fragmentary form. The task for this paper is to present it in a unified form as the foundation of the Orca C programming language.

2   A Parallel Machine Model

The parallel machine to be described is a hypothetical computer, or *type architecture* [16], idealizing the essential features of MIMD parallel computers. Just as the von Neumann model does not exactly describe sequential computers, the parallel type architecture need not exactly describe parallel computers. But it must be reasonably accurate or it will be useless to programmers in estimating the costs of their computations. In particular, the PRAM is not a suitable model because it does not accurately capture the costs of phenomena such as nonlocal memory references [3]. Because parallel computers are much more disparate than sequential machines, the "distance" between the CTA and some parallel computers will be greater than one expects in the sequential case. Nevertheless, it should be obvious how a given MIMD computer would efficiently implement the CTA model of computation. See section IV of Siegel et al. [15] for further benefits of "conceptual models."

Postulate a parallel computer, called the CTA^1, formed from a collection of P von Neumann machines, called *processors*. See Fig.1. Since these are sequential computers, they each have a fixed quantity of random access memory, called the *local memory*, and each has a program counter. This latter requirement implies that the CTA is a MIMD computer in Flynn's taxonomy. The local memory can store both instructions and data. The processors execute asynchronously. There is no "global" memory. It is possible to overlay a global addressing structure for referencing the local memories, but it is a convenience that does not change the local/nonlocal memory reference costs described below.

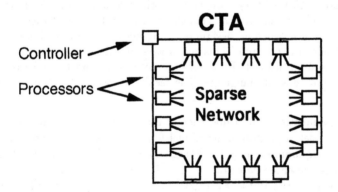

Fig. 1. CTA machine model

The processors are connected by a communication structure of unspecified, but sparse topology, called the *network*. The von Neumann processors are *nodes* in the topology. The node connection is via a communication coprocessor that contains a router, and "sparse" is used in a graph-theoretic sense to mean no

---

[1] Mnemonic for candidate type architecture [16].

more than log P node degree, i.e. no node is directly connected to more than log P other nodes.[2] Thus, the topology could be a mesh, a binary hypercube, shuffle exchange, indirect network or many others. The topology is not specified both because it changes from machine to machine and thus should not be relied upon to have any specific characteristics, and because there is as yet no agreement among architects as to the ideal communication structure [1]. However, the sparseness condition excludes unscalable alternatives such as the complete graph.

The connections establish *channels* over which *messages* are sent between processors. The latency of a message, L, is the time to transmit it and is large compared to a local memory access. The bandwidth, i.e. the number of words that can be transmitted to or from a processor per unit time, is small. It is at least limited by log P, but could be smaller since processors are often connected to the network by a single channel. Moreover, for messages beyond a certain size, transmission time is proportional to the size of the message. The quantities "large" and "small" are technology dependent, machine specific and vary widely. Though for a particular MIMD machine approximating the CTA it is possible to define these terms quantitatively, it is sufficient for the model to be qualitative. Specifically, the CTA's communication characteristics imply that execution referencing only local memory is fast, but sending information between processors is slow. This fact is intended to place a high premium on locality, which is beneficial even when the physical machine has shared memory [10, 14].

In addition to the processors, the CTA is postulated to contain another von Neumann machine, called the *controller*, connected to all of the processors via a "narrow" channel. This assists in implementing global activities, including barrier synchronization, broadcast of a limited amount of information, direct interrogation of the processors' memories, etc. The meaning of the term "narrow" is not easily quantified because the controller must support diverse tasks, but the intent is that it be implemented efficiently, and it be used only for control, not general computation. For example, an "AND-line" connecting all of the processors might assist in implementing barrier synchronization. Or a word-wide bus connecting all of the processors could implement the broadcast and interrogation.

Recall that the machine model provides an approximate description of execution engine to be used by the programmer to make performance estimates. What does the CTA say about the costs of parallel computation? To mention a few: Computations maximizing references to local memory will be more efficient than computations involving much nonlocal memory reference. The shortest time in which one processor could receive data from all others is at best proportional to P/log P, because of the sparseness condition, though it could well take more if the machine has a high diameter or the processor's connection to the network is narrower. However, data from one processor could be broadcast to all others

---

[2] The original CTA requires the degree to be bounded by a constant [16], which is an obvious requirement in the limit. There seems to be little harm in most cases in permitting the log P degree since the diameter of the network is at least that large.

quickly, using the controller. Barrier synchronization is reasonably fast and not directly related to network topology.

How faithfully does the CTA model contemporary MIMD computers? Every feature of the CTA has been implemented in some recent MIMD machines with cost characteristics as indicated. Moreover, most MIMD machines implement the features directly or can simulate them reasonably cheaply. Thus, like the von Neumann machine, the CTA captures a few crucial behavioral features – for example, the 1:L ratio between local and nonlocal memory reference time – while abstracting away most other characteristics.

3   A Parallel Programming Model

The Phase Abstractions programming model [17, 7, 2, 18] provides abstractions for formulating parallel algorithms that extend the capabilities of the CTA. It provides a modest enhancement of the CTA's capabilities analogously to the way the imperative-procedural programming model enhances the von Neumann machine model. Moreover, like the imperative-procedural model, Phase Abstractions presents a straightforward compilation setting that should lead to efficient compiled code for languages implementing it. The same benefits – transparency and efficiency – are expected to accrue to programs written in those languages.

The term "phase abstractions" refers to two types of programming constructs: the *XYZ programming levels* and *ensembles*. In essence, the XYZ programming levels partition the instructions of the program according to the roles they play in the computation. Ensembles are simply a specification mechanism for parallel algorithms. After the abstractions are introduced, an example will be presented.

3.1   The XYZ Programming Levels

A parallel computation can be structured by the roles its instructions play [17]. Three levels of structure are recognized, the process, phase and problem levels:

Process X level – the composition of instructions to be executed on a processor.

Phase Y level – the composition of processes to implement a parallel algorithm.

Problem Z level – the composition of phases to solve a user's application.

This decomposition allows programmers to use the standard computational tools of composition, hierarchical structuring, stepwise refinement, etc. in developing a parallel code. For example, viewed in the ZYX order, the computation is presented in a top down manner. Perhaps more importantly, this structuring gives the compiler valuable information needed for efficient compilation.

Processes X level describe computation analogously to the way procedures describe computation in the imperative-procedural model: Processes come into existence by invocations from the phase level that are external to themselves; though not recursive in the current formulation, they could be. Processes have sequential control flow semantics and generally process data that is external to themselves. Though sequential semantics are specified, it is assumed that standard fine-grain parallel compilation techniques VLIW, multi-threaded, etc. could be used if the target machine provides such capabilities. However, this is not intended as the source of the program's parallelism. The *scalable parallelism* is expressed in the phase level.

Phases Y level correspond to our informal notion of a parallel algorithm. They are the composition of process instances to perform an identifiable unit of concurrent computation. For example, the FFT computation might be expressed as a phase. By virtue of this composition in which process instances connect to other process instances with which they communicate, a phase has a characteristic graph, e.g. the butterfly for the FFT. A fundamental property of phases is they have variable size based on the number of process instances vertices in the graph and thus they define varying amounts of logical concurrency. Phases are defined using ensembles, as described in the next section.

The Problem or Z level controls how the phases are to be executed to realize the intended computation. In its simplest form, phase invocation proceeds sequentially with each phase "fully utilizing" the parallel machine. There is a logical barrier synchronization after each phase invocation, though in practice these are only occasionally needed and so are generally bypassed. The Problem level often encapsulates the solution methodology as the user sees it, e.g. an iterative approximation will typically be given by Z code that is a `while` loop with phase invocations in the body.

Notice the correlation between the Phase Abstraction programming model and the CTA machine model.

CTA Structure	Phase Abstraction
Processor	Process X
Parallel Engine	Phase Y
Controller	Problem Level Z

The Process level defines the code that executes on the processors and the Problem level logically defines the code that executes on the controller. The Phase level defines the concurrent execution of multiple processes and the characteristic graph specifies the communication topology that is logically implemented by the sparse network. In this way Phase Abstractions provide a thin layer of enhancement above the CTA machine model.

Standard programming concepts support the process and problem levels. That is, these levels can be expressed using standard features of the imperative-procedural model of sequential computation. Thus, one expects to use data structures, procedures, etc. when defining a process. Similarly, standard control structures, etc. are used in specifying the problem level, though standard procedure invocation is reinterpreted as phase invocation. The phase level, however, is the fundamentally different phenomenon of parallel computation and as such requires language concepts not needed in the imperative-procedural model. The requisite concepts are provided by ensembles.

3.2 The Ensemble Abstractions

Ensembles are concepts created to specify parallel algorithms. As such, they extend the usual programming repertoire developed for sequential computing.

An *ensemble* is a set with a partitioning. A partition of an ensemble is called a *section*. Ensembles are used in specifying phases, for which three kinds are required. There are other applications for ensembles not discussed here. The phase-defining ensemble varieties are:

> data ensemble – a data structure with a partitioning.
> code ensemble – a set of process instances with a partitioning.
> port ensemble – a graph with a vertex set partitioning.

Note that the set usually has some structure. The partitioning is critical to supporting the distributed structure of the CTA machine to which Phases Abstractions are targeted.

Data ensembles are the parallel analogue of sequential data structures. The data structure being partitioned to form the data ensemble is viewed globally and represents some component of the problem's global data space. For example, a row × col array A might be partitioned into an r × c array of contiguous subarrays. See Fig.2. The array partitionings, so common in current parallel programming research, are instances of data ensembles, though the ensemble concept applies to any data structure, not just arrays, making it more general.

a11 a12 a13 a14 a15 a16	a11 a12 a13 a14 a15 a16	a11 a12 a13 a14 a15 a16
a21 a22 a23 a24 a25 a26	a21 a22 a23 a24 a25 a26	a21 a22 a23 a24 a25 a26
a31 a32 a33 a34 a35 a36	a31 a32 a33 a34 a35 a36	a31 a32 a33 a34 a35 a36
a41 a42 a43 a44 a45 a56	a41 a42 a43 a44 a45 a46	a41 a42 a43 a44 a45 a46
a51 a52 a53 a54 a55 a56	a51 a52 a53 a54 a55 a56	a51 a52 a53 a54 a55 a56
a61 a62 a63 a64 a65 a66	a61 a62 a63 a64 a65 a66	a61 a62 a63 a64 a65 a66

Fig. 2. A row × col array A *left* and two ensembles created from it: A 2D section array r=2, c=3 of contiguous blocks *center* and a section array that could be defined either as a 1D array of n sections n=6 or a degenerate 2D array r=1, c=6 *right*.

Code ensembles are formed by partitioning a multi set of process instances. Since several different kinds of processes can be used, code ensembles support MIMD computation. If all process instances are the same, the computation is SPMD, single program, multiple data. SIMD computation is realized by a mechanism described below. Though the process instances could have a complex structure expressing such things as control dependence among different threads [7], the present formulation assumes the instances are unstructured, with one process per section.

Port ensembles specify the characteristic communication structure of the parallel algorithm, which is generally induced by the aggregate data dependencies of the phase. They are given as a partitioning of a scalable graph, where the nodes represent process instances and the edges represent communication channels for message exchange. Each section contains one vertex in the current formulation, so adjacencies in the graph define adjacencies among the sections.

A phase is defined by specifying one or more data ensembles, a code ensemble and a port ensemble that are conformable.[3] "Conformable" means that the partitionings have the same cardinality and the same naming structure.[4] As a result the ensembles can be placed into one-to-one correspondence, by associating sections with like names. The semantics of the phase are as follows: All process instances begin execution simultaneously and continue to execute asynchronously to completion; each process is applied to the data in the corresponding section s of the data ensemble s ; each process communicates with the processes in sections adjacent to it, as defined by the port ensemble. The phase completes execution when the last of its process instances completes execution.

The multiplicity of concepts introduced so far should be illustrated before proceeding further. Since the concepts are independent of the programming language, they will be illustrated in the next section using pseudocode.

3.3   A Simple Example

The Jacobi iteration is a common computation that makes a particularly easy example of the concepts just introduced [18]. This computation will be expressed more easily later when further concepts are available, but for now consider its formulation using the full capability of Phase Abstractions.

Given an array $A[1..N,1..N]$ of real values, iteratively update A by replacing, in parallel, each element by the average of its four nearest neighbors, where the boundaries are taken to be zero. The problem level specification can either treat the entire computation as a single phase and thus degenerate to the one operation of invoking that phase, or it can treat a single update of the entire array as a phase and iteratively apply it until convergence. Since the latter approach leads to a somewhat more interesting example, it is selected. See Fig.3.

This Z level code, after declaring the variables, reads the initial values into A, and then iterates until convergence. The capitalized names are phases, some of which are library routines, e.g. READ< and probably FINDMAX<, and some of which, e.g., JI< , are user defined using Y level concepts such as ensembles.

JI< , like all phases, is defined from data, code and port ensembles. This information is specified in the region of "other declarations" of the program in Fig.3.

To begin with the data ensemble definition, recall that it is a partitioning of the array A. Since the computation requires the average of the four nearest neighbors, the data reference pattern induces a NEWS communication structure,

---

[3] Note that if multiple communication structures are required for a single phase, they can be composed as graphs and then partitioned into ensembles, so a single port ensemble suffices.

[4] The "same naming structure," which is usually just an index set, is a convenience of the current formulation and can be simplified to "same cardinality"[18].

```
program Jacobi <N:integer, epsilon:real ;
    /* Configuration Goes Here */
    var err: real;
        A array [1..N,1..N] of real;
    /* Other declarations*/
    A := READ<;
    repeat {
            JI<A ;
            err := FINDMAX<A }
    until err < epsilon;
end.
```

Fig. 3. Problem level Z   program for Jacobi iteration in pseudocode.

i.e. to compute a set of points will require communication with neighbors to the north, east, west and south of the set. The array A could be decomposed in a variety of ways, but the choice of dividing it into blocks benefits from the surface-to-volume advantage, i.e. there are fewer edge elements to communicate when the decomposition is squarish. Thus, A will be partitioned, as illustrated in Fig.4, into a 2D array of sections containing rectangular subarrays. The declaration might take the form of

data_ensemble A Block[r,c];

indicating A is partitioned into rc blocks. Notice that even though A may be square, the blocks may not be, depending on the values of r and c, which depend on how many sections are to be created.

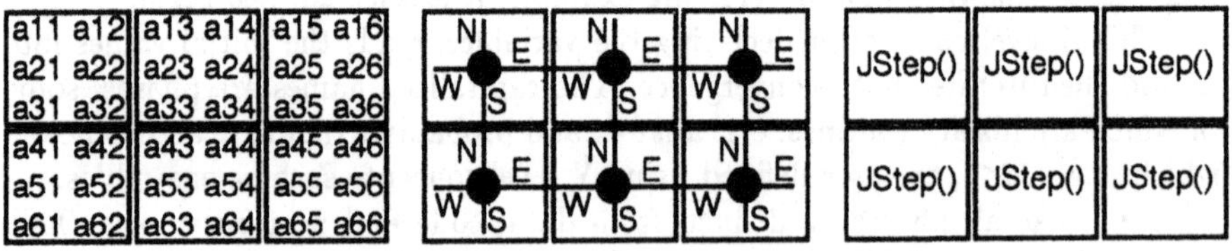

Fig. 4. Illustration of the data, port and code ensembles for the JI phase for a 6 section instance

The NEWS communication structure is specified by the port ensemble, which is simply a scalable mesh graph with one vertex per section. See Fig.4. The vertex represents the process executing in the section, and the adjacencies specify the other processes with which it will communicate. The labelings on the edges incident to a vertex, N, E, W and S, in this case, are called *port names* and they are used by the process corresponding to the vertex to refer to its neighbors. The declaration of the port ensemble might take the form

```
port_ensemble JI = N,E,W,S,
connect <N[i+1,j]=S[i,j], i=1..r-1;j=1..c ,
    <E[i,j] =W[i,j+1],i=1..r; j=1..c-1
```

indicating that each section has the four port names and that they are paired as shown into a mesh. The "dangling" port names, i.e. those incident to only one vertex, are discussed below.

The code ensemble specifies the partitioning of a set of process instances. For the Jacobi iteration instances of only a single process, called JStep< , are needed. That is, this is an SPMD computation. The code ensemble is easily specified, as shown in Fig.4. The declaration might be

```
code_ensemble JI = JStep[r,c];
```

JStep< is a process, that is, an X level programming form. It will compute a step of the Jacobi iteration on its local data the data assigned to its corresponding section in the data ensemble and communicate boundary values to the neighbors as specified by its corresponding section of the port ensemble. The code for the process is shown in Fig.5.

```
process JStep<LocA[1..m,1..n]:real ;
var    LocA array [0..m+1,0..n+1] of real;
        N, E, W, S: port;
    /* value derivative binding here */
begin /* send values to neighbors */
    N <- LocA[1,1:n]; E <- LocA[1:m,n];
    W <- LocA[1:m,1]; S <- LocA[m,1:n];
    /* receive values from neighbors */
    LocA[0,1:n] <- N; LocA[1:m,n+1] <- E;
    LocA[1:m,0] <- W; LocA[m+1,1:n] <- S;
    /* compute step */
    LocA[1:m,1:n] := <LocA[0:m-1,1:n] + LocA[1:m,2:n+1]
                    + LocA[1:m,0:n-1] + LocA[2,m+1,1:n]/4;
end.
```

Fig. 5. The process X level pseudocode for JStep< of the JI phase

As given in the JI invocation in the Jacobi program Fig.3 , the data ensemble is treated as an actual parameter for the LocA formal parameter with the indicated indexing. That is, references to the array section use local rather than global indexes. This indexing positions the data section into the local array which has been declared to be larger by one position on all sides. The extra space is used to cache values from adjacent sections. The send **portname <-id** and receive **id <- portname** statements fill this cache. Finally the averaging is performed. Notice that the use of array referencing : is a simplification in this pseudocode, but it could be an effective way to reduce the overhead of packetizing in the send/receive statements.

The remaining task in specifying the process is to handle the "dangling" edges in the port ensemble, i.e. edges incident to only one vertex in the port ensemble specification. These edges logically refer to the boundarys of the computation, which are to be treated as zero. Accordingly, the dangling edges are bound to *value derivatives*, special functions that behave like communicating neighbors, but which are locally computed. For **JStep**, the value derivative bound to a port is a no-op for sends and it returns zeroes for receive. The specification is given in the process definition at the indicated position; see Fig.5. Possible syntax might be

```
bind N,S = <nil, 0.0[1:n] ;
bind E,W = <nil, 0.0[1:m] ;
```

where the pair specifies the functions to be executed on send and receive. The result is that whenever data is sent to a port bound to a dangling edge it is ignored, and whenever it is received, a vector of zeroes of the proper length is returned.

Finally, the granularity control parameters of the Jacobi program, r and c, are defined on the second line of the program in Fig.3. The general topic of Phase Abstraction parameterization is discussed below. These parameters control the scalable concurrency of the program, i.e. the number and arrangement of sections. Let ProcNo be a keyword giving the number of logical processes.[5] Then the configuration code for the Jacobi program might be

```
var r,c: integer;
begin
    c := ceil<sqrt<ProcNo ;
    r := max<1, floor<ProcNo/c ;
end <r,c :
```

where the parameter list at the end of the block is thought of as parameterizing the program specification that follows it, i.e. the remainder of the Jacobi program.

Logically, the abstract interpretation is as follows. The configuration section is executed by the controller, thereby defining the configuration parameter list. It then executes the Z level logic of the program, performing control operations locally and invoking phases that execute on the parallel engine. One logical processor is assigned to each section. The ensembles of a phase, which are required

---

[5] The assumption is that ProcNo can be controlled externally to the program, e.g. as a command line parameter, which defaults to P, the number of processors on the machine. Assigning ProcNo values larger than P allows sections processes to be multiplexed; using smaller values underutilizes processors.

to have the same number of sections, provide to each section data, code and communication connections. The communication network of the CTA is logically the port ensemble during a phase execution. The logical processors execute the process code to completion, and when all sections are completed, the phase is complete.

The SIMPLE computation [11] provides a more complex application of phase abstractions and more complete explanations.

4 Programming Languages

The Phase Abstractions programming model covered in the previous section can be implemented in various programming language instantiations. One particular instance is the Orca family of languages, discussed below, but others are possible. In this section, a brief overview of the Orca family of languages will be provided to illustrate the third component of the machine model, programming model, programming language trichotomy. Full details are not necessary for the subsequent discussion.

To understand how Phase Abstractions have been implemented in Orca languages, consider the relationship between the three programming levels and sequential programming:

Process or X level – essentially programming of a sequential processor; standard sequential languages, properly extended, can suffice.

Phase or Y level – specifies the ensembles of a parallel algorithm; no programming structures for such specification exist in sequential languages.

Problem or Z level – essentially control intensive programming with phase invocation; extensions to standard sequential languages suffice, since it is the controller that is logically being programmed.

Thus, languages implementing Phase Abstractions can draw extensively from existing sequential languages. It is possible to amalgamate the three levels into one single extended sequential language, but maintaining the distinctions of the three levels greatly assists the compiler. Accordingly, keeping the three levels separate has been a design goal. A second design goal has been to enable the reuse of code from existing programs, where possible.

In Orca Λ an extended version of a standard sequential language Λ is used for X level programming. For example, Orca C [12] extends C with send/receive primitives, port specifications and value derivative bindings, as well as a means of interfacing to the local portion of the data ensemble. Orca Fortran extends Fortran analogously. By using an existing sequential language for the X level, portions of existing programs written in that language may be usable with only minor modification. The whole original program is not usable, of course, since it is sequential and Orca is explicitly parallel. However, it is often the case that the code of a process closely parallels that of a portion of the sequential program, especially in the "physics" portion, i.e. the floating point portions of the computation. The logical basis for this observation is that when the concurrency reduces to P=1, there is but one process and the computation is sequential. It is this "physics" code that could be reused with minor modification.

It would also be possible in principle for Orca Λ to use an extended version of Λ as the Z level language too, but this has not been done. The extensions are more substantial, as explained below, and the chances of using significant portions of an existing program are negligible. Rather, the Z level language is a new language designed with no consideration of making it compatible with an existing language, though it is in the style of the Modula languages. The benefit of using a single Z level language for every Orca Λ language is that it presents a standard interface and limits the distinctions only to the X level. Eventually, the distinctions should be removed and processes written in the Orca extensions of different sequential languages can be mixed.

An Orca program is logically viewed as a Z level code body with the Y level treated as a specification of the phases used in the Z level, and the X level treated as a specification of processes used in the Y level code ensemble. The program, therefore, has the following structure:

```
program <name> <parameter list>;
    <configuration section>
    <configuration parameter list>:
    <data structure declarations>;
    <data ensemble specifications>;    - - Y level
    <port ensemble specifications>;    - - Y level
    <code ensemble specifications>;    - - Y level
    <phase declarations>;              - - Y level
    <process definitions>;             - - X level
begin <Z level code> end.              - - Z level
```

The order of the specifications between the <configuration parameter list> and the **begin** is arbitrary, though the one given seems natural.

The <configuration section> is an essential feature of Orca programming languages. In it the programmer defines how the program is to be structured based on parameters describing the prevailing computational situation. Some parameters will be explicit, say from the command line or read in from a file. Examples include the size of data sets, characteristics of the data, etc. Other parameters will be implicit and may be provided by key words. Examples include the number of physical processors, level of processor multiplexing, number of vector registers, etc. The goal of the <configuration section> is to define the parameters of the <configuration parameter list> which in turn will determine the structure of the program. In the Jacobi example above, the implicit parameter ProcNo was used for the amount of logical concurrency, and the <configuration section> balanced r and c such that $rc \leq$ ProcNo. In general, more sophisticated configuration sections are to be expected.

The importance of the <configuration section> derives from the goal of portability and scalability, and it is embodied in the fact that a single parallel program generally does not fit all cases. Sometimes coarse grain is desirable;

other times medium or fine grain is preferable. A multitude of characteristics besides grain size can influence which program structure is best. The resulting programs, though often quite different, are usually instances of the same underlying logic. In view of the diversity of variants, it seems unlikely that a compiler will determine them automatically [2]. On the other hand, the programmer should not be embedding "if defs" or other case analysis in the logic of the program to respond to these different conditions, since this is poor software design and can lead to poor performance. Thus, in the Orca languages the programmer writes a parameterized program that covers a range of alternatives. The proper instances can then be produced by setting the parameters rather than modifying the logic of the program. Such external control of the structure of the program allows users to tune the program without knowing details of its logic. Furthermore, in case the original programmer did not anticipate all of the alternatives, as is likely, another programmer can encapsulate the modifications in terms of more parameters and a more sophisticated <configuration section>.

The Orca languages presently limit the data structures to statically declared arrays. This is sufficient for a substantial number of applications. The generalization to other data structures is direct, however, and is anticipated.

Conceptually, Phase Abstractions require the programmer to write a phase definition for every part of a parallel computation, since a phase expresses the scalable parallelism. Many aspects of a parallel computation can be expressed as phases in a simple and natural way. Two examples are standardized parallel abstractions, and data parallel computations.

Standardized parallel abstractions include such operations as global reduction operations, scans, data motion operations such as matrix transpose, etc. The **FINDMAX<** phase of the Jacobi computation in Fig.3 is an instance. It has been expressed as a "library call" in the pseudocode. This is often done since these parallel primitives benefit from implementations customized to a parallel machine. But from the compiler's point of view, library calls are usually treated as "black boxes." Orca supports the primitive operations as language constructs so that they can be incorporated into sophisticated code optimizations.

Data parallel constructs, such as $A := A + B - C$ where the variables are arrays and the operators apply elementwise, are widely appreciated as convenient facilities for expressing certain parallel computations. In the context of Phase Abstractions data parallel constructs can be viewed as tiny, compiler-produced phases in which a code segment is generated in each section to perform the indicated operations on the local section of data. Orca provides data parallel operations using this approach. In addition to the elementwise operations, shift operations are provided for array offset references. Using these facilities the **JI** phase can be easily written in two Z level lines, the first to initialize the boundary,

```
[North of R],[East of R],[West of R],[South of R] A:=0;
```

and the second in the loop to perform the computation:

```
[R] A:= <A@North + A@East + A@West + A@South /4;
```

where R is an index set [1..N,1..N] and A is declared [0..N+1,0..N+1][13].

The availability of such facilities greatly reduces the number of explicit phases that a programmer defines. Generally, explicit phase definitions will be needed only when complex MIMD concurrency is essential.

The final aspect of the Orca languages is the runtime virtual machine. Conceptually the programmer's Z level code directs the controller to invoke the Y level phases that execute on the parallel engine. An implementation for such a literal interpretation of Phase Abstractions might be suitable for a machine with a controller well integrated with the parallel engine, but it is not necessary. In the Orca languages, the Z level code is replicated on all of the processors. Duplicate copies of variables that are local to the controller, e.g. **err** in the Jacobi program, are kept in each processor. Assignments to these variables, e.g. the assignment of the result of **FINDMAX**, are broadcast so each processor has a current copy. The controller's computations are thus repeated on each processor. In this scheme, phases within a section reduce essentially to a procedure call. The local runtime virtual machine is whatever is suitable for the Λ language; for example Orca C simply uses the C runtime environment.

5 Discussion

An approach to parallel computation analogous to sequential computation has been outlined, using the CTA as the machine model, Phase Abstractions as the programming model and the Orca family as instances of programming languages. The consequences of pursuing this approach are now to be considered.

Evidence of Portability. Although a thorough study of the properties of this tripartite approach must await the completion of an Orca compiler, preliminary measurements of its portability have been gathered using the SIMPLE code [11]. SIMPLE is a much studied computational fluid dynamics benchmark developed at Livermore National Labs [6]. It has been written in a Phase Abstractions pseudocode and hand translated[6] to five diverse MIMD platforms: Sequent Symmetry, BBN Butterfly, Intel iPSC/2, nCUBE/7 and a simulated Transputer-based array machine. The results showed speedup for P processors of at least P/2 on all experiments on all machines [11]. A related study limited to shared memory machines was similarly successful [14]. These results support the claim of machine independence.

Granularity Control. The Phase Abstractions/Orca approach presented here is unique among parallel programming models and languages in providing control over process granularity and other essential characteristics of a parallel computation. Orca programs are logically meta-codes that can be instantiated to have many fine grain processes, or a few coarse grain processes, or some number of intermediate grain processes. Other adaptations are also possible: For example, one can convert a properly written binary tree code into one based on the

---

[6] The translation was simple, involving primarily macrosubstitution and interfacing to machine specific library routines, i.e. no complex compilation technology was presumed.

row/column properties of a mesh simply by providing a different communication topology; no program text need be modified [8]. It is evident both that such flexibility is essential if programs are to be portable and scalable, and that such flexibility cannot be achieved simply by compilation technology.

To be sure, granularity and other types of control rely on explicit consideration by the programmer of how the computation should change in response to changes in the computational environment. But the programming model provides key enabling mechanisms to make these properties malleable in a natural and straightforward way. In particular, an XYZ/ensembles program expresses the computation so that logical concurrency, granularity, communication topology, boundary conditions, etc. are all exposed. Thus, they can be easily changed parametrically. For example, when the programmer has explicitly stated the boundary conditions, it is then a simple matter for the compiler to provide for them when the program restructuring introduces them; see Fig.3, where reducing r=1 causes processes to have both north and south boundaries. The result is a versatile program that can be compiler customized to a spectrum of situations.

Such versatility seems essential if a single code is to adapt to the idiosyncrasies of different platforms, or the demands of scaling. The variations are implemented in the <configuration section> by changing the <configuration parameters>. Though a programmer may not initially anticipate all possible variations, subsequent revisions can be cleanly incorporated into the code by adding more parameters. In a sense the <configuration section> generalizes the concept of machine specific tuning that has always been a characteristic of high performance computing.

Comparative Properties. As already mentioned the CTA has a realism that the PRAM does not have, enabling the programmer to make practical decisions regarding program performance [3]. However, it is much more abstract than any physical machine, leaving most details implied or unexpressed. As mentioned in the introduction, a machine model must be descriptive enough to provide useful guidance on essential points, and it must be silent on everything else. Whether this is the correct balance between under-specification and over-specification will only become clear through extensive use.

Levels of Abstraction. The CTA employs "message passing" as the primitive communication mechanism of a parallel machine. This may equate to memory reference in a shared memory machine, since the message passing simply encapsulates the important fact of parallel computers that memory is physically distributed.

Message passing is retained in the Phase Abstractions as a means of transparently retaining the local/nonlocal memory distinction present in the CTA. The Phase Abstractions programming model is not a so-called "message passing" model, however, precisely because it provides global abstractions, for example data ensembles. These abstractions allow the programmer to view the computation globally rather than as a collection of unrelated concurrent processes. To emphasize this point, the data parallel subset of Orca C is a complete language founded on Phase Abstractions with arrays, primitive operations such as reduction, scan, shifts, elementwise data parallel operations, etc., but it does not contain **send** or **receive** [13]. Explicit message passing is not possible. Data communication is implemented implicitly in other language constructs, such as shift and reduce. The concept of message passing is essential to founding the models and languages in reality, but the programming language can hide it completely.

Further, it is possible to place a different set of abstractions on the CTA or to extend the Phase Abstractions with other features. The only condition is that the new abstractions' implementations be explained in terms of CTA operations, such as send and receive, with costs that are realistic with respect to the CTA. For example, by working out the details of a CTA-based implementation of distributed list processing, futures, etc. a machine independent MultiLisp-like language [9] could be formulated. The definition tells the programmer how expensive various operations are, and thus provides a guide for writing efficient programs. Additionally, the definition could serve as the basis for an implementation on a physical parallel machine.

Finally, it is possible to implement Phase Abstractions using languages other than the Orca languages.

Generality of Phase Abstractions. The concepts embodied in Phase Abstractions provide a firm foundation for solving parallel programming problems. As an example, consider the problem of supporting irregular data decompositions which, though static, are not known until runtime [19, 20]. The Orca C implementation of Phase Abstractions does not provide any specific support for this problem, but one can be imagined.

Postulate a program that produces an irregular data decomposition and executes as the first step of a numerical simulation. If the decomposition algorithm is sequential, it is conceptually executed by the controller, and if it is parallel it is treated simply as a phase.

The output of this decomposition step is the data ensemble for the main computation. In addition, the assignment of the data ensemble sections of this "irregular mesh" to processors induces the port ensemble. This is the graph whose vertices are the regions of the irregular mesh assigned to each processor, and whose edges are the induced adjacencies. Thus, two of the three constituents of a phase – the data and port ensembles – are not constructed until runtime. Nevertheless, the program can be written treating them as abstractions.

The data and port ensembles not only provide the conceptual basis for incorporating runtime decomposition into a parallel program, they provide standard compiler supported facilities. For example, the programmer need not build a runtime data structure to record the neighbors of a region of the "irregular mesh" and maintain it. Rather port vectors[7] are used in the program and instantiated by the system when the port ensemble is defined. With this approach comes the potential for automatic compiler supported caching of values from adjacent processes.

Unification of MIMD, SPMD and SIMD. The CTA is an MIMD machine

---

[7] A port vector is an indexed set of port names. If E[1..d] is a port vector, the value of d, the degree, and the contents are bound at runtime.

model and Phase Abstractions preserve the MIMD quality in the programming model. But the SPMD and SIMD models are seen to be important special cases. Specifically, when the code ensemble contains instances of more than one process, the execution is MIMD. When the code ensemble contains instances of a single nontrivial process, i.e. one with significant control flow, the model reduces to SPMD. When the process instances are all the same "straightline code," as when only the data parallel subset of Orca C is being used, then the implied barrier synchronization after each phase causes the model to reduce to SIMD.

The key point about the unification of the models is that, contrary to the seemingly widespread view that one model must be best or that programming languages can provide only a single model, Orca provides all three in a seamless manner. Moreover, our preliminary experience with Orca indicates that all but the most trivial programs will use all three models: The SIMD model is used for large quantities of routine computation having few dependencies; SPMD is used for most cases; MIMD is needed only when there is significant specialization among the concurrently executing processes.

6   Summary

Motivated by analogy with sequential computation, an approach to parallel computation founded on a machine model, a programming model and a programming language has been described. Though these three – the CTA machine model, the Phase Abstractions programming model, and the Orca C programming language – "reduce" to their sequential counterparts when there is but one processor, they are fundamentally parallel. Preliminary evidence has been cited indicating that this strategy produces high performance, portable programs.

Key properties of the triad are as follows:

The CTA is a simple machine model that distills the essential characteristics of physical parallel machines. It recognizes a performance difference between local and nonlocal memory reference, it does not specify the communication topology, although it mentions important constraints on it, and it promotes the use of certain global operations through the inclusion of a controller. The expectation is that the CTA specifies parallel computers at a level of detail analogous to the von Neumann machine's specification of sequential computers.

Phase Abstractions transparently extend the capability of the CTA. They provide the programmer with a single, global view of the computation while at the same time supporting its distributed nature with ensembles. Performance critical features are exposed in the Phase Abstractions, including locality, scalable concurrency, granularity, communication requirements, etc. This exposure should enable compilers to produce efficient object code for MIMD machines, due to the close correspondence with the machine model.

The Orca family of languages represents one approach to implementing the Phase Abstractions programming model. It provides direct support for ensembles and the XYZ programming levels. These "full MIMD" computational facilities are augmented with direct compiler support for data parallel operations as well as standard parallel constructs such as scan and reduction. In this way the Orca languages unify the SIMD, SPMD and MIMD models. Finally, the <configuration section> provides direct support for parameterizing such things as granularity, boundary conditions, etc.

Acknowledgments

This research spans many years, during which time numerous colleagues have critiqued the work and contributed to its advancement. I am grateful for the chance to work with such thoughtful scientists. Special thanks go to Gail Alverson, Bill Griswold, and David Notkin with whom the Phase Abstractions were developed. Also, Calvin Lin and Ton Ngo have been instrumental in testing these ideas experimentally as well as furthering the concepts; both contributions are greatly appreciated. Finally, the work presented has largely been funded by the Office of Naval Research under grant N00014-89-J-1007, and more recently by ARPA grant N00014-92-J-1824.

References

1. Agarwal, A.: Units on interconnection network performance. *IEEE Transactions on Parallel and Distributed Systems,* 2 4 :398–412, 1991.
2. Alverson, G.A., Griswold, W.G., Notkin, D., Snyder, L.: A Flexible Communication Abstraction for Nonshared Memory Parallel Computing. *Proceedings of Supercomputing 90,* pp. 584–593, 1990.
3. Anderson, R.J., Snyder, L.: A Comparison of Shared and Nonshared Memory Models of Parallel Computation. *Proceedings of IEEE,* 79 4 :480–487, 1991.
4. Bolding, K., Konstantinidou, S.: On the Comparison of Hypercubes and Torus Networks. *Proceedings of the International Conference on Parallel Processing,* 1992.
5. Carter, L.: The RAM Model and the Performance Programmer. Technical Report RC 16319, IBM Watson Research Labs, 1990.
6. Crowley, Hendrickson, Luby: Livermore SIMPLE program. 1978
7. Griswold W.G., Harrison, G.A., Notkin, D., Snyder, L.: Scalable Abstractions for Parallel Programming. *Proceedings of the Fifth Distributed Memory Computer Conference,* IEEE pp. 1008–1016, 1990.
8. Griswold, W.G., Harrison, G.A., Notkin, D., Snyder, L.: How Port Ensembles Aid the Efficient Retargeting of Reduction Algorithms. *Proceedings of the International Conference on Parallel Processing,* Vol. II pp. 286–287, 1990.
9. Halstead, R.H. Jr.: Multilisp: A Language for Concurrent Symbolic Computation. *ACM Transactions on Programming Languages and Systems,* 7 4 :501–538, 1985.
10. Lin, C., Snyder, L.: A Comparison of Programming Models for Shared Memory Multiprocessors. *Proceedings of the International Conference on Parallel Processing,* Penn State Vol. II, pp. 163–170, 1990.
11. Lin, C., Snyder, L.: A Portable Implementation of SIMPLE. *International Journal of Parallel Programming,* 20 5 :363–401, 1991.
12. Lin, C., Snyder, L.: Data Ensembles in Orca C. In eds. , *Languages and Compilers for Parallel Computing,* MIT Press, 1993 to appear .

13. Lin, C., Snyder, L.: ZPL: An Array Sublanguage. To appear in the *6th Workshop on Languages and Compilers for Parallel Computing,* Portland, OR, 1993.

14. Ngo, T., Snyder, L.: On the Influence of Programming Models on Shared Memory Computer Performance. *Proceedings of Scalable High Performance Computing Conference,* IEEE, pp. 284–291, 1992.

15. Siegel, H.J., et al.: Report on the Purdue Workshop on Grand Challenges in Computer Architecture. *Journal of Parallel and Distributed Computing,* 16:199–211, 1992.

16. Snyder, L.: Type Architecture, Shared Memory and the Corollary of Modest Potential. *Annual Review of Computer Science,* Vol. 1, Annual Review, Inc., pp. 289–318, 1986.

17. Snyder, L.: The XYZ Abstraction Levels of Poker-Like Languages. In David Gelernter, Alexandru Nicolau and David Padua eds. , *Languages and Compilers for Parallel Computing,* MIT Press, pp. 470–489, 1990.

18. Snyder, L.: Applications of the "Phase Abstractions" for Portable and Scalable Parallel Programming. In J. Saltz and P. Mehrotra eds. , *Languages, Compilers and Run-time Environments for Distributed Memory Machines,* Elsevier, pp. 79–102, 1992.

19. Venkatakrishnan, V., Simon, H., Barth, T.: A MIMD Implementation of a Parallel Euler Solver for Unstructured Grids. In J. Dongarra, et al. eds. , *Proceedings of the Fifth SIAM Conference on Parallel Processing for Scientific Computing,* SIAM, pp. 253–256, 1991.

20. Venkatakrishnan, V., Saltz, J., Mavriplis, D.: Solving Unstructured Mesh Problems with Domain Decomposed GMRES/ILU. In J. Dongarra, et al. eds. , *Proceedings of the Fifth SIAM Conference on Parallel Processing for Scientific Computing,* SIAM, pp. 257–262, 1991.

Prototyping Parallel Algorithms with ProSet-Linda

Wilhelm Hasselbring

University of Essen
Fachbereich Mathematik und Informatik — Software Engineering
Schützenbahn 70, 45117 Essen, Germany
willi@informatik.uni-essen.de

Abstract. ProSet is a procedural prototyping language based on the theory of finite sets. The coordination language Linda provides a distributed shared memory model, called tuple space, together with some atomic operations on this shared data space. Process communication and synchronization in Linda is called generative communication, because tuples are added to, removed from, and read from tuple space concurrently. Synchronization is done implicitly.

This paper presents ProSet-Linda which adapts the concept for process creation via Multilisp's futures to set-oriented programming and integrates Linda's concept for synchronization and communication via tuple space. This new approach to integrating futures and generative communication into a prototyping language extends the basic Linda model with multiple tuple spaces, the notion of limited tuple spaces, selection and customization for matching, specified fairness of choice, and the facility for changing tuples in tuple space.

The subject of this paper is the construction of prototypes and not the transformation of prototypes into production-quality programs. Therefore, we consider only the early phases in the process of software construction.

1 Introduction

Parallel programming is conceptually harder to undertake and to understand than sequential programming, because a programmer often has to focus on more than one process at a time. Furthermore, on most of today's parallel machines, programmers are forced to program at a low level to obtain performance — ease of use is sacrificed for efficiency. Consequently, developing parallel algorithms is in general considered as an awkward undertaking. The goal of ProSet-Linda is to overcome this nuisance by providing a tool for prototyping parallel algorithms.

As has been observed [5], no matter how effective the system software and hardware of a parallel machine are at delivering performance, it is only from new algorithms that orders of magnitude improvements in the complexity of a problem can be achieved:

> "An idea that changes an algorithm from n^2 to $n \log n$ operations, where n is proportionate to the number of input elements, is considerably more

spectacular than an improvement in machine organization, where only a constant factor of run-time is achieved." [5, page 250]

Thus, enabling rapid prototyping of parallel algorithms may serve as the basis for developing parallel, high-performance applications.

Current programming environments for distributed memory architectures provide inadequate support for mapping applications to the machine. In particular, the lack of a global name space forces algorithms to be specified at a relatively low level. This greatly increases the complexity of programs, and also stipulates algorithm design choices, inhibiting experimentation with alternate algorithm choices or problem decompositions.

Process communication and synchronization in Linda is reduced to concurrent access to a large data pool, thus relieving the programmer from the burden of having to consider all process inter-relations explicitly. The parallel processes are decoupled in time and space in a very simple way: processes do not have to execute at the same time and in the same address space. This scheme offers all advantages of a shared memory architecture, such as anonymous communication and easy load balancing. It adds a very flexible associative addressing mechanism and a natural synchronization paradigm and at the same time avoids the well-known access bottleneck for shared memory systems as far as possible. The shared data pool in the Linda concept is called *tuple space*. Its access unit is the tuple, similar to tuples in PROSET (Sect. 3). Tuples live in tuple space which is simply a collection of tuples. It may contain any number of copies of the same tuple: it is a multiset, not a set. The tuple space is the fundamental medium of communication in Linda.

Linda and PROSET both provide tuples thus it is quite natural to combine set-oriented programming with generative communication on the basis of this common feature to form a tool for prototyping parallel algorithms.

Programming in Linda provides a spatially and temporally unordered bag of processes. Each task in the computation can be programmed (more-or-less) independently of any other task. This enables the programmer to focus on one process at a time thus making parallel programming conceptually the same order of problem-solving complexity as conventional, sequential programming. The uncoupled and anonymous inter-process communication in Linda is in general not directly supported by the target machines. However, a *high-level* language must be able to reflect a particular top-down approach to building software, and not a particular machine architecture. This is also important to support portability across different machine architectures. Implementations of Linda have been performed on a wide variety of parallel architectures: on shared-memory multi-processors as well as on distributed memory architectures [3, 26]. Linda can be compared to explicit low-level parallel code such as message passing, in much the same way as high-level programming languages can be compared to assembly code.

C was the first computation language in which Linda has been integrated [11]. Meanwhile there exist also integrations into higher-level languages supporting the object-oriented, functional, and logic programming paradigm, respectively

[26]. The present paper presents the combination with a set-oriented language, where process creation via Multilisp's futures is adapted to set-oriented programming and combined with the concept for synchronization and communication via tuple spaces. We regard tuple spaces primary as a device for synchronization and communication between processes, and only secondary for process creation.

Sections 2 and 3 provide brief introductions to the prototyping process and to the language PROSET, respectively. In Sect. 4 the combination of PROSET with Linda will be presented. We refer to [4] for a full account to programming with C-Linda. Essential enhancements to the basic Linda model for this combination are multiple tuple spaces, the notion of limited tuple spaces, selection and customization for matching, specified fairness of choice, and the facility for changing tuples in tuple space. Section 5 sketches implementation issues and Sect. 6 draws some conclusions.

Henri Bal, Mike Factor, Jerry Leichter and Greg Wilson provided useful comments and suggestions on various aspects of this work. The comments on drafts of this paper by Ernst-Erich Doberkat are gratefully acknowledged.

2   The Prototyping Process and Parallel Programming

One of the more recent approaches for complementing the classical model of software production using the life cycle approach is rapid prototyping. Prototyping refers to the well defined phase in the production process of software in which a model is constructed which has all the essential properties of the final product, and which is taken into account when properties have to be checked, and when the further steps in the development have to be determined [10]. We want to note that a prototype is a model, and that this model taken as a program has to be executable so that at least part of the functionality of the desired end product may be demonstrated on a computer. Prototyping has been developed as an answer to deficiencies in the waterfall model, but it should not be considered as an alternative to this model. It is rather optimally useful when it complements the waterfall model. It is plausible that prototyping may be used during the early phases of the design.

The idea of prototyping is being adopted in software engineering for different purposes: prototypes are used *exploratively* to arrive at a feasible specification, *experimentally* to check different approaches, and *evolutionary* to build a system incrementally. Our approach to prototyping is an evolutionary development in versions. The prototype evolves in accordance with the changing environment. The linear ordering of development steps in the classical waterfall model is mapped here into successive development cycles. This implies that the users are involved in the system development process which supports the communication between users and developers.

PROSET also contains a Pascal-like subset that facilitates prototyping by allowing a program to be refined into successively finer detail while staying within the language. Prototypes should be built in very high level languages to make them rapidly available in the early phases of the production process. To be useful, prototypes must be built rapidly and designed in such a way that they can be modified rapidly. Consequently, a prototype is usually not a very efficient program since the runtime system has a heavy burden for executing the highly expressive constructs. To obtain a more efficient production-level version program transformations are desirable to refine the prototype design into a production-quality product [22]. The subject of this paper is the construction of prototypes and not the transformation of prototypes into production-quality programs. Therefore, we consider only the early phases in the process of software construction.

Prototyping means constructing a model. Since applications which are inherently parallel should be programmed in a parallel way, it is most natural to incorporate parallelism into the process of model building. Opportunities for automatic detection of parallelism in existing programs are limited and furthermore, in many cases the formulation of a parallel program is more natural and appropriate than a sequential one. Most systems in real life are of a parallel nature, thus the intent for integrating parallelism into a prototyping language is not only increased performance. If one wants to model an inherently parallel system, it is reasonable to have features for specifying (coarse-grained) processes that communicate and synchronize via a simple communication medium, and not to force such inherent parallelism into sequences. Our work intends to provide a tool for prototyping parallel algorithms and modeling parallel systems.

3 The Prototyping Language PROSET

The procedural, set-oriented language PROSET [8] is a successor to SETL [24]. This section will present a brief introduction to data and control structures of the language and a short example. The high-level structures that PROSET provides qualify the language for prototyping. For a full account to prototyping with set-oriented languages we refer to [7].

PROSET provides data types for atom, integer, real, string, Boolean, tuple, set, function, and module values. It is a *higher-order* language, because functions and modules have first-class rights. PROSET is weakly typed, i.e., the type of an object is in general not known at compile time. Atoms are unique with respect to one machine and across machines. They can only be created and compared. The unary **type** operator returns a predefined type atom corresponding to the type of its operand. Tuples and sets are compound data structures, which may be heterogeneously composed. Sets are unordered collections while tuples are ordered. There is also the undefined value **om** which indicates, e.g., selection of an element from an empty set. As an example consider the expression [123, "abc", true, {1.4, 1.5}] which creates a tuple consisting of an integer, a string, a Boolean, and a set of two reals. This is an example of what is called a *tuple former*. As another example consider the set forming expression {2*x: x in [1..10] | x>5} which yields the set {12, 14, 16, 18, 20}. Sets consisting only of tuples of length two are called maps. There is no genuine data type for maps, because set theory suggests handling them this way.

The control structures show that the language has ALGOL as one of its ancestors. There are **if**, **case**, **loop**, **while**, and **until** statements as usual, and the **for** and **whilefound** loops which are custom tailored for iteration over the compound data structures. The quantifiers (∃, ∀) of predicate calculus are provided.

In Fig. 1 a solution for the so-called *Queens' Problem* in PROSET is given. Informally, the problem may be stated as follows: "Is it possible to place n queens ($n \in \mathbb{N}$) on an $n \times n$ chessboard in such a way that they do not attack each other?". Anyone familiar with the basic rules of chess also knows what *attack* means in this context: in order to attack each other, two queens are placed in the same row, the same column, or the same diagonal. Our program does not solve the above problem directly. It prints out the set of all positions in which the n queens do not attack each other. If it is not possible to place n queens in non-attacking positions, this set will be empty. We denote fields on the chessboard by pairs of natural numbers for convenience (this is unusual in chess, where characters are used to denote the columns). [1,1] denotes the lower left corner.

Note that there are no explicit loops and that there is no recursion in the program. All iterations are done implicitly. One may regard this program also as a (executable) specification of the Queens' Problem.

4 Parallel Programming in PROSET

The following subsections will present and discuss process creation and tuple-space communication in PROSET.

4.1 Process Creation

In C-Linda [4] there is an inherent distinction between at least two classes of processes. Processes live inside and outside of tuple space: the main program is not part of an active tuple (thus it lives outside of tuple space) and all additional processes are created via C-Linda's **eval** operation as part of active tuples hence they live inside the tuple space.

But often it is not desired to put the return values of spawned processes (if after all available) into tuples in tuple space. This is for instance the case if a worker process executes in an infinite loop and deposits result tuples into a tuple space instead of returning only one result. It seems to be artificial to put such a worker process into an active tuple. In this section we will present an adaptation of the approach for process creation known from Multilisp to set-oriented programming, where new processes may be spawned inside and outside of tuple space.

Multilisp augments Scheme with the notion of *futures* where the programmer needs no knowledge about the underlying process model, inter-process communication, or synchronization to express parallelism. We refer to [14] for a full

```
program Queens;
   constant N := 4;
begin
   fields := {[x,y]: x in [1..N], y in [1..N]};
   put({NextPos: NextPos in npow(N, fields) | NonConflict(NextPos)});

   procedure NonConflict (Position);
   begin
      return forall F1 in Position, F2 in Position |
                   ((F1 /= F2) !implies
                    (F1(1) /= F2(1) and F1(2) /= F2(2) and
                    (abs(F2(1)-F1(1)) /= abs(F2(2)-F1(2)))));

      procedure implies (a, b); begin
         return not a or b;
      end implies;
   end NonConflict;
end Queens;
```

Fig. 1. Solution for the Queens' Problem.
The predefined function npow(k, s) yields the set of all subsets of the set
s which contain exactly k elements. The predefined function abs returns the
absolute value of its argument. NonConflict checks whether the queens in a
given position do not attack each other. It is possible to use procedures with
appropriate parameters as user-defined operators by prefixing their names with
the "!" symbol. This is done here with the procedure implies. T(i) selects
the ith element from tuple T.

This program produces this set as a result: $\{\{[1,3], [2,1], [4,2], [3,4]\},$
$\{[3,1], [1,2], [2,4], [4,3]\}\}$

which corresponds to these positions:

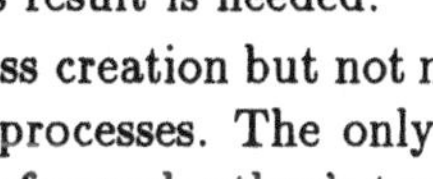

account to Multilisp. The semantics of futures is based on *lazy evaluation*, which
means that an expression is not evaluated until its result is needed.

Futures in Multilisp provide a method for process creation but not much help
for synchronization and communication between processes. The only synchronization and communication mechanism is waiting for each other's termination.
In our approach the concept for process creation via futures is adapted to set-
oriented programming and combined with the concept for synchronization and
communication using tuple spaces.

Multilisp is based on Scheme, which is a dialect of Lisp with lexical scoping. Lisp and Scheme manipulate pointers. This implies touching in a value-
requiring context and transmission in a value-ignoring context. This is in contrast to PROSET that uses value semantics, i.e., a value is never transmitted by
reference. However, there are a few cases where we can ignore the value of an

expression: if the value of an expression is assigned to a variable, we do not need this value immediately, but possibly in the *future*.

Process creation in PROSET is provided through the unary operator | |, which may be applied to an expression (preferably a function call). A new process will be spawned to compute the value of this expression concurrently with the spawning process analogously to futures in Multilisp. If this *process creator* | | is applied to an expression that is assigned to a variable, the spawning process continues execution without waiting for the termination of the newly spawned process. At any time the *value* of this variable is needed, the requesting process will be suspended until the future resolves (the corresponding process terminates) thus allowing concurrency between the *computation* and the *use* of a value. Consider the following statement sequence to see an example:

```
x := || p();      -- Statement 1
...               -- Some computations without access to x
y := x;           -- Statement 2
```

After statement 1 is executed the process p() runs in parallel with the spawning process. Statement 2 will be suspended until p() terminates, because a copy is needed (value semantics). This is in contrast to Lisp where an assignment would copy the address and ignore the value. If p() resolves before statement 2 has started execution, then the resulting value will be assigned immediately. Also, if a compound data structure is constructed via a set or tuple forming enumeration, and this data structure is assigned to a variable, we do not need the values of the enumerated components immediately, thus allowing concurrency as above. Additionally, statements such as "| | p();", which spawn new processes, are allowed.

4.2   Tuple-Space Operations

PROSET provides three tuple-space operations. The **deposit** operation deposits a new tuple into a tuple space, the **fetch** operation fetches and removes a tuple from a tuple space, and the **meet** operation *meets* and leaves a tuple in a tuple space. It is possible to change the tuple's value while meeting it.

Depositing Tuples. The **deposit** operation deposits a tuple into a specified tuple space. We distinguish between passive and active tuples in tuple space. If there are no executing processes in a tuple, then this tuple is added as a passive one (cp. out of C-Linda [4]):

```
deposit [ 123, "mystring", 3.14 ] at TS end deposit;
```

TS is the tuple space at which the specified tuple has to be deposited. See Sect. 4.4 for a discussion of multiple tuple spaces in PROSET. If there are executing processes in a tuple, then this tuple is added as an active one to the tuple space:

```
deposit [ "myprocess", || p() ] at TS end deposit;
```

Depositing a tuple into a tuple space does not touch the value. When all processes in an active tuple have terminated their execution, then this tuple converts into a passive one with the return values of these processes in the corresponding tuple fields. Active tuples are invisible to the other tuple-space operations until they convert into passive tuples. The other two tuple-space operations apply only to passive tuples (see the following subsections).

Limited Tuple Spaces. Because every existing computing system has only finite memory, the memory for tuple spaces will also be limited. Pure tuple-space communication does not deal with *full* tuple spaces: there is always enough room available. Thus most runtime systems for Linda hide the fact of limited memory from the programmer.

In PROSET, the predefined exception `ts_is_full` will be raised by default when no memory is available for a **deposit** operation. This exception is raised with the **signal** statement of PROSET. Signal exceptions permit the operation raising the exception to be either terminated or resumed at the handler's discretion. We refer to [13] for a discussion of exception handling in general and to [8] for a discussion of exception handling in PROSET. It is possible to specify a handler for an exception by annotating a statement with a new binding between exception name and handler name. If the associated handler then executes a **return** statement, the statement following the **deposit** will be executed and the tuple of the respective **deposit** will not be deposited. If the handler executes a **resume** statement, then the **deposit** operation tries again to deposit the tuple.

Optionally, the programmer may specify that a **deposit** operation will be suspended on a full tuple space until space is available again. The suitable handling of full tuple spaces depends on the application to program. Thus a general setting does not seem to be appropriate. Blocking is useful, e.g., in a producer-consumer application. In a master-worker application you might prefer to collect some results by your own handler before producing more tasks, when your tuple space is full.

Fetching Tuples. A **fetch** operation tries to fetch and remove exactly one tuple from a tuple space. It is possible to specify several templates for the specified tuple space in a statement, but only one template may be selected nondeterministically (see also Sect. 4.3). We start with a first example for a **fetch** operation with a single template:

```
fetch ( "name", ? x |(type $(2) = integer) ) at TS end fetch;
```

This template only matches tuples with integer values in the second field and the string **"name"** in the first field. The symbol **$** may be used like an expression as a placeholder for the values of corresponding tuples in tuple space. The expression (i) then selects the ith element from such tuples. As usual in PROSET | means *such that*. The Boolean expression behind | may be used to customize matching by restricting the set of possibly matching tuples. PROSET employs *conditional* *value matching* and not the type matching known from C-Linda and similar embeddings of Linda into statically typed languages. A tuple and a template match iff all the following conditions hold:

- The tuple is passive.
- The arities are equal.
- Values of actuals in templates are equal to the corresponding tuple fields.
- The Boolean expression after | in the template evaluates to **true**. If no such expression is specified, then **true** is the default.

The *l*-values specified in the formals (the variable **x** in our example) are assigned the values of the corresponding tuple fields, provided matching succeeds. The selected tuple is removed from tuple space. If there are no **else** statements specified as in the above example then the statement suspends until a match occurs. If statements are specified for the selected template, these statements are executed. An example with multiple templates, associated statements, and an **else** statement:

```
fetch ( "name", ? x |(type $(2) = integer) ) => put("Integer fetched");
  xor ( "name", ? x |(type $(2) = set) )     => put("Set fetched");
    at TS
  else put("Nothing fetched");
end fetch;
```

Here both templates consist of an *actual* (the expression **"name"**), a so-called *formal* preceded by a question mark, and a template condition. The template lists are enclosed in parentheses and not in brackets in order to set the templates apart from tuples. The **else** statement will be executed, if none of the templates matches. We will use the notion *non-blocking matching* if **else** statements are specified as opposed to *blocking matching* if no **else** statements are specified.

Meeting Tuples. The **meet** operation *meets* and leaves one tuple in tuple space. It is possible to change the tuple while meeting it. Except for the fact that a **meet** operation, which does not change the met tuple, leaves the tuple it found in tuple space, it works like the **fetch** operation.

Changing Tuples. The absence of support for user-defined high-level operations on shared data in Linda is criticized [1]. We agree that this is a shortcoming. For overcoming it we allow to change tuples while meeting them in tuple space. This is done by specifying expressions **into** which specific tuple fields will be changed. Tuples, which are met in tuple space, may be regarded as shared data since they remain in tuple space; irrespective of changing them or not. Consider

meet ("name", ? into $(2)+1) at TS end meet;

which is equivalent to the series of statements with **x** as a fresh name:

```
fetch ( "name", ? x ) at TS end fetch;
deposit [ "name", x+1 ] at TS end deposit;
```

If there are **intos** specified after the formals as in this example then the tuple is at first fetched from the tuple space as it would be done with the **fetch** operation. Afterwards a tuple will be deposited into the same tuple space, where all the tuple fields without **intos** are unchanged and all the tuple fields with **intos** are updated with the values of the respective expressions.

Indivisibility is guaranteed, because fetching the passive tuple at starting and depositing the new passive or active one at the end of the user-defined operation on shared data are atomic operations. Note that the tuple is not really removed from the tuple space. The above equivalence is only introduced to specify the semantics, not the implementation. Therefore, with the **meet** operation expensive copying of compound data may be avoided.

4.3 Nondeterminism and Fairness while Matching

There are two sources for nondeterminism while matching:

1. Several matching tuples exist for a given template: one tuple will be selected nondeterministically.
2. A tuple matches several templates: one template will be selected nondeterministically.

If in any case there is only one candidate available, this one will be selected. There are several ways for handling fairness while selecting tuples or templates that match if there are multiple candidates available. We will now discuss *fairness of choice* which is important for handling the nondeterminism derived from matching. There exist some fairness notions [18]. Weak fairness means that, if a process is enabled continuously from some point onwards then it eventually will be selected. Weak fairness is also called *justice*. Strong fairness means that, if a process is enabled infinitely often then it will be selected infinitely often. In PROSET the following fairness guarantees are given for the two sources for nondeterminism as mentioned above:

1. Tuples will be selected without any consideration of fairness.
2. Templates will be selected in a weakly fair way.

Since deposited tuples are no longer connected with processes, it is reasonable to select them without any consideration of fairness. Linda's semantics do not guarantee tuple ordering — this aspect remains the responsibility of the programmer. If a specific order in selection is necessary, it has to be enforced via appropriate tuple contents. Fairness is also important for processes which are blocked on full tuple spaces:

3. Processes which are blocked on full tuple spaces are selected in a weakly fair way when tuples are fetched from the respective tuple spaces.

In cases (2.) and (3.) processes are involved and enabled after selection, whereas in case (1.) this is not the case for deposited tuples. Therefore, it is reasonable to employ weakly fair selection in cases (2.) and (3.), and unfair selection in case (1.). These fairness properties are specified formally by means of temporal logic in [16].

Weakly fair selection of templates applies only to blocking matching: if a template that is used for non-blocking matching does match immediately then this one is excluded of further matching and the corresponding process is informed of this fact. If we would guarantee strongly fair selection of templates then the system would have to retain non-blocking matching operations of processes, for which no matching tuples were available. We see no justification to guarantee strong fairness.

4.4 Multiple Tuple Spaces

Atoms are used to identify tuple spaces. As mentioned in Sect. 3 atoms are unique for one machine and across machines. They have first-class rights.

PROSET provides several library functions for handling multiple tuple spaces dynamically. The function `CreateTS(limit)` creates a new tuple space and returns its identity (an atom). Since one has exclusive access to a fresh created tuple-space identity, `CreateTS` supports information hiding. The integer parameter `limit` specifies a limit on the expected or desired size of the new tuple space. This size limit denotes the total number of passive and active tuples, which are allowed in a tuple space at the same time. `CreateTS(om)` would instead indicate that the expected or wanted size is unlimited regarding user-defined limits, not regarding physical limits. The function `ExistsTS(TS)` yields `true`, if `TS` is an atom that identifies an existing tuple space; else `false`. The function `ClearTS(TS)` removes all active and passive tuples from the specified tuple space. This function appears to be useful, e.g., in a master-worker application: when the work has been done, the master can remove garbage and abandon the workers. The function `RemoveTS(TS)` calls `ClearTS(TS)` and removes `TS` from the list of existing tuple spaces.

Every PROSET program has its own tuple-space manager. Tuple spaces are not persistent. They exist only until all processes of an application have terminated their execution. Tuple space communication in PROSET as presented in this paper is designed for *multiprocessing* (single application running on multiple processors) as opposed to *multiprogramming* (separate applications). Multiprogramming in PROSET is done via a separate mechanism for handling persistent data objects [6].

4.5 The Queens' Problem Revisited

In Sect. 3 the Queens' Problem was introduced together with a sequential solution. In Fig. 2 a parallel solution based on the master-worker model with limited tuple spaces is given. It is recommended to examine the sequential solution in Fig. 1 again. In a master-worker application, the task to be solved is partitioned into independent subtasks. These subtasks are placed into the tuple space, and each process in a pool of identical workers then repeatedly retrieves a subtask description from the tuple space, solves it, and deposits the solutions into the tuple space. In our example, these subtasks are the possible positions. The master process then can collect the results. Among the advantages of this programming approach are load balancing and transparent scalability.

4.6 Discussion

This section discusses some design issues for the presented language constructs. A more detailed discussion of these and other issues may be found in [16].

Process Creation. The **deposit** operation comprises the **out** and **eval** operations of C-Linda [4]. You might compare depositing of active tuples with **eval**, but it is not exactly the same, however, because all fields of an **eval** tuple are executed concurrently and not only fields which were selected by the programmer. This is a noteworthy difference: according to the semantics of **eval** *each* field of a tuple is evaluated concurrently. But probably no system will create a new process to compute, e.g., a plain integer constant. In the Yale Linda Implementation, only expressions consisting of a single function call are evaluated within new processes [4]. The system has to decide, which fields to compute concurrently and which sequentially. Similar problems arise in automatic parallelization of functional languages: here you have to reduce the existing parallelism to a reasonable granularity. In our approach the programmer has to communicate his knowledge about the granularity of his application to the system. Furthermore, the semantics of **eval** is not always well understood: some current implementations in fact evaluate all fields of an **eval** tuple sequentially within a single new process. This may cause deadlocks if processes within an **eval** tuple communicate with each other.

Extending the Type System. As Linda relies heavily on type matching, the type system of the computation language has a notable effect on tuple-space implementation and semantics. E.g., in C the equivalence of types is not that obvious. Under which conditions are structures resp. unions equivalent? Are pointers equivalent to array-names? In [19] it has been proposed to extend the type system of C to overcome some of the problems thus caused: each expression has two distinct types associated with it, its *C type* and its *Linda type*. The Linda type follows stricter rules and is significant only in tuple matching, thus these type extensions only influence the matching process and not the type system of C. In PROSET there is no necessity for extending the type system for obtaining a smooth integration of Linda: firstly, since PROSET provides a well-formed type system with clear semantics for type equivalence, there exists no necessity to extend the basic type system for tuple matching. Secondly, since there exist no difference between PROSET-tuples and Linda-tuples, a combination on the basis of this common feature becomes straightforward.

```
program ParallelQueens;
   constant N := 8, NumWorker := argv(2), -- program argument
           TS := CreateTS(om);  -- no limit specified
begin
  for i in [1 .. NumWorker] do      -- spawn the worker processes
     deposit [ || Worker(TS) ] at TS end deposit;
  end for;
  deposit [ {} ] at TS end deposit;  -- initialize the result set
  deposit [ 0 ] at TS end deposit;   -- initialize the counter

  Positions := npow(N, {[x,y]: x in [1..N], y in [1..N]});
  for NextPosition in Positions do
     deposit [ NextPosition ] at TS end deposit;
  end for;

  fetch ( #Positions ) at TS end fetch;  -- wait for the workers
  fetch ( ? ResultPos |(type $(1) = set) ) at TS end fetch;
  put (ResultPos);
  ClearTS(TS);

  procedure Worker (MyTS); begin
     loop
        fetch ( ? MyPosition |(type $(1) = set) ) at MyTS end fetch;
        if NonConflict (MyPosition) then
           -- add the position:
           meet ( ? into ($(1) with MyPosition) |(type $(1) = set) )
             at MyTS
           end meet;
        end if;
        -- increase the counter of evaluated positions:
        meet ( ? into ($(1) + 1) |(type $(1) = integer) )
          at MyTS
        end meet;
  end Worker;
end ParallelQueens;
```

Fig. 2. Parallel Solution for the Queens' Problem.
See Fig. 1 for the procedure NonConflict. The resulting set of non-conflicting
positions is built up in tuple space via changing meet operations. The master
program spawns NumWorker worker processes. This number is an argument to
the main program. The counter in tuple space is necessary to let the master
wait until all positions are evaluated. The unary operator "#" returns the
number of elements in a compound data structure. The tuple space is cleared
after work has been done thus also terminating the workers.

Multiple Tuple Spaces. Multiple tuple spaces allow the programmer to partition the communication medium as he sees fit. The representation of individual tuple spaces can be customized based on their contents and usage. Compile-time analysis is simplified with respect to partioning of tuple space, and modularity and information hiding is supported. The idea of splitting the tuple space into multiple spaces is frequently applied. New data types and classes are often proposed to organize them [26]. In most proposals for introducing multiple tuple spaces, values of objects of these types are used as identifiers/references to tuple spaces and not as the value of a tuple space itself. Conversely, in [12] operations on tuple spaces as first-class objects are supported (e.g. suspension). However, because of concurrent access it is rarely possible to make any sensible statement with respect to the *actual value* of a tuple space (tuple-space constants make not much sense, except for the creation of tuple spaces). A tuple space may be viewed as the dynamic envelope of a growing and shrinking multiset of passive and active tuples that controls the communication and synchronization of parallel processes. This dynamic communication device has *no* first-class rights in PROSET. Atoms as tuple-space identities already have first-class rights.

5 Implementation Issues

The definition of C-Linda has been presented informally [11] and, as a result, has included several ambiguities. E.g., [20] summarizes four basic types of process creation used in implementations of C-Linda's **eval** operation. These are different interpretations of the informal specification of the **eval** operation. Additional discussions of problems with the semantics of the **eval** operation may also be found in [19] and in [16]. Such a situation demands a more precise definition.

In [15], a formal semantics of tuple spaces in PROSET by means of the formal specification language Z [25] has been presented to avoid such problems. We refined this formal specification into an implementation design and implemented a prototype from the formal specification. The prototype allows immediate validation of the specification by execution, and provides us with a *touch-and-feel* experience necessary to test the specification. The prototype enables us to avoid the large time lag between specification of a system and its validation in the traditional model of software production using the life cycle approach.

We can only sketch some implementation issues here. An implementation of a graphical debugger [23], and an implementation on a network of workstations [21] are in progress. Multiple tuple spaces provide a direct approach for distributing the tuple space on a distributed memory architecture. The representation of individual tuple spaces can be customized according to their contents and usage.

6 Conclusions

In this paper, we presented PROSET-Linda which adapts the concept for process creation via Multilisp's futures to set-oriented programming and integrates

Linda's concept for synchronization and communication via tuple space. The basic Linda model is enhanced with multiple tuple spaces, the notion of limited tuple spaces, selection and customization for matching, specified fairness of choice, and the facility for changing tuples in tuple space. It is fairly natural to combine set-oriented programming with generative communication on the basis of tuples, as both models, PROSET and Linda, provide tuples.

The small example presented here did not fully demonstrate the advantages of multiple tuple spaces. However, in more sophisticated problem domains such as process trellises [9] the advantage of information hiding is obvious, since processes may communicate within isolated tuple spaces independent of communication in other tuple spaces. The enhanced facilities for nondeterminism will support distributed implementation of backtracking such as branch-and-bound applications, where selective waiting for multiple events is often desired [17].

We implement PROSET-Linda in a somewhat unconventional way: the informal specification is followed by a formal specification, which serves as the basis for a prototype implementation before the production-level implementation is undertaken. Applying formal methods early in the design stage of computer systems and software can increase the designer's productivity by clarifying issues and eliminating errors in the design. A side effect is that very few design errors will prevail at the implementation stage; design errors detected at the implementation stage are often more expensive to correct. When formal methods are systematically applied to all stages of design and implementation, we can increase our confidence that the software is robust and correct. A formal development process is more expensive in terms of time and education, but much cheaper in terms of maintenance. There may be bugs, but they are less likely to be at the conceptual level.

Our goal is to make parallel program design easier through prototyping of parallel algorithms. The high level of PROSET's constructs for parallel programming enables us to rapidly develop prototypes of parallel programs and to experiment with parallel algorithms.

References

1. H.E. Bal. A comparative study of five parallel programming languages. *Future Generations Computer Systems*, 8:121–135, 1992.
2. R. Budde, K. Kuhlenkamp, L. Mathiassen, and H. Züllighoven, editors. *Approaches to Prototyping*. Springer-Verlag, 1984.
3. N. Carriero. *Implementation of tuple space machines*. PhD thesis, Yale University, New Haven, CT, December 1987.
4. N. Carriero and D. Gelernter. *How to write parallel programs*. MIT Press, 1990.
5. J. Cocke. The search for performance in scientific processors. *Communications of the ACM*, 31(3):249–253, 1988.
6. E.-E. Doberkat. Integrating persistence into a set-oriented prototyping language. *Structured Programming*, 13(3):137–153, 1992.
7. E.-E. Doberkat and D. Fox. *Software Prototyping mit SETL*. Leitfäden und Monographien der Informatik. Teubner-Verlag, 1989.

8. E.-E. Doberkat, W. Franke, U. Gutenbeil, W. Hasselbring, U. Lammers, and C. Pahl. PROSET — A Language for Prototyping with Sets. In N. Kanopoulos, editor, *Proc. Third International Workshop on Rapid System Prototyping*, pages 235–248, Research Triangle Park, NC, June 1992. IEEE Computer Society Press.

9. M. Factor. The process trellis software architecture for real-time monitors. In *Proc. Second ACM SIGPLAN Symposium on Principles and Practice of Parallel Programming (PPoPP)*, pages 147–155, Seattle, WA, March 1990.

10. C. Floyd. A systematic look at prototyping. In Budde et al. [2], pages 1–18.

11. D. Gelernter. Generative communication in Linda. *ACM Transactions on Programming Languages and Systems*, 7(1):80–112, 1985.

12. D. Gelernter. Multiple tuple spaces in Linda. In *Proc. Parallel Architectures and Languages Europe (PARLE'89)*, volume 366 of *Lecture Notes in Computer Science*, pages 20–27. Springer-Verlag, June 1989.

13. J.B. Goodenough. Exception handling: Issues and a proposed notation. *Communications of the ACM*, 18(12):683–696, 1975.

14. R.H. Halstead. Multilisp: A language for concurrent symbolic computation. *ACM Transactions on Programming Languages and Systems*, 7(4):501–538, 1985.

15. W. Hasselbring. A Formal Z Specification of PROSET-Linda. Informatik-Bericht 04-92, University of Essen, September 1992.

16. W. Hasselbring. *Prototyping Parallel Algorithms in a Set-Oriented Language*. PhD thesis, University of Essen, 1993. (in preparation).

17. M.F. Kaashoek, H.E. Bal, and A.S. Tanenbaum. Experience with the distributed data structure paradigm in Linda. In *USENIX/SERC Workshop on Experiences with Building Distributed and Multiprocessor Systems*, pages 175–191, Ft. Lauderdale, FL, October 1989.

18. M.Z. Kwiatkowska. Survey of fairness notions. *Information and Software Technology*, 31(7):371–386, 1989.

19. J.S. Leichter. *Shared tuple memories, buses and LAN's — Linda implementations across the spectrum of connectivity*. PhD thesis, Yale University, New Haven, CT, July 1989.

20. J.E. Narem. An informal operational semantics of C-Linda V2.3.5. Technical Report 839, Yale University, New Haven, CT, December 1989.

21. R. Naujokat. Entwurf und Implementierung einer Laufzeitbibliothek für PROSET-Linda auf einem lokalen Netzwerk. Master's thesis, University of Essen, 1993. (in preparation).

22. H.A. Partsch. *Specification and Transformation of Programs*. Springer-Verlag, 1990.

23. H. Pohland. Entwurf und Implementierung eines graphischen Debuggers für PROSET-Linda. Master's thesis, University of Essen, 1993. (in preparation).

24. J.T. Schwartz, R.B.K. Dewar, E. Dubinsky, and E. Schonberg. *Programming with Sets - An Introduction to SETL*. Springer-Verlag, 1986.

25. J.M. Spivey. *The Z Notation: A Reference Manual*. Prentice-Hall, 2nd edition, 1992.

26. G. Wilson, editor. *Proc. Workshop on Linda-Like Systems and Their Implementation*. Edinburgh Parallel Computing Centre TR91-13, June 1991.

Identifying the Available Parallelism Using Static Analysis

Spiridon Kalogeropulos

INMOS Software Group,
1000 Aztec West, Almondsbury,
BRISTOL BS12 4SQ
e-mail sk@inmos.co.uk

Abstract. In this paper we present a technique for identifying the available parallelism in a sequential *Lisp* program which is related to the data dependences between program constructs. Our technique first removes some of the data dependences due to assignments to scalar variables in a *Lisp* program to increase its available parallelism and consequently computes the required precedence constraints necessary for the creation of a parallel program, which is semantically equivalent to the sequential one, by detecting the data dependences between expressions using static analysis. We remove some of the data dependences due to assignments to scalar variables by transforming a *Lisp* program into Static Single Assignment (SSA) form.

Key Words Static Single Assignment, Data Depentence, Precedence Constrains.

1 Introduction

The compile-time transformation of a sequential *Lisp* program into a faster parallel one which will be executed on a multiprocessor involves the development of techniques capable of solving the problems of identifying the available parallelism, partitioning the program into tasks with optimal task granularity, and scheduling these tasks for concurrent execution.

In this paper we present a technique for identifying the available parallelism in a sequential *Lisp* program. The identification of the available parallelism in a *Lisp* program involves the computation of the required precedence constraints due to data dependences between program's expressions in order the resulting parallel program to be semantically equivalent to the sequential one. Most of the current research reveals concurrency in a sequential program by detecting data dependences between program constructs. Our technique, however, first removes some of the data dependences due to assignments to scalar variables in a *Lisp* program to increase its available parallelism by transforming it into Static Single Assignment (SSA) form. Subsequently, our technique computes the required precedence constraints by detecting the data dependences existing in the evaluation of expressions using static analysis.

In the following sections, we describe the transformation of a *Lisp* program into Static Single Assignment (SSA) form. Furthermore, different frameworks are discussed for the run-time mapping of variables and pointers to memory locations, which will aid the detection of data dependences between expressions that manipulate and access aggregate objects. We continue by introducing a method for conservatively approximating the above mentioned data dependences between expressions. Finally we present our method for identifying the available parallelism using an intermediate program representation called Graphical Representation Model which expresses the available concurrency.

2 Classifying Data Dependences

A data dependence between two expressions imposes a precedence constraint on their evaluation, because both anticipate the use of a common storage location holding only one value at a time. Thus, the program's computation might be changed, if the relative order in the evaluation of two expressions is reversed. Consequently, for the concurrent execution of a sequential program on a multiprocessor, it is necessary to compute the program's data dependences between expressions to relax its sequential execution order and allow some operations to be performed in parallel.

The following three kinds of data dependences have been identified when expressions e_1 and e_2 either read from or write to a memory location l and there exists a path in the control flow graph that joins e_1 and e_2 with no intervening writing into l:

- e_2 has a *Flow Dependence* on e_1 over the memory location l if e_1 writes a value into the location l that is subsequently read by e_2;
- e_2 has an *Anti-Dependence* on e_1 over the memory location l if e_1 reads a value from the location l that is subsequently modified by e_2;
- e_2 has an *Output Dependence* on e_1 over the memory location l if e_1 writes a value to the location l that is subsequently modified by e_2.

We transform a *Lisp* program into SSA form to eliminate the *Anti-Dependences* and *Output Dependences* caused by assignments to scalar variables.

3 SSA Form

A program is in SSA form if each variable is assigned only once in the program text. Dynamically, a program with loops may assign to the same variable many times, even if only one assignment appears in the program text.

In order to transform a program to SSA form, we construct its control flow graph. This is a directed graph, in which each node corresponds to a basic block in the program, that is a sequence of consecutive statements, which may be entered only at the beginning, and when entered are executed in sequence without halt or possibility of branch (except at the end of the basic block). Furthermore, each edge corresponds to a branch in the program.

The transformation of a program to SSA form involves the renaming of variables throughout the program, so that each variable is assigned exactly once in the program text. Each assignment to a variable X will be replaced by an assignment to X_i, where i is an integer. The new name X_i will replace the uses of X along every execution path that starts from the assignment to X_i until an assignment to variable X is met. At join nodes in the control flow graph, if there are two inedges of the join node reached by two different new names for X, a new type of assignment statement to one of the new names X_k for X is added. The new assignment ensures that the variable X_k is assigned the value of the appropriate new variable name, if control enters along a certain inedge. After renaming, every point in the program will be reached by exactly one of the new names for X, which represents whatever value X has, when control reaches that point. The new variable names are to be generated and assigned so as to satisfy the SSA rules [10].

The SSA form of a program is semantically equivalent to the original program, since any new variable name X_i for X that reaches a point in the transformed program has always the same value as the value of X at the same point in the original program. The SSA transformation of a simple program is shown in figure 1. In a program which is in SSA form, trivial assignments in which one variable gets the value of another can be removed, simply by changing all uses of the assignment's target to uses of the variable on the right-hand side of the assignment.

After defining the SSA form of a program, we are ready to discuss the SSA transformation of a $Lisp$ program in details.

3.1 Transforming Lisp Programs

We have mentioned in the last section that the SSA transformation of a program involves the renaming of variables throughout the program, in order for each variable to be assigned exactly once in the program text. Within $Common$ $Lisp$ a symbol can name more than one variables at a time. When a symbol is evaluated the question arises which variable it refers to. In $Common$ $Lisp$ the variables can be classified into the following three categories.

- Global variables, which can be referred to at any time and have indefinite scope.

- Dynamic variables, which have dynamic extent and indefinite scope. A dynamically bound variable can be referred to at any time, starting from the variable's binding until the evaluation of the construct that binds the variable terminates.

- Local lexical variables, which have lexical scope. A lexically bound variable can be referred to only by forms occurring at any place textually, within the program construct that binds the variable.

When a symbol is evaluated, the variable it refers to depends on the context of evaluation. The general rule is that, if the symbol occurs textually within a program construct that creates a binding for a variable of the same name,

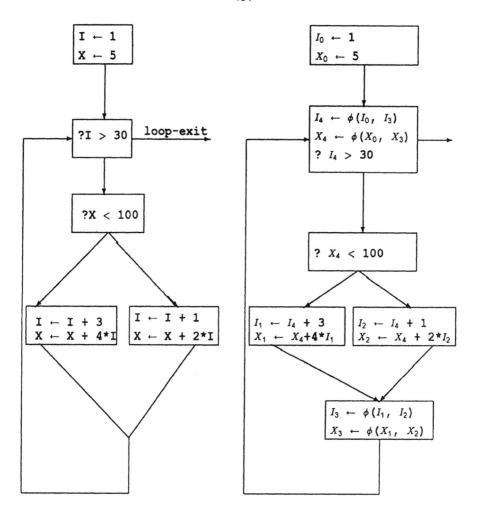

Fig. 1. The Control Flow Graph of a Simple Program and its SSA form

then the reference is to the variable specified by the binding; if no such program construct exists, then the symbol is taken as dynamic variable or global depending on the existence or not of a program construct which creates a dynamic binding for a variable of the same name and has not been terminated. In the above rule we did not consider the possibility of two textually nested constructs binding either lexical or dynamic variables with the same name. In the case of lexical variables, references within the inner construct refer to the variable bound by the inner one; while a reference to a dynamic variable will always refer to the one that is bound most recently and has not been disestablished.

From the above discussion, we conclude that it is necessary to know during the static analysis of the program the active dynamic variables and their order of establishment to determine the variable referred to by a symbol. This information about dynamic variables can be derived at compile-time only if the functions invoked at each call site are known at compile-time. We use the following approach for the SSA transformation of a $Lisp$ program, by assuming that $Lisp$ programs do not pass functional values and use language constructs with run-time behaviour that can be analysed at compile-time. The first step in transforming a $Lisp$ program to SSA form is to construct the function call graph of the program; that is a directed graph in which the nodes represent functions and the edges represent calls to functions. Then we start the transformation from the function that is the entry node in the function call graph, and we proceed by transforming recursively each called function and then invoking its SSA form.

For the transformation of each function to SSA form the following information about the active variables is maintained.

- A list that holds the names of the global variables.
- A stack in which each element is a list that holds the dynamic variables, which are established within a certain construct of a certain function.
- A stack in which each element is a list of local variables established within a certain establishing construct.
- A list for each category of variables in which each element is a list that contains the new introduced names for each read or written variable.

Consequently, the control flow analysis and the renaming of the variables throughout each function to be put into SSA form is done by recursive decomposition of the function.

The control flow analysis aids in identifying the join nodes, which can be classified according to whether they are, or not, loop headers. If a join node is a loop header, then in a second pass, after renaming the variables according to the SSA rules [10], we insert at the point immediately after the loop header a new assignment, for each modified variable X see figure 1. The new assignment has the form $X_k \leftarrow \phi(X_i, X_j)$ where X_k is a unique new name for X, X_i is the name for X that reaches the loop header from a program point which precedes the loop header and X_j is the name of X that reaches the loop backedge which points at the loop header (we suppose one backedge to minimize notation). Finally, we replace each mention of X_i within the loop with X_k.

We implement the new introduced type of assignment $X_j \leftarrow \phi(X_a, X_b)$ by inserting the assignments $X_j \leftarrow X_a$, $X_i \leftarrow X_b$ correspondingly to the left and right inedges of the join node so that these assignments are the last statements that reach the join node from left and right inedges.

In a function that is being transformed to SSA form, for each mention of a symbol we identify the variable it is referred to, by examining successively the stacks of local lexical, dynamic variables and the list of global variables. Then we rename the variable, so as to satisfy the SSA rules and update the list that holds the new introduced names for that variable. During the function body transformation to SSA form, it is necessary to introduce a communication mechanism for the connection of the new variable names between a calling and a called function. This communication mechanism provides information about the last new introduced name for each variable, before the function call, which is read within a called function; as well as the last new introduced name for each variable that exits from the called function. The communication mechanism is implemented by introducing in each function additional parameters X_r and X_{out} for each free variable X that is read and written within the function.

For each category of variables we proceed as follows.

Global variables. For a function other than the entry in the function call graph, each global variable X that is read by the function and is not yet written within the function is replaced by a new name X_r, which is a new parameter to the function. In addition, a new parameter X_{out} is introduced for each global variable X that is written within the function body. The parameter X_{out} refers to the new variable name for X which will be used after the function call in the calling function and it is set by the called function to the value of the last new introduced name for variable X that exits from the called function.

After renaming the global variables throughout the function according to SSA rules, we bind the new introduced names locally within the function body. Furthermore, for each global variable X that is read or written we insert the new parameters X_r, X_{out} correspondingly in the formal parameter list of the function. When the function is called, the value of the last new name X_i for X in the calling function is passed to X_r. Furthermore, we pass the environment of the new dynamic variable X_{i+1} for X to the formal parameter X_{out} and update the calling function's list that holds the new introduced names for X. The variable name X_{i+1} is the one that is referred to and replaces any references to the variable X at the point P immediately after the function call and any other point Q such that every path from P to Q does not include any assignments to names of X.

In the case of direct recursive functions, a second pass is necessary to provide the arguments for the X_r and X_{out} parameters of any direct recursive function calls, since we may have to analyse the whole function body before being able to infer that a global variable is read or written. The variable name X_k for X, which is bound to the parameter X_{out} at a certain recursive function call, is the one that reaches any point P after the function call such that every path from the function call to P does not include any assignments to names of X.

The SSA transformation of mutually recursive functions is more complicated. The mutually recursive functions can be grouped in Strongly Connected Components ($SCCs$). The algorithms which determines the $SCCs$ [12] partitions the set of functions into equivalence classes S_i for $1 \leq i \leq k$ such that S_i's functions v_1 and v_2 are equivalent if and only if there is a path from v_1 to v_2 and a path from v_2 to v_1. The graphs $G_i = (S_i, E_i)$ are the strongly connected components where E_i for $1 \leq i \leq k$ is the set of edges with head and tail in S_i. Consequently, we distinguish function calls to either externals or internals according to whether they are between functions in different SCC's, or between functions in the same SCC.

After identifying the $SCCs$, the SSA transformation of a SCC can be performed in two phases. In the first phase, we transform each function in the SCC to SSA form without inserting the new parameters for each global variable that is referred in the function's formal parameter list. In the second phase for each global variable X that is read or written by any function in the SCC we insert the new parameters X_r or X_{out} correspondingly in the formal parameter list of each function belonging to the SCC. Subsequently, we pass the right arguments to X_r and X_{out} in each internal function call.

Dynamic variables. We treat them in a similar fashion as the global variables; but we remove them from the stack that holds the dynamic variables, when their establishing construct is terminated, and we bind the new introduced names for the dynamic variables within their establishing construct.

Local lexical variables. We treat them in a similar fashion as the global variables; but we bind the new names locally within their establishing construct and remove them from the stack that holds the local variables, when their establishing construct is terminated.

The SSA transformation of a $Lisp$ program is a tool for exposing as well as for increasing the available parallelism in a program related with data dependences on scalar variables. Therefore after creating the parallel tasks by applying a partitioning algorithm [7, 6] on the intermediate program representation described in section 5, we are interested only for the free variables which are written by one task and are read by another one. Consequently we can optimise the code of each task, which is executed sequentially, by removing some of the new introduced variable names which are referred in the task's body.

4 Data Dependences in expressions using Pointer Variables

After considering data dependences in expressions using scalar variables, we will discuss about the data dependences in expressions using aggregate objects connected by pointers. This data dependence problem involves an analysis to determine whether two different names access the same memory location. The analysis is complicated since the unbounded data structures have to be represented in some finite way.

In the next subsections we start with defining some terminology; subsequently we introduce the memory approximation scheme for data structures that arise at run-time which will be extended for the detection of data dependences. Finally, we present our extension to the above memory approximation scheme and describe our method for detecting data dependences in pointer variables.

4.1 Definitions

A structure is a memory located object composed of a collection of named fields (structures are called "records" in some programming languages). Each field can have as values either a pointer to a structure or a non-pointer value. We can represent a collection of structures and pointer variables by using a labelled, directed graph $G = (N, E)$. Each node, $n_i \in N$, corresponds to either an instance of a certain type structure or a pointer variable. An edge in G has the form (n_i, f, n_j) and indicates that the structure n_i contains a pointer in field f to the structure n_j. An *access path* in G, $n.a$, consists of a starting node $n = n_0$ and a string of fields $a = a_0...a_l$ for $l \geq 0$ such that $\{(n_0, a_0, n_1), (n_1, a_1, n_2), ..., (n_l, a_l, n_{l+1})\} \subseteq E$. We also define $a_{0..l}$ to be the sequence of fields $a_0...a_l$. The node n_{l+1} is the destination of the path, denoted by $dest(n.a)$. While the node n_l is the destination of the access path up to its last field, denoted by $predest(n.a)$.

In the case of more than one edges leaving a field from a node, a path can lead to more than one nodes. Consequently, $dest(n.a)$ and $predest(n.a)$ are the sets of nodes being the destination of the path and the destination of the path up to its last field respectively. We define a location $loc(n.a)$ to be the set of pairs $(predest\ (n.a) \otimes a_l)$. Two access paths $x.a$, $y.b$ in G are aliases, if $dest(x.a) = dest(y.b)$.

4.2 Memory Approximation Schemes for Data Structures

The first step in the computation of the data dependences in expressions for languages using data structures to manipulate heap allocated storage is the approximation of the run-time mapping of variables and pointers to memory locations. Exact information about this mapping is generally undecidable or at least very difficult to compute. In addition, further information is lost because of the finite representation of unbounded data structures.

The current techniques approximate the actual memory layouts which exist at each program expression during execution using two different summarising approaches for the data structures which grow unboundly. The work of [9, 8, 4, 5, 11] view the program as a generator of data structures. Their techniques are based on the symbolic execution of the program and on a separate summarising process that limits the size of the data structures, which exceed some bound K. Hence, they are called *K-bounded* techniques. On the other hand, the work of [1] summarises the data structures that will be created at run-time by each expression in the program.

We choose the memory approximation technique proposed by Chase *et. al.* [1] for the mapping of variables and pointers to memory locations because the *K-bounded* techniques have several disadvantages. The fixed choice for the maximum acyclic path length in the structure graph does not capture the periodic pattern of a recursively defined data structure. The reason is that different components of the pattern, which are allocated by different expressions in the program below a depth of K, are grouped into a summary node destroying the repeated pattern of a recursively defined data structure. The choice of K cannot be large enough for one structure because other structures will be expanded uselessly and an exponential explosion may be possible. In addition, the truncation process in *K-bounded* techniques is fairly complex. On the other hand, the summarising process [1] which groups data structures allocated by the same expression at run-time not only preserves the pattern of data structures but also makes the truncation process unnecessary.

The Chase *et. al.* [1] approach in computing a finite static approximation of the storage's shape at each expression is based on a static analysis of the program. The data structure that is used, is a directed graph called *storage shape graph* (*SSG*). Its nodes correspond to either variables (*variable* nodes) or to heap allocated structure instances by constructs like *cons* in *Lisp* (*heap* nodes). Each *heap* node in the *SSG* that is created from the symbolic evaluation of an expression e is the summary of all the structure instances created at run-time by the expression e. Edges in the graph correspond to pointers from *variable* nodes and fields within *heap* nodes towards *heap* nodes. Each node can have more than one edges leaving a field or variable because the directed graph conservatively approximates all data structures arising at run-time. Each expression in the program has its own SSG. The initial optimistic approximation for an expression's SSG is the graph with no edges. The most conservative approximation is the SSG with all possible edges.

The algorithm used for the approximation of run-time mapping of variables and pointers to memory locations is a modification of Wegbreit's iterative data flow analysis technique [13]. It iteratively removes the first expression from the worklist, which is initialised to the entry expression in the program, and updates the graph upon entry to the expression by adding new edges in a manner that models its evaluation semantics. Subsequently the successors of the expression in the control flow graph of the program are inserted into the worklist. The algorithm terminates when a fixed point is achieved in each expression's graph. The entry graph to an expression is the union of the graphs for each of the immediate predecessor expressions. For example, the evaluation of **cons** (e_1, e_2) expression updates the graph by adding a new node n_i. The *car* and *cdr* fields of node n_i point to the set of nodes n_1 and n_2 that result from evaluation of e_1 and e_2 correspondingly. Thus, we add to the graph the edges directed from the *car* field of n_i to nodes in n_1, and the edges directed from the *cdr* field of n_i to nodes in n_2.

Cycles in the graph may either represent a cycle in a data structure at run-time or an unbounded acyclic data structure. When the analysis is complete, the *SSG* graph of each expression e is a conservative approximation of all pointer paths that could arise after executing the expression e.

The *storage shape graph (SSG)* after the execution of the following loop example is shown in figure 2.

while $X \neq \emptyset$ **do**
    $Y \leftarrow cons\ (X.car, Y);$
    $X \leftarrow X.cdr$

The following kinds of update operations are applied to an *SSG* graph.

- A *strong update* reflects the fact that after a variable or a field in a node has been changed, due to either an assignment or a structure modification, it must point to a new location rather than the old one. It is not always correct to perform a *strong update*.
- A *weak update* adds the new edges from a variable node or a field in a node to their previous set of edges. It is always correct to perform a weak update, but it provides poor information.

In *SSG* graphs, the appropriate condition for a strong update is the assigned pointer to point to a unique node.

All the techniques which approximate the memory layouts during the program's execution do not analyze unrestricted pointer arithmetic that is possible in languages such as C.

4.3 Computing Data Dependences in Dynamically Allocated Objects

We extend the memory analysis model proposed by Chase *et. al.* [1] by labelling each edge that is emanating from either a field in a *heap* node or a *variable* node with a label which is the last expression either setting the content of the field in the node or assigning to the variable respectively. We also introduce a label for each node to be able to distinguish nodes that are local to a function from nodes that are globally accessible. Thus, if a node is pointed to by either a global variable or a pointer field in a global node it is considered global; otherwise it is considered local.

In order to detect dependences we compute for each expression e the set of locations read by e, R_e, and the set of locations written by e, W_e. A location is written, either if it is first allocated as the result of evaluating a *cons*, or if it is updated in a store. A location can have the value of either a constant or a pointer. The R_e and W_e are computed upon the *SSG* entering the expression e. This entry graph is the union of the graphs for each of the immediate predecessor expressions. As an example, we consider an expression e that has the form $x \leftarrow z$ where x, z are pointers with *access paths* $x.a_{0..n}$, $z.b_{0..l}$ respectively. The R_e and W_e are computed by the following equations using

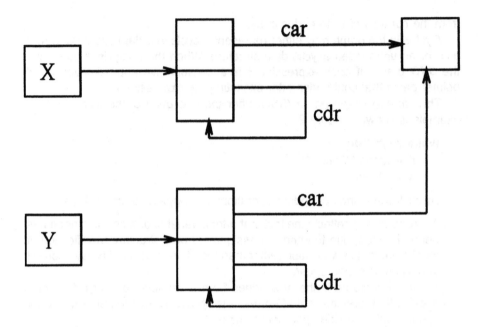

Fig. 2. The Storage Shape Graph

the definitions in subsection 4.1:

$$R_e = \bigcup_{i=0}^{n-1} loc(x.a_{1..i}) \cup \bigcup_{j=0}^{l} loc(z.b_{1..j}) \tag{1}$$

$$W_e = loc(x.a_{0..n}) \tag{2}$$

The SSG graph of a function call is computed as follows: We update the SSG graph that enters the function call by adding new edges emanating from the formal parameters of the function to their bindings in order to model the parameter passing; subsequently we propagate the updated SSG graph through the function's code and we modify it in a manner that models the evaluation semantics of the function's code. Finally we introduce a new variable node which points to the returned value from the function call. For each function call we compute the set of globally accessed locations read by the function, R_e, and the set of globally accessed locations written by the function, W_e. Our approach works on the function's use differing form the Larus's technique [8] which works on the function's definition. By working on the function's definition the union of the memory approximating graphs which are reaching all the function's invocations in a program is propagated through the function's body making indistinguishable the data dependences caused by different invocations. Hence our method is more precise than Larus's method at the expense of using more computer resources.

According to the data dependence definitions in section (2) the conservative approximation of the dependences is computed as follows:

- the flow dependences for each expression e with $R_e \neq \emptyset$ are determined by the labels of the edges that are emanating from the locations in the R_e set;
- the output dependences for each expression e with $W_e \neq \emptyset$ are computed by finding the edges that come out from the locations written by the expression e. The labels of the edges conservatively approximate the output dependences of the expression e;
- we determine the anti-dependences for each expression e with $W_e \neq \emptyset$ by examining the R_{e_i} sets of the expressions e_i that are *predecessors* of e in the control flow graph. The expression e has an anti-dependence on e_i, if the following condition is satisfied: the expression e_i reads a location written by e and the location has an emanating edge labelled with an expression on which e is a potentially output dependent.

5   Identifying the available Parallelism

We identify the available parallelism in a program by computing the required precedence constraints in order the parallel execution of a program to be compatible with the semantics of sequential execution. For the identification of the available parallelism, we employ an intermediate program representation called Graphical Representation Model GRM that is able to express the *Lisp* program's performance characteristics, such as available concurrency [6]. The transformation of a *Lisp* program into a GRM involves the construction of a GRM graph for each function in the *Lisp* program. A GRM graph is a 2-tuple $G = (N, E_{pc})$, Where:

N is a set of nodes. GRM graphs have the following five kinds of nodes: a *simple* node, a *function call* node, an *iteration* node, a *conditional* node, and a *composite* node. We define $id : N \rightarrow Z^+$ so that $id(n)$ results in a unique identifier for node n over all GRM graphs in the program. Each node carries the following additional information:

- IMP, is the set of variables and parameters of a function which enter a node and are read by it. Each variable and parameter is accompanied by its type and its average size;
- EXP, is a set of variables and parameters that are written and exit from a node. In addition we declare that a node is an argument to a function call by including the parameter of the function that is bound to that argument along with the function name in the node's EXP;
- S_{pc}, is a set that defines the precedence constrains of the node due to destructive operations on structures in the node and is calculated using the method described in the subsection 4.3;

- H_d, is a flag which becomes "true" when we cannot analyze the effects of the node. The flag H_d of any node which has a graph containing a node with its H_d flag having the value "true" is set to "true".

E_{pc} is the set of edges that enforces precedence constraints and identifies the available parallelism. The edge (n_a, n_b) denotes that the node n_a has to complete execution before the node n_b starts. The E_{pc} imposes a partial order $\prec$ on N that is respected in the following sense:

- if $n_a \prec n_b$ then n_b cannot be started until n_a has been completed.

We compute the set of precedence constraints E_{pc} by assuming sequential execution and specify only the required precedence constraints that result from the semantics of the sequential execution. The computation uses information that is provided by the flag H_d and the sets IMP, EXP, S_{pc} in each GRM graph g's node; and the fact that the order in g's set of nodes N is compatible with the semantics of sequential execution. Consequently, we examine each node n_i in N whether it is considered *hard* to analyse by checking the value of the flag H_d. If the flag H_d has the value "true", then n_i has to complete execution before any other node n_m that follows n_i in N. Otherwise n_i precedes in execution any node n_k which results from the set of precedence constraints $n_i.S_{pc}$ and any node n_j that follows n_i in N and n_j has got a variable or parameter x in its set $n_j.IMP$ which is also in $n_i.EXP$.

6 Related Work

Cytron *et. al.* [2] propose a method for eliminating some storage related data dependences by introducing variable instances specific to processes for variables which are written more than once. This technique is referred to as privatisation. If a variable X is privatised in a set of processes, then each process in the set computes a value for an instance of X which is referred to in the process allowing the processes to be executed concurrently. A variable X can be privatised in a set of processes if it can be decided at compile-time which process provides the value for X that will be used after the termination of the processes. This decision cannot be made at compile-time for processes which are inedges at a join node in the control flow graph of a program, hence their sequentialisation is unavoidable. The SSA transformation of a program overcomes this problem by introducing a new instance of a variable X at join nodes (see 5th SSA rule) and therefore exposes more parallelism.

Larus and Hilfinger describe a technique in [9] for detecting conflicts between expressions which access data structures. The analysis uses a *K-bounded* technique to approximate the run time mapping of variables and pointers to memory locations. Conflict analysis is less precise than data dependence analysis because as defined in [9] two expressions e_1 and e_2 conflict if both potentially access the same memory location l and at least one of them writes into l, even if there is an intervening write into l along the execution path that joins e_1 and e_2.

In [8], Larus proposes a technique for data dependence analysis based again on a *K-bounded* memory approximation technique. However, his technique is less efficient in precision and performance than the technique proposed in this paper. His labelling scheme does not provide any information about the last expression that modifies a particular memory location. Hence his technique has to compute for each expression e the set of definitions – expressions and the locations they modify– that reach e.

Horwitz *et. al.* in [3] propose a data dependence analysis technique that is based on Jones and Muchnick *K-bounded* technique for approximating the memory layouts which could arise at each program point. They use similar labelling scheme, but they do not consider the interprocedural aspect of the dependence analysis.

All the techniques discussed in this paper share the drawback of introducing spurious data dependences because they are based on a finite representation of unbounded data structures.

7 Conclusions

In this paper, first we have presented our approach for exposing the available parallelism in a *Lisp* program which consists of:

- the transformation of a *Lisp* program into *SSA* form in order to eliminate the *Anti-Dependences* and *Output Dependences* caused by assignments to scalar variables, thus revealing more parallelism than the "privatization" technique proposed by Cytron *et. al.* [2];
- the detection of the data dependences due to destructive updates to data structures based on our development of the memory approximation technique proposed by Chase *et. al.* [1] which is more precise than Larus's method [8].

Consequently, we have presented our method for identifying the available parallelism in a *Lisp* program by computing the necessary precedence constrains due to data dependences.

References

1. David R. Chase, Mark Wegman, and F. Kenneth Zadeck. Analysis of Pointers and Structures. *SIGPLAN'90 Conference on Programming Language Design and Implementation, Vol. 25, Num. 6, pages 296-310*, June 1990.
2. Ron Cytron, Michael Hind, and Wilson Hsieh. Automatic Generation of DAG Parallelism. *SIGPLAN notices, volume 25, number 7, pages 54-68*, July 1989.
3. Susan Horwitz, Phil Pfeiffer, and Thomas Reps. Dependence Analysis for Pointer Variables. *Proceedings of the SIGPLAN '89 Symposium on Compiler Construction, Vol. 24, Num. 7, pages 28-40*, June 1989.
4. N. D. Jones and S. S. Muchnick. Flow Analysis and Optimization of LISP-like Strutures. *Program Flow Analysis: Theory and Applications, chapter 4, pages 102-131, Prentice-Hall*, 1981.

5. N. D. Jones and S. S. Muchnick. A Flexible Approach to Interprocedural Data Flow Analysis and Programs with Recursive Data Structures. *9th Annual ACM Symposium on Principles of Programming Languages, pages 66-74*, January 1982.
6. Spiridon Kalogeropulos. Compiling Techniques for the Parallel Execution of Lisp Programs. Technical report, Bath University, 1990.
7. Spiridon Kalogeropulos. On partitioning lisp programs. *Proceedings of the 1990 EUROPAL: High Performance and Parallel Computing in Lisp Conference*, November 1990.
8. James R Larus. Restructuring Symbolic Programs for Concurrent Execution on Multiprocessors. Technical Report UCB/CSD 89/502, University of California, 1989.
9. James R. Larus and Paul N. Hilfinger. Detecting Conflicts Between Structure Accesses. *Proceedings of the SIGPLAN '88 Conference on Programming Language Design and Implementation Atlanta, Georgia, pages 21-34*, June 1988.
10. B. K. Rosen, Mark N. Wegman, and F. Kenneth Zadeck. Global Value Numbers and Redundant Computations. *Proceeding of the Fifteenth Annual ACM SIGACT-SIGPLAN Symposium on Principles of Programming Languages, p. 12-27*, 1988.
11. C. Ruggieri and T. P. Murtagh. Lifetime Analysis of Dynamically Allocated Objects. *Fifteenth Annual ACM Symposium on Principles of Programming Languages, pages 285-293*, January 1988.
12. Robert Tarjan. Depth-First Search and Linear Graph Algorithms. *SIAM Journal on Comput. Vol. 1, No. 2, p. 146-160*, June 1972.
13. Ben Wegbreit. Property Extraction in Well-founded Property Sets. *IEEE Transactions on Software Engineering, SE-1 (3), pages 270-285*, September 1975.

Automatic Parallelization by Pattern–Matching

Christoph W. Keßler*** and Wolfgang J. Paul

Fachbereich Informatik
Universität Saarbrücken
Postfach 1150
D-66041 Saarbrücken, Germany

Abstract. We present the top–down design of a new system which performs automatic parallelization of numerical Fortran 77 or C source programs for execution on distributed-memory message – passing multiprocessors such as e.g. the INTEL iPSC860 or the TMC CM-5.
The key idea is a high–level pattern-matching approach which in some useful way permits partial restructuring of a wide class of numerical programs. With only a few hundred patterns, we will be able to completely match many important numerical algorithms. Together with mathematical background knowledge and parallel compiler engineering experience, this opens access to a new potential for automatic parallelization that has never been exploited before.

1   Introduction and Overview

Current distributed memory multiprocessers are hard to program, and predicting the performance of a nontrivial parallel program is not easy either. Thus it is a natural consequence to leave as much as possible of this tedious work to an optimizing parallelizing compiler. The programmer wants to feed in just the sequential program and get out optimized parallel code.

Today, truly automatic parallelization is yet a dream (and some people believe it will remain so forever). Currently, research concentrates more on parallel programming languages for distributed memory systems (such as e.g. Fortran–D ([HKT91]) or Vienna Fortran ([CMZ92])) than on parallelizing compilers.

The state of the art in both parallelizing compilers and compilers for parallel programming languages for distributed memory multiprocessors is semiautomatic parallelization: The programmer supplies the compiler with array distribution specifications (e.g. in the form of directives, as in Fortran–D), and the job of the compiler is to insert masks and communication statements according to this specification. This enables the programmer to write his code in the single–program–multiple–data programming paradigm which is well suited for scientific (numeric) applications. However, the efficiency of the generated parallel code is heavily dependent on the chosen data distribution.

---

* Research funded by Graduiertenkolleg Informatik at Saarbrücken University
** email: kessler@cs.uni-sb.de

This user interaction seems inevitable since the problem of determining optimal array distributions is a hard one, and only the user seems to possess sufficient knowledge of his program in order to decide which distributions to choose to maintain parallel program efficiency.

However, for large application programs with lots of arrays and complex distribution relations between them, this becomes impracticable because the user cannot solve this optimization problem either. Moreover, detailed knowledge of the target machine must be available at this step, and different parts of the application program may require different data partitioning schemes to perform efficiently. Where may redistribution be useful, and where not? Furthermore, the quality of a given data distribution is also dependent on the underlying hardware. Changing the hardware platform means repeating the whole parallelization procedure.

Recently some research has been done on automatic derivation of data distribution ([KLS90, GB90, LC90, Who91, KK91]), but we are missing a really automatic approach which leaves no partial work to the programmer any more and requires no user interaction.

Some recent research has recommended to apply pattern matching on a quite low level to facilitate parallelization and optimizations ([GB90, PP91, CHZ91a, CHZ91b]). We claim that pattern matching can be usefully applied to entire programs as the *core* of an automatic parallelization system.

How can pattern recognition techniques be motivated? In order to answer this question, we have examined lots of numerical application algorithms that are typically run on distributed memory multiprocessors, e.g. the algorithms considered in [Mül89] or the algorithms occurring in a parallel numerics course [Lou92]. These algorithms contain basic linear algebra subroutines (see also [LHKK79, DDHH88]), direct solvers for linear equation systems (such as Gaussian Elimination, LU, QR or Cholesky decomposition), Simplex, iterative linear equation solvers (such as Jacobi, Gauß–Seidel, JOR, SOR and Conjugate–Gradient solver), fixpoint iterations (e.g. square–rooting a matrix), grid relaxations (used e.g. for numerical solution of differential equations), interpolation problems, numerical integration and differentiation, and multigrid algorithms.

We observed that these numerical algorithms are made up of only a few (around 100) characteristic programming schemes (called *patterns*) such as e.g. vector and matrix operations, simple recurrences, relaxation operations or simple reduction operations. We describe these patterns in more detail in section 3.

We claim that these few patterns cover a broad range of numerical application codes that are actually run on distributed–memory multiprocessors. We exemplify this in section 3 by examining the source codes of actual application programs.

Faced with these real–world codes, the pattern matcher must be robust against semantics preserving code transformations, in order to maintain acceptability. In general, there are several different implementations (called *templates*) of the same pattern which is, in some way, a normal form of all its templates. The job of pattern matching is to compare a given piece of the source program with the templates, to choose the corresponding pattern and to replace this program piece by an instance of that pattern. We will describe our pattern matching algorithm in detail in section 4.

Once this pattern matching tool performs well, the rest is quite simple: locally find out what the programmer's intention was, and then select well–suited and highly optimized target code for this piece of the application. If necessary, these code pieces must be connected by appropriate redistribution operations.

The remaining sections describe the other components of our parallelization system called PARAMAT ("PARallelize Automatically by pattern MATching") that use the pattern matcher's output in order to generate efficient parallel code.

2 Preprocessing the Source Code

It is very important that the program is rather explicit when it is submitted to automatic parallelization by pattern matching. Beyond a sophisticated dependence analysis, the following transformations[3] should be carried out in order to facilitate pattern matching:

- procedure inlining[4]
- constant propagation
- induction variable recognition (substitution, if possible)
- temporary variable recognition (substitution or temporary scalar expansion)
- dead code elimination
- conversion of GOTO's into if–then–else or while statements, where possible
- loop distribution

Furthermore we disallow constructs causing run–time dependencies which cannot be recognized by the prototype version of PARAMAT. This especially concerns index vectors, so programs containing indirect array references will be rejected just at the beginning. For these cases, dynamic techniques must be applied (see e.g. [SCMB90]). In this work we restrict ourselves to static parallelization.

3 Which Patterns are Supported?

Now, let us describe which patterns should be included into the pattern library of PARAMAT. On the one hand, we want to cover a very high percentage of numerical programs, on the other hand we must not use too many patterns, leading to inacceptable compile times.

---

[3] For a detailed description of optimizing transformations, see e.g. [ZC90].

[4] This is only for a prototype version of PARAMAT in order to make the implementation easier. Interprocedural analysis is currently evolving, and we will include interprocedural analysis tools into the final system as soon as they become adequately reliable. Our case studies have shown that for purely numerical programs, procedure inlining will blow up program size by only a small constant factor. Since this only appears at compile time, it can be tolerated.

Of course we cannot go beyond a certain level — one single pattern for a whole application program of several hundred lines would be nonsense. If a piece of program is too exotic and occurs very seldom, then it is not worth becoming a pattern. Thus the philosophy is to have as many patterns as necessary, and as few as possible.

The basic algorithms considered in [Mül89] and [Lou92] suggest that a rather small number of patterns will suffice to cover large parts — especially the time-critical ones — of real application programs. In order to exemplify this assumption, we took a closer look to some real-world codes (after being normalized by the transformations described in the last section):

- the Livermore Loops (cf. [McM86]),
- some kernels from the NAS Benchmark program (cf. [BB86]),
- a LU decomposition code from the netlib,
- a least-square Conjugate Gradient solver[5] from [Lou92],
- selected codes from the Perfect Club Benchmarks
- and others.

Faced with these codes, we created appropriate patterns, subpatterns and templates while carefully making the patterns robust against many possible semantics-preserving code modifications. The result of this research, the current version of the Basic PARAMAT Library, unfortunately cannot presented here for lack of space, but it is listed in [Keß93a]. A brief summary of the patterns is given in Tab. 1. Some ideas for the efficient distributed-memory parallel implementation of all the patterns occurring in these algorithms are summarized in [Mül89].

As one can see from Tab. 1, the number of low-level patterns (statement level) is rather limited; so is the number of medium-level patterns (loop level, e.g. vector instructions). The number of medium-level patterns can additionally be restricted by maintaining loop normal forms generated by loop distribution; we will discuss this following the example of section 4.4. The most critical point is how many *high*-level patterns (and which) to include in the library; they are often too specific to include them into the Basic Library. This question will later be alleviated by introducing a modular concept where the pattern library may be individually composed from the basic and other more specific sub-libraries in a hierarchically organized database.

With the current version of the Basic Pattern Library — containing only 100 patterns — we are able to cover *completely* (and thus, to parallelize automatically) a lot of the basic numerical codes from [Mül89] and [Lou92], e.g. Gaussian Elimination (with pivoting), LU decomposition, Simplex, Jacobi relaxation, Gauß-Seidel relaxation, JOR, SOR and CG, iteratively square-rooting a matrix, and others. The results for the Livermore Loops are given in Tab. 2. We obtained similar results for the other application codes listed above.

---

[5] E.g. the main patterns generally contained in CG-algorithms are $CGINIT^{(1)}$, $MV^{(2)}$ or $VM^{(2)}$ (vector-matrix multiply), $VADD^{(1)}$, $VADDMUL^{(1)}$ (vector instructions), $SSP^{(1)}$ (standard scalar product) and $SV^{(1)}$ (scalar-vector multiply).

order	patterns	number
0	scalar arithm. operations, init, max, min, swap, assign, read write	20
	difference stars and substars (first and second order)	3
1	vector instructions, v-init/-assign/-copy/-swap, v-read/write, SV	16
	reductions: v-sum, scalarproducts, vector norms	8
	reductions: vector maximization/minimizations	6
	1D relaxation steps	2
	first order linear recurrences	2
2	matrix operations, m-init/-assign/-copy, m-read/-write, SM	12
	vector/matrix multiplication patterns	4
	2D-reductions: m-sum, concurrent v-sum, matrix norms	5
	2D-reductions: m-max/min, row/col-max/min	8
	diverse relaxation steps	4
	global matrix updates (GJstep, GRstep,..., MSOLVEL/-U)	6
3	matrix multiplication	2
	matrix inversion, GReduce	2

Table 1. A brief summary of the patterns included into the current version of the Basic PARAMAT Pattern Library. No pattern has more than three different templates, most patterns have only one or two. All BLAS routines operating on dense real matrices have been entered.

4 Pattern–Matching

Pattern Matching is done in a rather intuitive way. It is supported by a suitable hierarchical representation of the input program and the complexity is diminished by a suitable hierarchical ordering of the possible patterns. For each template of each pattern there exists a small procedure which tests whether a given piece of program matches this pattern, and if yes, it returns an *instance* of this pattern where the formal pattern parameters are bound to the corresponding actual parameters occurring in the program piece.

4.1 Program Representation

The source program is represented by an attributed syntax tree. The nodes are control statements (do, if, etc.), assignment statements, or expression operators ($+, -, *, /$ etc.). There is one root node called main which represents the highest program control level.

We distinguish between two kinds of directed edges between nodes:

1. *vertical edges:* these are the edges contained in the syntax tree representation of the program, e.g. from all statement nodes corresponding to the body of a do statement to the do node, from the then resp. else statement nodes to the corresponding if node, from expression tree nodes to their parent nodes and so on.

LL	Name	recognized patterns	recogn. loops
1	Hydrofragment	$GVOP^{(1)}$	1 from 1
3	Inner Product	$SSP^{(1)}$	1 from 1
5	tri-diag. elim., below diagonal	$FOLRO^{(1)}$	1 from 1
8	A.D.I Integration	$VDIF^{(1)}(3x)$, $GVOP^{(1)}(3x)$	6 from 6
9	Numerical Integration	$GVOP^{(1)}$	1 from 1
10	Numerical Differentiation	$GVOP^{(1)}$	19 from 19
11	First Sum	$FOLR^{(1)}$	1 from 1
12	First Difference	$VDIF^{(1)}$	1 from 1
13	2D particle in a cell	$VCOPY^{(1)}(4x)$, $VADD^{(1)}$ $(2x)$, $GVOP^{(1)}(4x)$	10 from 17
14	1D particle in a cell	$GVOP^{(1)}(3x)$, $VCOPY^{(1)}$ $(1x)$, $VADD^{(1)}(2x)$	6 from 12
18	2D explicit hydrodyn. fragment	$MADDMUL^{(2)}(2x)$	2 from 6
21	Matrix Product	$MMO^{(3)}$	1 from 1
22	Planckian Distribution	$GVOP^{(1)}(2x)$	2 from 2
23	2D implicit hydrodyn. fragment	$GAUSSSEIDEL^{(2)}$	1 from 1
24	1D Minimization	$VMINLOC^{(1)}$	1 from 1

Table 2. Analysis of the Livermore Loops: currently recognizable patterns. The right–hand column indicates how many loops (after applying loop distribution) can be covered by patterns from the Library. $GVOP^{(1)}$ denotes a general vector operation, $FOLRO^{(1)}$ and $FOLR^{(1)}$ first order linear recurrences, $VDIF^{(1)}$ a 1D difference star; $VMINLOC^{(1)}$ finds in a vector the location with minimal absolute value.

2. *horizontal edges:* these edges establish a partial execution order among several child nodes of the same parent node; they are caused by data dependency. If there might exist a loop–independent[6] data dependence from a statement S_1 to another statement S_2, then a horizontal edge e must be drawn in the following way: Let v be the lowest common vertical successor of both S_1 and S_2, and let u_1, u_2 be direct vertical predecessors (*'son statements'*) of v such that u_1 is a vertical successor of S_1 (but not of S_2) and u_2 is a vertical successor of S_2 (but not of S_1), see the figure below:

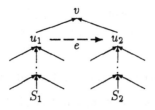

---

[6] We do not consider loop–carried dependences here because all patterns provided so far allow dependence cycles only from a statement to itself. This is sufficient for most applications if we have applied the restructuring transformations listed in section 2 before.

Then the horizontal edge e must be drawn from u_1 to u_2, implying a partial execution order on the son statements of v. Note that S_1 may be equal to u_1 and S_2 equal to u_2. If $S_1 = S_2$ then there is no edge necessary, of course. If it is not clear at compile time which of several statements is the source of a dependence, then all of them are to be connected with the target node by the way just described. The order among these possible source nodes must be maintained by inserting horizontal edges following the textual order of the statements in the source program.

Thus the vertical edges form a tree while the horizontal edges form a directed acyclic graph on each control hierarchy level. For an example, see section 4.4.

The horizontal edges may be extremely useful when trying to recognize patterns from subpatterns which are textually separated by other pieces of code not affecting the relations between these subpatterns.

4.2 Pattern Hierarchy Graph

The Pattern Hierarchy Graph (PHG) consists of all possible predefined patterns as its nodes. There is a directed edge from one pattern p_1 to another pattern p_2 if p_1 may occur as a subpattern of p_2 (see Fig. 1 for an example). Thus the PHG is acyclic.

Each pattern has an *order* number which indicates how many loop nests it contains. Thus an edge from p_1 to p_2 in the PHG implies that $order(p_1) \leq order(p_2)$.

The PHG is called *complete* for a pattern p if it contains p and all possible subpatterns p_i of p and is complete for all p_i.

Usually, a pattern has only a few predecessors and a few successors in the PHG. The pattern matching algorithm only needs to inspect the PHG successor's templates of an already matched pattern p when looking for a possible pattern containing p as a subpattern. That results in a large increase in matching speed compared with simple testing of all predefined templates.

4.3 The Matching Algorithm

The matching algorithm descends the syntax tree as follows:

```
function stmtdescend(node)
if node is not a leaf
then forall sons s of node (in textual order)
     do stmtdescend(s) od
fi
forall expressions e occurring in node
do exprdescend(e) od
/* now all vertical predecessors (substmt's, subexpr's) of node are known */
/* possible patterns p of node are all direct PHG successors (superpatterns)
   of the patterns already computed for the sons s of node */
```

forall possible patterns p for *node*

do   test by $match(p, node)$ whether there is an instance q of p
      that matches *node* **od**

replace *node* by q just computed

reset pointers to and from *node* correctly

repeat

      forall direct predecessors x of *node* in this block

      do /$\star$ x has been visited earlier than *node* $\star$/

          test by $merge(x, node)$ whether there is an instance y
          of a pattern that consists exactly of x and *node*

      od

      replace x and *node* by y just computed;

      reset edges to or from x and *node* to or from y, respectively;

      rename y by *node*

until there are no mergeable predecessors for *node* left.

The function $exprdescend()$ traverses the expression trees in a similar way.

This pattern matcher is similar to other bottom–up pattern matching algorithms such as used in automatically generated code generators, e.g. BURG ([FHP92]). These systems automatically[7] generate a tree automaton whose state table corresponds to our PHG. Unfortunately, all automatic systems work only on (syntax) trees; this disables matching along horizontal edges as required here. Another advantage of our simple pattern matcher is that it can locally deviate from the general scheme to save patterns and matching time, such as we did for matching difference stars (see [Keß93a]).

4.4 A simple example

Let us start with a simple example. Matrix multiplication is well suited for this purpose since it is not so trivial but is not made up of too many subpatterns so that its pattern hierarchy graph (Fig. 1) remains quite handy.

Suppose the programmer has coded a matrix multiplication in the following way:

---

[7] This would make the pattern specification easier if there were many intermediate patterns which only propagate information upwards and never occur in a final matched program. But this does not really occur in our case.

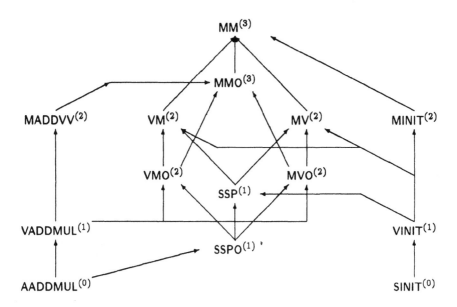

Fig. 1. The pattern hierarchy graph of Matrix Multiplication. It covers all possible ways how matrix multiplication may be coded without using an auxiliary variable.

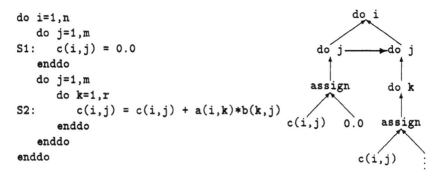

The pattern matcher traverses the syntax tree (see above) by a leftmost depth–first–search. First the assignment node ASSIGN[(0)] corresponding to S1 will be replaced by the pattern instance SINIT[(0)]$(c, i, j, 0.0)$ since this is the leftmost leaf of the syntax tree (determined by the horizontal edge caused by the data flow dependence from S1 to S2).

Pursuing this back towards the root, the do j loop around S1 will be matched with the SINIT[(0)] node, resulting in a new pattern instance VINIT[(1)]$(c(i, *), j, m, 0.0)$ (vector initialization).

Then the algorithm descends further towards S2, replaces the assignment statement leaf corresponding to S2 by a pattern instance AADDMUL[(0)]$(c(i,j), a(i,k), b(k,j))$ (accumulatively adding products) and, following the suitable edge in the PHG, merges this with the do k loop giving the instance SSPO[(1)]$(c(i,j),$

$a(i, *)$, $b(*, j)$, k, r) (standard scalar product with offset). Now the program corresponding to the modified syntax tree looks as follows:

```
do i=1,n
   VINIT(c(i,*), j, m, 0.0)
   do j=1,m
      SSPO(c(i,j), a(i,*), b(*,j), k, r)
   enddo
enddo
```

The do j loop can be merged with the $\mathrm{SSPO}^{(1)}$ instance resulting in an instance $\mathrm{VMO}^{(2)}(c(i, *), a(i, *), b, k, r, j, m)$ (vector–matrix multiply with offset). Now the $\mathrm{VINIT}^{(1)}$ instance is a mergeable horizontal predecessor of the $\mathrm{VMO}^{(2)}$ instance. Merging them yields a new pattern instance $\mathrm{VM}^{(2)}(c(i, *), a(i, *), b, k, r, j, m)$ (vector–matrix multiply), which, in turn, can be matched with the do i loop resulting in an instance $\mathrm{MM}^{(3)}(c, a, b, k, r, j, m, i, n)$ (matrix multiply) representing this entire piece of code.

We remark that in this small example, no loop distribution had been applied before. This did not matter since the PHG covers all sensible codings of matrix multiplication, with and without loops being distributed, at the expense of a few more patterns and edges in the PHG. In general, we will have to test whether it is more useful to put more intelligence into the PHG (and thus, perhaps, wasting some space and (compile) time), or to rely on non–failing basic transformations such as loop distribution.

5 A Parallel Algorithm for each Pattern

For each predefined pattern there exists a suitable parallel algorithm implementing this pattern, parameterized by the problem size (e.g. matrix extents) and, if necessary, also by the data partitionings for the arrays involved in this pattern.

A major benefit of this technique is that once the pattern is recognized, the best possible algorithm for this pattern will be chosen. If e.g. the programmer has implemented a Gauß–Seidel relaxation in a wave–front manner, the system should choose another implementation which is better suited for efficient parallelization, e.g. a red–black scheme (which has the same convergence property as the wavefront scheme) or to replace it by the double number of Jacobi– or Gauß–Seidel–Jacobi hybrid iterations[8].

Another occasion for algorithm replacement are simple linear recurrences. Consider for instance the following piece of code:

```
X[1] = A[1]
```

---

[8] The latter replacements should be a priori allowed by the user. We expect that the average user does not want to compare Gauß–Seidel with Jacobi but to get the actually fastest parallel implementation — independent of a particular relaxation coding.

```
      DO 1 I=2,1000
        X[I] = A[I] + B[I] * X[I-1]
1     CONTINUE
```

Independent of the data partitioning, this code is doomed to sequential execution due to the loop–carried data dependence on array X. Once recognized as an instance of the FOLR pattern (First Order Linear Recurrence), this piece of code will be replaced by recursive doubling techniques[9] described in [KS73].

For a lot of patterns, the programming environment supplies highly optimized parallel algorithms, e.g. for VSUM (global summation of vector elements). In these cases the parallel algorithm simply consists of a runtime library call.

For each parallel implementation of a pattern (located in a large algorithm library) there is an assigned cost function which is also parameterized by problem size and array partitionings. This function models the run time behaviour of the algorithm under consideration. Section 7 explains how it is determined.

6 Alignment and Partitioning

The problem of array partitioning consists of two steps. First, it must be determined how arrays should be *aligned* with each other, i.e. which elements of different arrays should be mapped together to the same (virtual) processor (if possible) to minimize interprocessor communication. The alignment preferences are induced by the array references occurring in the source program. Second, the array elements must be *distributed*, i.e. actually mapped to a concrete processing element of the (physical) target machine. At this stage, aligned array sections can be handled as an entity.

For alignment and partitioning issues, we will use well–known techniques introduced by Li and Chen ([LC90]), Knobe et al. ([KLS90, KN90]) or Wholey ([Who91]). The cost estimate functions in these approaches will be replaced by our own cost functions being described in the next section.

The problem of determining optimal data alignment and distribution is well-known to be NP–complete (cf. [LC90]), thus automatic partitioning may take exponential time in the worst case. That is why we intend to limit the number of distribution alternatives severely[10]. Furthermore, we limit the number of partitionable array dimensions to 2. Together with the simplification of the source program by pattern matching, these restrictions enable the application of a branch–and–bound search for the optimal distribution, as done in [Hay93].

For each pattern there generally exists one locally optimal data distribution scheme. E.g. for matrix multiplication $C = A \cdot B$, matrix A should be distributed by row and matrix B should be distributed by column, and furthermore,

---

[9] The optimal number of recursive doubling steps depends on the number of iterations and on the message startup time of the target machine. For small problem sizes, sequential execution will be faster.

[10] In fact we will only allow the following five possibilities (for two-dimensional arrays): row-/column-/block-contiguous and row- or column–cyclic (cf. e.g. [GB90]). For all the applications considered so far these are enough to supply good distributions.

C should be aligned with either A or B. PARAMAT provides a default recommendation for alignment and one for array distribution for each pattern[11]. If these recommendations cause an alignment or distribution conflict throughout the program (and they will usually do), the given recommendations will be the first choices when searching for the optimal data distribution.

Some recommendation examples are summarized in Tab. 3.

The points between the pattern instances in the final matched program representation are natural places for possible redistribution of arrays. In [KK91] an interesting method for (static) redistribution has been presented; we will include it into the PARAMAT system with small modifications. The details will be given in a later paper.

pattern	algorithm	alignment recomm.	distribution recomm.
$A = \text{MCOPY}^{(2)}(B)$	matrix copy	$A \equiv B$	arbitrarily
$V = \text{VCOPY}^{(1)}(W)$	vector copy	$V \equiv W$	arbitrarily
$A = \text{MJACOBI}^{(2)}(B)$	one Jacobi step	$A \equiv B$	quadratic blocks
$C = \text{MM}^{(3)}(A, B)$	matrix multiply	$A \equiv C \lor B \equiv C$	A by row, B by col.
$s = \text{VSUM}^{(1)}(V)$	vector sum	arbitrarily	arbitrarily
$s = \text{SSP}^{(1)}(V, W)$	dot product	$V \equiv W$	arbitrarily

Table 3. Array alignment and distribution recommendations for some patterns

7 Determining Cost Functions: Estimating and Benchmarking

A simple way to determine the run time of a given parallel algorithm parameterized by problem size and array partitions is to estimate it from the basic computation and communication statements occurring in that algorithm (see e.g. [FBZ92]).

In reality, however, it seems that these estimations very rarely meet the actual run time since a parallel computer such as the INTEL iPSC860 behaves as a chaotic system, its performance heavily depending on the actual network traffic, which, in turn, depends on the algorithm under consideration. This problem has been adressed in [BFKK91]. There performance estimation is based on benchmarking of simple communication patterns and propagating this information 'up' through the program's syntax tree.

Our parallelizer will be able to inspect precomputed tables of *really measured* run times for all patterns (especially, the high–level patterns!), as indicated

---

[11] Note that the alignment recommendation depends only on the pattern itself whereas the distribution recommendation is, in general, also dependent on the target machine and on the problem size (cf. [KK91]).

above. We expect the accuracy of performance prediction being substantially improved by this method.

8 Implementation and Future Extensions

The overall PARAMAT system is outlined in Fig. 2. Note that the time–consuming work concerning parallel algorithm development (either optimized SPMD routines or just operating system calls like GLOBALSUM) and benchmarking their run times for all possible array distributions has not to be performed at compile time but at an earlier stage (at compiler generation time). We intend to develop an automatic benchmarking tool that does this tedious job for us.

Furthermore it will be useful to arrange the Pattern Library as a hierarchical collection of modules which may be individually composed for the special application area.

Up to now, the pattern recognizer and the PARAMAT Basic Pattern Library have been implemented. The results for the Livermore Loops and for the CG solver (cf. Tab. 2, [Lou92]) have been confirmed by the implementation. Currently, the functionality of our pattern recognition tool already exceeds the features presented in this paper (e.g., the pattern recognizer is able to perform loop re-rolling, loop unblocking and similar operations). More details can be found in [Keß93b] and [Keß93a].

9 Conclusions

We have outlined the PARAMAT system which performs automatic parallelization of a restricted but quite important class of numerical programs. Local parallelization is done by pattern matching and algorithm replacement. The pattern matching algorithm with the hierarchical pattern base described above is robust enough to perform its job well. Pattern matching simplifies the program graph and thus alleviates global optimizations such as determining optimal array alignment and partitioning. Pattern matching enables optimal use of the highly optimized operating system routines supplied with the hardware environment. It also supports better performance prediction accuracy by benchmarking higher-level patterns. Beyond automatic parallelization, pattern matching may be of great use at reengineering sequential dusty–deck codes for porting them to other languages or target machines.

The PARAMAT system is limited in some ways. First, it is unable to process *all* source programs. This is taken into account to obtain a really automatic parallelizing compiler *without any* interaction or directives supplied by the user at compile time. Second, the search space for possible array distributions has to be severely restricted to maintain acceptable compile time. In general, heuristics will have to be applied.

A prototype of PARAMAT is currently being implemented at Saarbrücken university. The first target machine will be the Intel iPSC860. The Pattern recognition tool and the Basic Pattern Library are already implemented.

source code: F77.F (later on also F90.f, C.c)

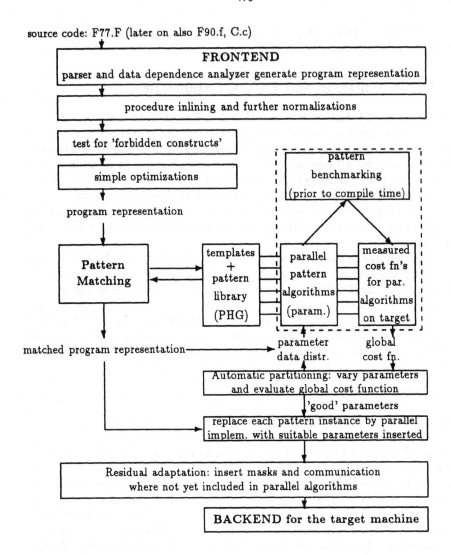

Fig. 2. Block diagram of the overall PARAMAT system. Only the components enclosed in the dashed rectangle (and the back end, of course) are dependent on the target machine. Parallel algorithms for each pattern and their run-time approximations, parameterized by the data partitionings of the arrays involved in the resp. pattern instance, have to be precomputed once for each hardware constellation (pattern benchmarking) *before* compile time.

The PARAMAT system is open for extensions. The pattern library can be extended by adding more pattern modules according to individual application areas. The computation of the run time approximation functions can be automated by a universal benchmarking tool. Changing the hardware platform means only to load another base of parallel algorithms and their run time functions. Thus the PARAMAT system will always be up to date for the latest hardware environments available.

References

[BB86]   David H. Bailey and John T. Barton. The NAS Kernel Benchmark Program. Numerical Aerodynamic Simulations Systems Division, NASA Ames Research Center, June 1986.

[BFKK91] Vasanth Balasundaram, Geoffrey Fox, Ken Kennedy, and Ulrich Kremer. A Static Performance Estimator to Guide Data Partitioning Decisions. In *ACM SIGPLAN Symposium on Principles and Practices of Parallel Programming*, volume 3, pages 213–223, 1991.

[CHZ91a] Barbara M. Chapman, Heinz Herbeck, and Hans P. Zima. Automatic Support for Data Distribution. Technical Report ACPC/TR 91-14, Austrian Center for Parallel Computation, July 1991.

[CHZ91b] Barbara M. Chapman, Heinz Herbeck, and Hans P. Zima. Knowledge-based Parallelization for Distributed Memory Systems. Technical Report ACPC/TR 91-11, Austrian Center for Parallel Computation, April 1991.

[CMZ92]   Barbara Chapman, Piyush Mehrotra, and Hans Zima. Programming in Vienna Fortran. In *Third Workshop on Compilers for Parallel Computers*, 1992.

[DDHH88] J. J. Dongarra, J. DuCroz, S. Hammarling, and R. Hanson. An Extended Set of Fortran Basic Linear Algebra Subprograms. *ACM Trans. on Math. Software*, 14(1):1–32, 1988.

[FBZ92]   Thomas Fahringer, Roman Blasko, and Hans Zima. Automatic Performance Prediction to Support Parallelization of Fortran Programs for Massively Parallel Systems. In *Int. ACM Conference on Supercomputing*, 1992. Washington DC.

[FHP92]   Christopher W. Fraser, Robert R. Henry, and Todd A. Proebsting. BURG — Fast Optimal Instruction Selection and Tree Parsing. *SIGPLAN Notices*, 27(4):68–76, April 1992.

[GB90]   Manish Gupta and Prithviraj Banerjee. Automatic Data Partitioning on Distributed Memory Multiprocessors. Technical Report CRHC-90-14, Center for Reliable and High-Performance Computing, University of Illinois at Urbana-Champaign, Oct. 1990.

[Hay93]   Roman Hayer. Automatische Parallelisierung, Teil 2: Automatische Datenaufteilung für Parallelrechner mit verteiltem Speicher. Master thesis, Universität Saarbrücken, 1993.

[HKT91]   Seema Hiranandani, Ken Kennedy, and Chau-Wen Tseng. Compiler-Support for Machine–Independent Parallel Programming in Fortran-D. Technical Report Rice COMP TR91-149, Rice University, March 1991.

[Keß93a] Christoph W. Keßler. The Basic PARAMAT Pattern Library, May 1993.

[Keß93b] Christoph W. Keßler. Knowledge–Based Automatic Parallelization by Pattern Recognition. In *Proc. of AP'93 Int. Workshop on Automatic Distributed Memory Parallelization, Automatic Data Distribution and Automatic Parallel Performance Prediction, Saarbrücken, Germany*, pages 89–107, 1993.

[KK91] Ken Kennedy and Ulrich Kremer. Automatic Data Alignment and Distribution for Loosely Synchronous Problems in an Interactive Programming Environment. Technical Report COMP TR91-155, Rice University, April 1991.

[KLS90] Kathleen Knobe, Joan D. Lukas, and Guy L. Steele. Data Optimization: Allocation of Arrays to Reduce Communication on SIMD Machines. *Journal of Parallel and Distributed Computing*, 8:102–118, 1990.

[KN90] Kathleen Knobe and Venkataraman Natarajan. Data Optimization: Minimizing Residual Interprocessor Data Motion on SIMD machines. In *Third Symposium on the Frontiers of Massively Parallel Computation*, pages 416–423, 1990.

[KS73] Peter M. Kogge and Harold S. Stone. A Parallel Algorithm for the Efficient Solution of a General Class of Recurrence Equations. *IEEE Transactions on Computers*, C-22(8), August 1973.

[LC90] Jingke Li and Marina Chen. Index Domain Alignment: Minimizing Cost of Cross–referencing between Distributed Arrays. In *Third Symposium on the Frontiers of Massively Parallel Computation*, pages 424–433, 1990.

[LHKK79] C. Lawson, R. Hanson, D. Kincaid, and F. Krogh. Basic Linear Algebra Subprograms for Fortran Usage. *ACM Trans. on Math. Software*, 5:308–325, 1979.

[Lou92] A. K. Louis. Parallele Numerik. Course script and selected programs, unpublished, Universität Saarbrücken, 1992.

[McM86] Frank McMahon. The Livermore Fortran Kernels: A Test of the Numeric Performance Range. Technical report, Lawrence Livermore National Laboratory, 1986.

[Mül89] Silvia M. Müller. Die Auswirkung der Startup-Zeit auf die Leistung paralleler Rechner bei numerischen Anwendungen. Master thesis, Universität Saarbrücken, 1989.

[PP91] Shlomit S. Pinter and Ron Y. Pinter. Program Optimization and Parallelization Using Idioms. In *Principles of Programming Languages*, pages 79–92, 1991.

[SCMB90] J. Saltz, K. Crowley, R. Mirchandaney, and H. Berryman. Runtime Scheduling and Execution of Loops on Message Passing Machines. *Journal of Parallel and Distributed Computing*, 8:303–312, 1990.

[Who91] Skef Wholey. *Automatic Data Mapping for Distributed-Memory Parallel Computers*. PhD thesis, Carnegie Mellon University, Pittsburgh, PA 15213, 1991.

[ZC90] Hans Zima and Barbara Chapman. *Supercompilers for Parallel and Vector Computers*. ACM Press Frontier Series. Addison–Wesley, 1990.

Parallelization - A Case Study

Jürgen Lampe

Dept. of Mathematics, TU Dresden
Mommsenstr.13, D-01062 Dresden
Email: lampe@mathematik.tu-dresden.dbp.de

Abstract. Parallelization of non-regular organised algorithms has turned out to be a very complicated task. Due to the hierarchical structure of context-free languages compiling is an illustrative example for these issues. Thus, the suggested technique may serve as an example for how to develop efficient parallel programs.

Starting from fundamental technical requirements of parallel computers, a list of essentials is compiled which every algorithm has to fulfil. Based on these demands, the concept of local parsability forms the theoretical base for a new approach on parallel parsing. Although the presented method applies only for a subclass of context-free languages it proved to be strong enough to handle nearly all programming languages.

1   Introduction

During the last years innovative hardware developments, the Transputer chip or Intel's i860, e.g., have caused a refreshed interest in parallelization. However, practical experience shows that this is still an intellectual challenge. There is, up to now, no easy way to transform results obtained for abstract parallel computer models like the PRAM-machine in an efficient manner to real world parallel computers.

Compiling is a favourable field for research in algorithmics. Building a compiler is a task large enough to demand for sophisticated tools and it is, on the other hand, well understood and specified with mathematical rigour. However, the situation concerning the design of parallel compilers can be seen to be typically and so this task may serve as a testbed for developing parallel algorithms in general.

In contrast with most of published theoretical advances the few practical experiments showed "...*with a surprising agreement, that a speedup factor of about three can be achieved with about five processors, assuming that the source program is not very small. Increasing the number of processors from five does not seem to essentially raise this factor...*" [1, p.1]

To overwhelm this discrepancy, the reasons for have to be investigated. Here one has to distinguish between the hardware's impact and the problems inseparable connected with the application.

At first we have to state our model of a parallel processing computer. This is a crucial point because the difficulty to transpose theoretical work into practice is originated to a large degree by weakness of claims. Especially the influence of communication is usually underestimated. An analysis of existing papers leads to the conclusion that the efforts for communication should be focussed on when constructing parallel algorithms. In difference to sequential processes the implementation of theoretical computer models by layered virtual machines causes an unacceptable performance degradation.

Here we will take a tightly coupled multiprocessor of the so-called MIMD architecture consisting of a number of processors, data areas and an interconnecting network. The number of data areas is assumed to be remarkable bigger than that of processors. Each processor has access to all the program code. Besides it may own some of the data areas and only in this case it may access them freely. Communication takes place by exchanging the ownership of data areas. Getting and delivering such blocks can consume some relevant amount of time while actual memory access does not cause any additional delay. Parallel computers of this kind can be constructed based on today's technologies making advantage of special hardware designed intentionally for aiding virtual memory management. Lundberg describes in [2] a rather similar experimental configuration for exploiting inherent parallelism in Ada programs.

Alternative implementations taking data blocks as messages for example are imaginable, too.

Compiling is constituted from the tasks lexical analysis, parsing, and, so-called, semantic processing, which comprises simple code generators as well as highly sophisticated optimising back-ends. As attribute grammars have proved useful in numerous investigations we will also refer to this formalism. So the semantic phase corresponds to attribute evaluation. Let us mention, that the division into subtasks does not imply any assumption concerning the actual proceeding, e.g., sequentiality.

Finally, the application of algorithms for processing formal defined languages is not restricted to compiling. There is a growing interest in utilising these techniques in other areas such as describing two-dimensional structures [3], software specifications [4], and proof checkers [5].

2 Locality

A crucial point for the efficiency of each parallel computation is the overhead and the remainder of non-parallelized tasks. (To the latter usually belongs - but is very rarely mentioned - the down-loading of code.) To gain efficient parallel procedures, we have to minimise as both of them as, of course, communication.

Thus, it is not a good idea to take some sequential technique and to turn it into a parallel one, because the intuitive concept of parallelism differs substantially from the class of parallelism that may be utilised by real multiprocessor-computers.

Another awkward direction is the restriction of parallelization efforts to certain parts of an algorithm. Although this may be useful for reasons of methodology, there is a real danger of misleading further investigations. The interlocking of the single processing steps plays a very similar role to those of communication on the next level.

Usually parallel parsing approaches are classified with respect to their processing model (pipeline, SIMD, MIMD, etc.) and to the data partitioning strategy (e.g., free, bounded, static). This may serve for discriminating, but it does not aid potential users in estimating practical applicability. It lacks in stating limits of parallelization and identifying the limiting features.

The most serious boundary for parallelization on MIMD-computers is induced by connectivity and communication. That is why we suggest *locality* of computations to be the most important criterion here.

In detail, one can separate communications in:

(i) control communication, resulting from, e.g., central control by a master processor or using a central common data structure, and

(ii) data communication to near (neighbouring) and/or far processors, caused by the demands of the application.

With the term *locality* we will designate the property of the processes of a parallel algorithm to proceed with as less as possible communication (preferably of type ii). Methods with good locality do not suffer from communicational bottlenecks. Their suitable degree of parallelization is limited by the task's size and the unavoidable *distributed* overhead.

A comparison of parallel compilers known from literature shows very poor results with respect to locality [6, p.33]. This can be interpreted as an explanation for the unsatisfactory behaviour observed in practical experiments.

3 Local Grammars

To achieve a realistic evaluation of potential parallelism in formal language processing we will start with a new approach for parsing. It is based on a concept of localitiy in context-free (cf) languages' theory.

In fact, already the phrase *context free* suggests some kind of independence from the surroundings, of some *locality*. It is also a matter of experience, that usually a human has no problem to determine the syntactical structure of fragmentary program texts or even in the much more complex case of natural language texts. The following is built on an attempt to formalise those features, that assist in parsing fragments of a given text locally in an always correct way.

At first, we have to introduce some notation. Let A be a (finite) alphabet. For every word $w = a_1 a_2 ... a_n$ from elements of A (i.e. $w \in A^+$) let $|w| = n$ denote the *length* of w and w[i:j] the factor (sub-word) $a_i a_{i+1} ... a_j$, with w[i:]=w[i:|w|] for short. As usually, the empty word is denoted by ε, with $|\varepsilon| = 0$ and $A^* = A^+ \cup \{\varepsilon\}$.

Now, let $L \subseteq A^*$ be a decidable formal language over A. Then a word $u \in A^+$ is called a *L-factor of w*, if there exist words x and y in A^* such that w=xuy and $u \in L$.

So for every $w \in A^+$ it is possible to compute the function:

$$rm_L(w,i) = \max_{j=i...|w|} \{0, j \mid w[i:j] \in L\} .$$

I.e., it delivers the length of the longest L-factor of word w, starting at letter i of w.

Definition: Let $w \in A^*$ and $L \subseteq A^*$. Every factor $w[i:rm_L(w,i)]$ such that $rm_L(w, i) \neq 0$ holds, is called a *right-maximal L-factor* of w at point i.

Before continuing, we will specify the notational conventions for grammars and languages that will be used in the remainder.

The tuple $G = (N, T, P, n_0)$ is said to be a context-free grammar, with:

$N = \{n_0, n_1, \ldots n_l\}$ finite set of non-terminal symbols
$T = \{t_0, t_1, \ldots t_k\}$ finite set of terminal symbols
$V = T \cup N$ vocabulary
$P \subseteq N \times V^*$ productions
n_0 root.

Relations $\rightarrow$ (produces directly) and $\xrightarrow{*}$ (produces) are defined as usually. For every $v \in V^*$ is $L(v) = \{w \in T | v \xrightarrow{*} w\}$ the language generated by v, and $LS(v) = \{z \in V^* | v \xrightarrow{*} z\}$ its sentential forms. The language generated by G is $L(n_0)$.

Let R be an operator that reduces a given cf-grammar.

Definition: Let $G = (N, T, P, n_0)$ be a cf-grammar. Then for every $n \in N$ the grammar $G_n = (N_n, T_n, P_n, n) = \mathsf{R}((N, T, P, n))$ is called a *local grammar* of G. In addition, the language generated by G_n is $L(n)$ and called a *local language* of L.

Let $\mathcal{G} = \{G_n | n \in N\}$ be the set of local grammars of some cf-grammar G. Then a reflexive quasi-order $\leq_G$ in $\mathcal{G}$ may be defined by $G_n \leq_G G_m \Leftrightarrow N_n \subseteq N_m$. The derived irreflexive quasi-order is described by $<_G$.

One can conclude from the equivalence relation $\sim_G$ induced by $\leq_G$:

(1) $G_n \sim_G G_m \Rightarrow T_n = T_m \wedge P_n = P_m$

(2) $\forall m \in N_n : G_m \sim_G G_n \vee G_m <_G G_n$

(3) $G_m \leq_G G_n \Leftrightarrow \forall m' \in N_m : \exists u, v \in V^* : n \rightarrow u m' v$

These rules will be used later when designing a parsing strategy.

There is a group of symbols that play a key role in identifying certain L-factors because they allow unambiguous conclusions concerning the productions involved in deriving the string.

Definition: A Symbol $v \in V$ is called to be *characteristic* for G_n (resp. $L(n)$), iff
$$\forall u, w \in V^*, m \in N : (m, uvw) \in P \Rightarrow m = n \text{ holds.}$$

The set of characteristic symbols of a local grammar G_n is described by $CH_V(n)$. The elements of the set $CH_T(n) = CH_V(n) \cap T$ are called characteristc terminals.

It follows from this definition that for every $w \in L$ such that there exists some i with $1 \leq i \leq |w|$ and $w[i] \in CH_T(n)$, then $\exists k < i, j > i : w[:k]nw[j:] \in LS$ is true.

Characteristic terminals are of good use in parsing. They allow excellent error recovery and may support the stack management by confirming the analysis state. The development of modern programming languages shows increasing sets of characteristic terminals from Pascal over Modula to Ada.

As a rule, words belonging to the local languages under consideration appear as factors in words of the base language $L = L(n_0)$. So it makes sense to have a look at their environments.

Definition: A word $v \in T^*$ is called a (textual) *predecessor* of length $k>0$ of $L(n)$ in L, iff $|v|=k$ and $\exists x, y \in T^*: xvny \in LS$.

The set of predecessors of length k is written $PRD_k(n)$, and, in addition, we define $PRD_k^*(n) = PRD_k(n) \cup \{ v \in T^* \mid |v| \leq k \wedge \exists y \in T^*: vny \in LS \}$.

Similarly the notions of a (textual) successor and the sets $PST_k(n)$ and $PST_k^*(n)$ are defined.

In practice it seems almost sufficient to consider environments of length one (or two sometimes).

This leads to the next definition for local languages (grammars resp.).

Definition: A local language is said to be *(right-k-) bounded* in L, iff there exists a $k \geq 0$ such that

$$\forall w \in L(n): \big(\forall x \in PST_k(n): \forall t \in T^*: wxt \notin L(n)\big) \wedge \forall x \in PST_{k-1}^*(n) \backslash \{\varepsilon\}: wx \notin L(n).$$

It can be shown that boundedness is undecidable in general and the following holds:

(i) Let $L(n)$ be a local language and it holds

$$\forall w, x \in T_n^+: w \in L \Rightarrow wx \notin L(n) \text{ or}$$
$$\forall w, x \in T_n^+: w \in L \wedge wx \in L \Rightarrow x[1] \notin PST_1(n)$$

then $L(n)$ is (right-) bounded.

(ii) Let $G=(N, T, P, N_0)$ be a strong LL(k)-grammar. Then for every $n \in N$ holds:

$$\exists k_n: k_n \leq k \wedge L(n) \text{ is right-bounded by } k_n.$$

With this, we have the prerequisites for a closer look on parsing. We will continue abstracting, as much as possible, from details not essential for parallelizing, even from a certain parsing direction, i.e., top-down resp. bottom-up, by a functional view on the topic.

4   Local Parsability

A parse function $A_L \mid T^* \to T'^*$ with $T'=T \cup \{z\}$, where z is a new symbol $(z \notin T)$ may be defined for some $L \subseteq T^*$ by

$$A_L(w) = \begin{cases} w[1]A_L(w[2:]) & \text{if } rm_L(w,1) = 0 \\ \varepsilon & \text{if } w = \varepsilon \\ zw[rm_L(w,1) + 1:] & \text{else} \end{cases}$$

Now let again $L \subseteq T^*$ be the language generated by the grammar G and $n \in N$ an arbitrary nonterminal symbol. Then the mapping $A_{L(n)} \mid T^* \to (T \cup \{n\})^*$ is called a *locale parse function* of G.

Definition: Let $A_{L(n)}$ a local parse function of the cf-grammar $G = (N, T, P, n_0)$. Then a local language (grammar) is said to be *local parsable* in $L(n_0)$, iff for every $w \in L$ the following holds: $\forall i = 1 \ldots |w|$: $w[1 : i-1]A_{L(n)}(w[i:]) \in LS(n_0)$.

That means, a language is local parsable just in those cases if right maximal $L(n)$-factors can be derived only from the nonterminal n.

Another characterisation of local parsability can be given for unambiguous grammars: A local language $L(n)$ is local parsable in $L(n_0)$, iff for every $w \in L$ the following holds: $\forall i = 1, \ldots, |w|$: $r m_{L(n)}(w, i) = 0 \lor w[1:i-1] n w[r m_{L(n)}(w, i)+1:] \in LS$.

Considering other properties of cf-grammars resp. languages, it is not surprising that local parsability is also undecidable in general. It can be shown (cf. [7]) that the decidability of local parsability would enable one, to construct a method to decide whether the intersection of two cf-languages is empty or not, which is a famous problem proved to be undecidable.

The following two theorems state some necessary preconditions for local parsability.

Theorem: Let G be an unambiguous grammar, and let $n \in N$ be some (direct or indirect) recursive nonterminal such that

$$\exists v, v_1 \in V^*: n \xrightarrow{+} nv \land n \xrightarrow{+} v_1 \land L(v) \cap L(v_1) \neq \emptyset \text{ holds.}$$

Then $L(n)$ is not local parsable in L.

Proof: We assume the grammar G to be reduced as usually. Then, there exist words $w, x, y \in T^*$, $w \in L(v) \cap L(v_1)$, such that $n_0 \xrightarrow{*} xny \xrightarrow{+} xnvy \xrightarrow{+} xnwy \xrightarrow{+} xv_1wy \xrightarrow{+} xwwy$ and $x w A_{L(n)}(wy) = x w n y_1$ with $y_1 = y[i:]$ holds for some $i = 1 \ldots |y|$. Because G was said to be unambiguous, $x w n y \notin LS$ must hold, i.e., $L(n)$ is not local parsable in L.

Theorem: Let $L(n)$ be a local language of an unambiguous grammar G. If there exists at least one word $w \in L$ and $i < j$ such that $j \leq r m_{L(n)}(w, i) < r m_{L(n)}(w, j)$ then $L(n)$ is not local parsable in L.

(The proofs for this and the following theorems are omitted here. They may be found in detail in [6].)

This means, if $L(n)$ is local parsable in L, then no word of L may contain intersecting right-maximal $L(n)$-factors.

We will continue with some sufficient condition for determining local parsable languages of a given cf-grammar G. The aim will be achieved by use of characteristic terminal symbols of certain productions.

Theorem: Let G_n be a local grammar of some unambiguous cf-grammar G, where
  (i) $L(n)$ is right-bounded by $k = 0$ or $k = 1$ and
  (ii) $\forall (n, p) \in P_n$: $p[1] \in CH_T(n)$ and $p[2:] \in (V_n \backslash CH_T(n))^*$.
  Then G_n is local parsable.

One can give easily several modifications to weaken the preconditions but in cases of practical interest it will often be easier to verify the property of local parsability directly than by use of such criteria.

Finally, there exist no relations to other classes of cf-grammars such as LL(k) or LR(k). This is due to the fact that for local parsability the embedding in the base language is of superior importance.

Although always assumed, it is not really necessary to have some unambiguous grammar.

5 Parallel Parsing

We will continue to assume some unambiguous cf-grammar $G=(N, T, P, n_0)$. One can show, from $L(n)$ is local parsable in $L(n_0)$ follows this is also true for $LS(n)$ in $LS(n_0)$.

In the remainder of this section the existence of a special end-marker sign '#' ($\# \notin T \cup N$) is assumed. It is also taken for granted, that the word considered is of sufficient length.

Besides a function cp is defined that indicates the possibility of continuations of right-maximal factors:

Let $L \subseteq T^*$, $w \in T^*$, $M_L = \{ i \mid i=1,\ldots,|w| \text{ and } \exists x \in T^+ : w[i:]x \in L \}$ then

$$cp_L(w) = \begin{cases} \min(M_L) & \text{if } M_L \neq \varnothing \\ 0 & \text{if } M_L = \varnothing \end{cases}.$$

This helps in defining a modified parse function, applicable on fragments:

$$\overline{A}_L(w) = \begin{cases} w[1]\overline{A}_L(w[2:]) & \text{if } rm_L(w,1) = 0 \text{ or } cp_{L(n)}(w) = 1 \\ \varepsilon & \text{if } w = \varepsilon \text{ or } w = \# \\ zw[rm_L(w+1)+1:] & \text{else} \end{cases}.$$

To take advantage from the potential parallelism one has to include all local parsable sublanguages. Thus, let $\mathcal{L} = \{L(n) \mid n \in N \text{ and } L(n) \text{ local parsable in } L\}$ be the set of local parsable sublanguages of L.

A local parse function may be defined as follows:

$$P_{\mathcal{L}}(w) = \begin{cases} \varepsilon & \text{if } w = \varepsilon \text{ or } w = \# \\ w[1]P_{\mathcal{L}}(w[2:]) & \text{if } \forall L(m) \in \mathcal{L} : \\ & \quad rm_{L(m)}(w,1) = 0 \text{ or } cp_{L(m)}(w) = 1 \\ nP_{\mathcal{L}}(w[rm_{L(n)}(w,1)+1:]) & \text{else with n satisfies } (*) \end{cases}$$

$(*)$: $L(n) \in \mathcal{L} \wedge cp_{L(n)}(w) \neq 1 \wedge rm_{L(n)}(w,1) > 0$
$\wedge \forall L(m) \in \mathcal{L} : (rm_{L(m)} \leq rm_{L(n)} \vee cp_{L(m)}(w) = 1)$

Theorem: Let G an unambiguous grammar. For every word $w \in L(n)$ and every partition $w = w_1 w_2 \ldots w_k$ holds: $P_{\mathcal{L}}(w_1)P_{\mathcal{L}}(w_2)\ldots P_{\mathcal{L}}(w_k) \in LS(n_0)$.

When designing the algorithmic implementation of local parse functions, this can be based on some specific properties of local parsable languages and by use of the relations in the set of local grammars defined in par. 3.

Theorem: Let L be the set of local parsable languages of some unambigous cf-grammar G. Then, for any $w \in L$, $i=1...|w|$, and $L(n), L(m) \in L$:

(1) $L(n) <_G L(m) \Rightarrow rm_{L(n)}(w, i) \leq rm_{L(m)}(w, i)$

(2) $L(n) \sim_G L(m) \wedge (\neg \exists v \in T^* : mv \in LS(n)) \Rightarrow rm_{L(n)}(w, i) \leq rm_{L(m)}(w, i)$.

With that, we have got the needed prerequisites for the formulation of the parallel parsing algorithm. It works by the scheme:

(i)   Partitioning the source

(ii) Local parsing of the fragments (i.e., computing $P_L(w_i)$)

(iii) Combination of parsed fragments.

Steps (ii) and (iii) are repeated until the number of fragments is reduced to one.

The algorithm in more detail:

Let $z = b^k$ and $w = w_1^{(0)} w_2^{(0)} ... w_z^{(0)}$ a partition of the source text (word) to analyse.

1. Parallel computing of the z parse functions

$$w_1^{(1)} = P_{LS(no)}(w_1^{(0)})$$

$$w_j^{(1)} = P_L(w_j^{(1)}) \qquad\qquad \text{for } j = 2,...,z$$

2. Set $i = 2$

3. Parallel computation of the parse functions

$$w_1^{(i)} = P_{LS(no)}(w_1^{(i-1)} w_2^{(i-1)} ... w_b^{(i-1)})$$

$$w_j^{(i)} = P_{LS}(w_{b*j-b+1}^{(i-1)} w_{b*j-b+2}^{(i-1)} ... w_{b*j}^{(i-1)}) \qquad \text{for } j=2,...,\frac{z}{b^{i-1}}$$

4. Set $i = i+1$

5. If $i \leq k$ then goto step 3 else ready.

Any implementation requires the extraction of operational descriptions from the specifications above. The parse functions may be computed as follows:

Let $w \in T^+$ be a word over T and $L \subseteq T^*$ a cf-language. Then $rm_L(w,1)$ is fixed by[1]:

1. Try to verify the hypothesis $w \in L$ by use of a known parsing technique (e.g. recursive descent, LR(1)-, SLR(1)-algorithm).

2. This will end in one of the following three states:

   a) After accepting the first i-1 characters (symbols), the analyser reaches a state, which is not a final one and it is unable to accept w[i]. Then the hypothesis is falsified.

   b) The analyser reaches a stable final state after accepting i characters, i.e. $w[:i] \in L$ and with this $rm_L(w,1) = i$.

---

[1] $rm_L(w,i)$ equals $rm_L(w[i-1:],1)$ and can be attributed to this.

c) The word w can be accepted but the analyser ends up in a non-final state or a non-stable final state, i.e., there exist transitions. Thus, the value of $rm_L(w,1)$ has to be determined in the next cycle, after combination with the following subword.

The efficiency of the method as a whole depends heavily form the expense needed to get the statement $rm_L(w,1)=0$.

6   Estimating Efficiency

The parallel processor model is based on the following assumptions:

1. Each processor has fast access to its own data.

2. The time needed to transfer blocks of data between processors may be estimated by a constant.

3. Initially the source text is distributed on n $(=2^k : k$ natural) processors.

We also assume a deterministic parsable grammar and local parsable sublanguages with characteristical terminals in starting position. Then the time required for computing the local parse functions and doing lexical analysis depends linearly from the text length.

Designations:

- h   : cost to transfer a result string to another processor
- s   : length of source text (characters)
- a_L : cost of lexical analysis (per character)
- v_L : average ratio token per character for source texts $(v_L<1)$
- a_p : cost of syntactical analysis (per token)
- v   : average reduction of token number through application of a local parse function $(v<1)$

Thus, we get for a simple parse $t_1 = a_L*s+a_p*v_L*s = s*(a_L+a_p*v_L)$

and for a parallel parse with $n=2^k$ processors

$$t_n = a_L\frac{s}{n} + a_p v_L(1+v+2v^2+K+2^{k-1}v^k)\frac{s}{n} + k*h$$

$$= \frac{s}{n}(a_L + \frac{a_p v_L}{2}(\frac{2v-(2v)^{k+1}}{1-2v}+2)) + k*h \quad .$$

k∗h is the overhead for data exchange, i.e., for the transfer of the pre-parsed string to the next processor. The sum constitutes from the stepwise combination of two factors of length s_i (on average) into one word of length $2*s_i*v$ of which only the second half of length s_i*v has still to be parsed.

With n processors, one can achieve an speedup of

$$c_n = \frac{t_1}{t_n} = \frac{s(a_L + a_p v_L)}{\frac{s}{n}(a_L+a_p v_L(1+\frac{2v-(2v)^{k+1}}{2(1-2v)}))+k*h} \quad .$$

In good agreement with the results of practical experiments, the speedup is as a function of n non-monotone and has a maximum value.

Noteworthy, the influence of the source text size s is proportional on c_n, but unfortunately in cases of interest of minor impact.

This estimate refers to mean values only. To get a slight impression from the order of magnitude a set of data concerning the ratios of lexical to syntactical analysis's cost and the mean number of characters per token, had been compiled from various published papers, see [6, p.110]. The obtainment of sound data for the on average reduction v is a little bit harder. It depends closely on the very syntactic structure (e.g., a plain list of statements versus a deep nested if-then-else construct). Own computations indicate that there is a rapid reduction especially during the first steps. With Modula-2 programs, we found a ratio between 0.01 and 0.03 in the first step. Of course, this drops drastically in the following steps. Altogether, assuming v=0.4 as a mean value seems to be not too optimistic. Thus giving the following survey (a_L=1 is taken as a base):

					Speedup for			
s	h	v_L	a_p	v	n=4	n=16	n=128	n=4096
2000	1.0	0.1	2.5	0.4	3.5	12.7	76.4	195
20000	0.1	0.1	1.0	0.4	3.8	14.4	112.0	2940
20000	0.1	0.1	2.5	0.4	3.5	12.9	97.0	2610
20000	1.0	0.1	2.5	0.4	3.5	12.9	94.7	1230
20000	1.0	0.5	2.5	0.4	2.9	9.6	67.4	1310
20000	1.0	0.5	2.5	0.7	2.1	4.2	12.4	72
200000	1.0	0.5	2.5	0.4	2.9	9.6	68.1	1910

As expected, the presented algorithm will fit for a small number of processors (say 10 to 100) and large texts. There is a great influence of the structure of the singular string: "...*the amount of concurrence which exists in the compiler is determined to a greater extend by the characteristics of the source program being compiled and the underlying hardware, rather than by the structure of the compiler.*"[8, p. 8]

7   Conclusion

It turned out that parallelization of parsing resp. compiling is an outstanding complicated task because of the various hierarchical dependencies. Up to now there is no satisfying solution. By this, it is typically for a wide group of algorithms. Therefore, the outlined approach may be of exemplary importance.

Starting from some basic assumptions concerning the design of real world multiprocessor computers, we discovered locality to be an essential criterion. As a next step, base conditions for any efficient parallel algorithm had been stated. In difference to many other attempts the development of the method started from these conditions - not from a classification of the field of application. Consequently the concept of locality is introduced in formal language theory and, additionally, in parsing methods. The definition of the so-called *parse functions* enables us to abstract from certain parsing strategies thus saving freedom for particular implementations.

The algorithm developed this way, seems to be comparably efficient.

After this, it was possible to determine the category of formal languages which can be handled by the suggested method. It is not surprising that it is just a fairly special subclass not related to other known subclasses (also defined by specific parsing efforts, e.g., deterministic parsable languages). As one can verify easily any attempt to enlarge the covered class will degrade the efficiency of parallelization. But, fortunately, a broad group of today's programming languages has a sufficient number of local parsable sublanguages and those that fail, for example PL/I will belong very probably to them, are of bad convenience for the human, too. From this we are quite confident that our algorithm will meet practical needs. Experience shows that even hard restrictions like the LL(1)-property will lead to powerful tools, sometimes with the aid of some supplementation. (cf. e.g. [9, p.8]: *It is attractive to consider the precise way in which the context-free languages shoul be restricted to make them easy to compile in parallel.*)

Further investigations will have to tackle the problem of including the subsequent processing into the parallelization. Although there exist some results for attribute grammar based systems, which fit rather well in the framework of local parsing a lot of work is still to be done (cf. [10, 11]).

Further developments will possibly be initiated by the so-called virtual shared memory architectures and distributed file systems.

Besides its fundamental implications, this research raises the question whether there is really the need to parallelize compiling resp. related language processing tasks. But, a look back into history shows that even great improvements in processing speed will be used up by grown areas of application. Along with the growing complexity of software systems the importance of lingual interfaces among their components will increase rapidly. So we will be faced soon with the demand for fast, parallel language processing methods. Then the described technique should be useful.

References

1. E. Klein, K. Koskimies: The Parallelization of One-Pass-Compilers. GMD Sankt Augustin. Arbeitspapiere 416. 1989

2. L. Lundberg: A Parallel Ada System on an Experimental Multiprocessor. Softw.Pract.Exper. 8, 787-800 (1989)

3. L.A. Barford, B.T. van der Zanden: Attribute Grammars in Constraint-based Graphic Systems. Softw.Pract.Expr. 4, 309-328 (1989)

4. P. Rechenburg: Attributierte Grammatiken als Methode der Softwaretechnik. Elektr. Rechenanlagen 3, 111-118 (1984)

5. B. Alpern, T. Reps: Interactive Proof Checking. In ACM Symp. on Principles of Programming Languages. 1984.

6. J. Lampe: Zur parallelen Verarbeitung formal definierter Sprachen. Habilit. TU Dresden 1991

7. J. Lampe: Local Parse - A Base for Realistic Parallelization of Compilers. J. Inf. Process. Cybern. EIK 1/2, 75-84 (1990)

8. R.o.d. Akker *et al.*: An Annotated Bibliography on Parallel Parsing. Enschede: University of Twente. Mem. Informatica 89-67. 1989

9. D.B. Skillicorn, D.T. Barnard: A Survey of Parallel Compilation. Kingston (Canada): Queen's University, Dept. of Computing and Information Science, Sept. 12, 1990

10. M.F. Kuiper, A. Dijkstra: Attribute evaluation on a network of transputers. In J. Wexler (ed.): Developing Transputer Applications. Amsterdam: 1989, 142-149

11. J. Lampe: Ein Lokalitätskonzept für die parallele Sprachverarbeitung mit Attributgrammatiken. Wiss. Z. Techn. Univers. Dresden 4, 57-60 (1992)

PVM 3 Beyond Network Computing [*]

G. A. Geist

Oak Ridge National Laboratory
P.O. Box 2008 Oak Ridge, TN 37831-6367

Abstract. PVM (Parallel Virtual Machine) is a byproduct of the heterogeneous network research project going on at Oak Ridge National Laboratory and the University of Tennessee. It is a software package that permits a user defined collection of serial, parallel, and vector computers to appear as one large distributed memory computer. PVM's popularity is quickly making it the worldwide de facto standard for distributed computing. Applications, which can be written in FORTRAN or C, can be parallelized by using simple message-passing constructs common to most distributed-memory computers. By sending and receiving messages, subtasks of an application can cooperate to solve a problem in parallel. This paper describes the features of the latest release of PVM (version 3.1) and explains the major new research areas we are beginning to explore in heterogeneous network computing. The new features of PVM version 3 open many new opportunities to go beyond simple network computing, but several technical and social issues must be addressed before we can make the next big leap in distributed computing.

1 Introduction

Imagine having a computer with more power than a dozen supercomputer centers, more memory than a disk farm, and more disk space than a tape library. This is the dream of distributed computing. By exploiting the existing infrastructure of computer networks, collections of machines that represent an enormous computational resource can be tied together. Just as important is the perception (mostly true) that distributed computing is more cost effective than mainframe computing. The argument is that distributed computing utilizes "wasted" cycles on exiting machines while delivering the power of a supercomputer.

We are just beginning to see sophisticated scheduling software that only uses otherwise idle cycles and schedules jobs so they do not compete for the same resources. In the next couple years this scheduling software will be integrated into packages such as PVM making them much more useful to large organizations trying to manage multiple distributed jobs over hundreds of individual computers.

---

[*] This work was supported in part by the Applied Mathematical Sciences subprogram of the Office of Energy Research, U.S. Department of Energy, under Contract DE-AC05-84OR21400, and in part by the the National Science Foundation Science and Technology Center Cooperative Agreement No. CCR-8809615.

PVM was initially developed at Oak Ridge National Laboratory as a research tool to explore heterogeneous network computing. The project has since expanded to include several other institutions including the University of Tennessee, Emory University, and CMU. Under PVM, a user defined collection of serial, parallel, and vector computers appears as one large distributed-memory computer. Throughout this report the term *virtual machine* will be used to designate this logical distributed-memory computer, and *host* will be used to designate one of the member computers. PVM supplies the functions to automatically start up tasks on the virtual machine and allows the tasks to communicate and synchronize with each other. A *task* is defined as a unit of computation in PVM analogous to a Unix process. Applications, which can be written in Fortran77, C, or C++, can be parallelized by using message-passing constructs common to most distributed-memory computers. By sending and receiving messages, multiple tasks of an application can cooperate to solve a problem in parallel.

PVM supports heterogeneity at the application, machine, and network level. In other words, PVM allows application tasks to exploit the architecture best suited to their solution. PVM handles all data conversion that may be required if two computers use different integer or floating point representations. And PVM allows the virtual machine to be interconnected by a variety of different networks.

In the next section we describe the basic features available in version 3.1 of PVM. In section 3 we discuss how the latest version of PVM is allowing researchers to go beyond simple network computing. Section 4 presents some of our future research plans in heterogeneous network computing, and section 5 describes some of the social issues that must be addressed to expand the scope of distributed computing. Conclusions are presented in section 6.

2   PVM 3 features

2.1   Task Identification

All processes that enroll in PVM 3 are represented by an integer task identifier. Throughout this report the task identifier is represented by *tid*. The tid is the primary and most efficient method of identifying processes in PVM. It allows fast message routing because the location of the task is encoded into the tid. This turned out to be necessary for efficiency when porting PVM to massively parallel processors (MPP). Since tids must be unique across the entire virtual machine, they are supplied by the local processor and are not user chosen. This improves the scalability of PVM since the assigning of a tid to a new task does not require global communication to guarantee uniqueness. PVM 3 contains several routines that return tid values so that the user application can identify other processes in the system.

Although less efficient, processes can also be identified by a name and instance number by joining a group. A user defines a group name and PVM returns a unique instance number for this process in this group.

2.2 Process Control

PVM supplies routines that enable a user process to become a PVM task and to become a normal process again. There are routines to add and delete hosts from the virtual machine, routines to start up and terminate PVM tasks, routines to send signals to other PVM tasks, and routines to find out information about the virtual machine configuration and active PVM tasks.

2.3 Fault Tolerance

If a host fails, PVM will automatically detect this and delete the host from the virtual machine. The status of hosts can be requested by the application, and if required a replacement host can be added by the application. It is still the responsibility of the application developer to make his application tolerant of host failure. PVM makes no attempt to automatically recover tasks that are killed because of a host failure, but this is a future research area. Another use of this feature would be to add more hosts as they become available, for example on a weekend, or if the application dynamically determines it could use more computational power.

2.4 Dynamic Process Groups

Dynamic process groups are implemented on top of PVM 3. In this implementation, a process can belong to multiple groups, and groups can change dynamically at any time during a computation.

Functions that logically deal with groups of tasks such as broadcast and barrier use the user's explicitly defined group names as arguments. Routines are provided for tasks to join and leave a named group. Tasks can also query for information about other group members. Future research will add more group communication functions such as global max and total exchange to the PVM group library.

2.5 Signaling

PVM provides two methods of signaling other PVM tasks. One method sends a Unix signal to another task. The second method notifies a set of tasks about an event by sending them a message with a user-specified tag that the application can check for. The notification events include the exiting of a task, the deletion (or failure) of a host, and the addition of a host.

2.6 Communication

PVM provides routines for packing and sending messages between tasks. The model assumes that any task can send a message to any other PVM task, and that there is no limit to the size or number of such messages. While all hosts have physical memory limitations which limit potential buffer space, the communication model does not restrict itself to a particular machine's limitations and assumes sufficient memory is available. The PVM communication model provides asynchronous blocking send, asynchronous blocking receive, and non-blocking receive functions. In our terminology, a blocking send returns as soon as the send buffer is free for reuse regardless of the state of the receiver. A non-blocking receive immediately returns with either the data or a flag that the data has not arrived, while a blocking receive returns only when the data is in the receive buffer. In addition to these point-to-point communication functions the model supports multicast to a set of tasks and broadcast to a user defined group of tasks. Wildcards can be specified in the receive for the source and message "type" allowing either or both of these contexts to be ignored. A routine can be called to return information about received messages.

The PVM model guarantees that message order is preserved. If task 1 sends message A to task 2, then task 1 sends message B to task 2, message A will arrive at task 2 before message B. Moreover, if both messages arrive before task 2 does a receive, then a wildcard receive will always return message A.

Message buffers are allocated dynamically. So the maximum message size is limited only by the amount of available memory on a given host. PVM includes routines to create and manipulate multiple message buffers. For example, a message can be forwarded by switching the receive buffer to the send buffer. The principle reason for using multiple message buffers is to allow libraries and graphical interfaces to interact with an application without interfering with messages the application is sending or receiving.

2.7 Multiprocessor Integration

PVM 3 is designed to use native communication calls within a multiprocessor. Messages between two nodes of a multiprocessor go directly between them while messages destined for a machine out on the network go to the user's single PVM daemon on the multiprocessor for further routing.

The Intel iPSC/860 and Paragon have been integrated into PVM 3.1 so that Intel's NX message-passing routines are used for inter-node communication. Cray, Convex, Intel, TMC, SGI, DEC, KSR, and IBM have announced they are supplying PVM 3 compatibility with their respective multiprocessors as they become available. Thus programs written in PVM 3 can run on a network of SUN's, on a group of nodes on an Intel Paragon, on multiple Paragons connected by a network, or a heterogeneous combination of multiprocessor computers distributed around the world without having to write any vendor specific message-passing code.

3 Beyond network computing

The most common form of distributed computing utilizes 10 to 50 powerful workstations hooked together on a local area network like ethernet. Over the next two years we see this view changing as high performance wide area networks make it possible to tie together machines located at several collaborating institutions. And these machines may include MPPs with performance in the hundreds of Gigaflops.

3.1 Geographically distributed computing

We have done experiments at ORNL to study the viability of tying together supercomputers geographically distributed across the USA. In these experiments we were calculating the electronic structure of high temperature superconductors from first principles [5]. This was the first large application parallelized with PVM. Over the years this application has evolved to include dynamic load balancing and better portability. In a series of tests combining Cray YMP and C90 supercomputers, performance as high ,as 9.5 Gigaflops was reached using a total of 27 processors. The maximum number of processors tried during the series was 54, and in one test a Cray located in Europe was tied into the USA configuration. Because of the communication to computation ratio of this application, it performed well in all these tests with performance related more to the size of the problem being solved rather than the geographic distribution of the hosts. The most negative result that came from this test series was the time it took to start up many tasks. It took several minutes before all 54 tasks were running. The typical run submitted to a C90 does not take this long to execute, so some common sense should be used in designing computational applications that utilize multiple supercomputers.

In other experiments applications have run across workstations at ORNL and Florida State University. More recently, the Paragon and iPSC/860 at ORNL with the CM5 at the University of Tennessee formed the virtual machine used to run a large scientific code.

There are reasons other than computational performance that make geographically distributed computing attractive. There are applications in business and the military where fault tolerance is of utmost importance. By using machines distributed over a wide area, the application can continue to run even if parts of the virtual machine are incapacitated by disasters such as lightning strikes and city-wide blackouts.

Another reason geographically distributed computing will become more popular is to utilize computational and data base information not locally available. For example, a climate modeling code may need to access a remote weather data base for input, compute on a collection of hosts (some local, some remote), and then write the results to another site for storage. Similarly, the computational resources required, for example, a Paragon for atmospheric calculations and a C90 for solar radiation modeling, may not be located at the same site, which again leads to the need for geographically distributed computing.

A less grandiose but more practical use for this form of distributed computing is in research collaborations between universities and also between universities and businesses. In this case researchers at several different sites are collaborating on a single computational problem. Each institution has some hardware dedicated to the project, but by pooling all the institutions' project resources, bigger more realistic problems can be solved. This scheme of distributed computing also promotes closer collaborations.

3.2 Integration of massively parallel processors

We envision distributed computing to begin to incorporate more MPP hosts into the virtual machines. Presently, we see people who run their application on a workstation network for development and debugging and then make production runs on an MPP. In the future we will see more of an integration. One or more MPPs may be used to do the majority of the computational work, but the results may be fed to a graphical workstation for real time display, to another host for archive storage, and there may be another host feeding input to the MPPs from a remote data base. The ability to tailor virtual machines to match the needs of an application and at the same time supply more computational power than that of any one computer will revolutionize computing and the scope of problems we can solve.

PVM 3 is designed to make the virtual machine hardware transparent to the user. The user can write his application using PVM calls knowing that if this call is made on an MPP then PVM makes sure the right thing gets done. If the call is made from a workstation a different but equally correct operation is performed, each tuned to the particular environment. From the user's perspective he does not have to learn how to use each MPP, and he does not have to change his source to run over a variety of virtual machines.

As a proof-of-principle researchers at ORNL ran an advanced version of the electronic structures code written in PVM on several virtual machines containing MPPs. The four virtual machines consisted of:

10 IBM RS/6000 workstations,
32 nodes of a Pargon,
8 nodes of an iPSC/860 and 16 nodes of a Paragon,
64 nodes of an iPSC/860, 32 nodes of a Paragon, and 32 nodes of a CM5.

3.3 Distributed visualization

Visualization is a compute intensive and often embarrassingly parallel application, making it an ideal candidate for distributed computing. We predict that this area of distributed computing will grow at least as fast as scientific computing over the next three years.

As the problems being solved get more complex so do the results. In order to understand or find important features of the results scientists are increasingly turning to visualization for help. Output visualization allows the scientist to look at the data in several different ways and even to explore the data by "flying" through it.

Developing video presentations of important results can also be very time consuming. In many cases individual frames must be calculated and stored. Distributed computing allows more computational and display hardware to be focused on the creation of such videos.

Interactive application interfaces will change the way we do computing. Instead of just running a week-long simulation and looking at the results, researchers will be able to steer the calculations towards interesting solutions. By being able to visualize and change the parameters of a simulation while it runs, researchers can ask "what if..." questions. It gives them another method to discover the important phenomena in their scientific study. Researchers at ORNL are developing materials science applications that run in a distributed environment and use PVM for interactive steering of the simulations as well as for sending back visualization data for real time display.

4 Future research

Network technology will be rapidly changing over the next few years. Network backbone speeds will reach and exceed a gigabit per second, and more gigabit LANs will appear. Initially several protocols will be available such as ATM, FCS, and HIPPI. In order to prepare for these coming changes, the PVM plan calls for the development of a high-speed interface layer in PVM. The idea is to add a smart routing layer into PVM that can determine the best or fastest method to move data between two tasks. Vaidy Sunderam has developed a prototype that switches to lower protocol layers when possible and showed potential performance improvements of 2-3 times TCP [4]. The more general layer planed for PVM would do this as well as choose an alternate network if appropriate and available. For example, if some of the hosts are connected by ethernet and a high-speed network like HIPPI, then PVM may decide to move data between these hosts over the faster network using a high-speed, low-level protocol. The MPP port where PVM moves the data over the multiprocessor's built in network is an early prototype of this more general research topic.

Multimedia is a growing trend in computer interface development. As the speeds of wide area networks grows the capability to do video conferencing, hypertext searches of remote data bases, and transmission of audio/video data will grow.

Our PVM plan calls for expanding the existing capabilities of PVM to allow it to be used to develop multimedia applications that can utilize the computational and storage capacities of a virtual machine. Distributed multimedia requires dedicated real time streams of data unlike most of scientific computing which relies on packages of data. Typically computer networks are not set up to handle real time data streams, but as the network speeds grow they have the appearance of having dedicated streams. Our efforts will be in providing a mechanism in PVM for "best effort" delivery of data streams as the closest approximation to real time given network constraints.

As the popularity of PVM grows so does the need to administer and schedule the PVM jobs to get the best utilization of existing resources. Several groups around the world have been working on adapting existing distributed batch schedulers to be able to handle parallel PVM applications. The DQS package developed at Florida State University was the first to be able to use PVM, followed by the Condor package developed at the University of Wisconsin [2,3].

Part of our future PVM development plan is to define a clean interface between PVM and scheduler packages. This will allow organizations that wish to set up a single scheduler that controls a organization-wide virtual machine to do so. Their users could submit serial or PVM jobs to the scheduler with a suggested number of machines to use. The scheduler keeps track of which machines are idle and which are being used. The scheduler assigns tasks to the virtual machine and migrates them in a way that yields a high utilization of the available resources. The goal is to achieve a high utilization without impacting researchers who are actually typing on their workstations. Trials done at Florida State and Wisconsin have shown that utilizations over 85% are possible on configurations consisting of hundreds of machines.

In the development of concurrent applications for heterogeneous target environments, large grained sub-task partitioning and processor allocation are critical issues. Additionally, the construction of program modules, specification of interdependencies and synchronization, and the management of multiple objects for different architectures are tedious activities that are prone to errors. To address these issues and to provide at least partial solutions, we are developing two packages on top of PVM to aid in the use, programming, and analysis of parallel computers. These packages are called XPVM and HeNCE.

XPVM is a X-window based tool for run-time monitoring of PVM programs. Using XPVM, the network traffic, host loads, and PVM activities inside an application can be easily monitored.

HeNCE (Heterogeneous Network Computing Environment) is an environment that is concerned with the development of high level techniques for programming concurrent virtual machines of the type provided by PVM. The HeNCE philosophy of parallel programming is to have the programmer explicitly specify the parallelism of a computation by drawing a graph of his application. The nodes of the graph represent standard serial subroutines and the arcs in the graph represent data dependencies. Special nodes are supplied with HeNCE to represent looping, conditional execution, and parallel DO constructs. Once the graph and the hosts in the virtual machine are specified, HeNCE then automates, as much as possible, the tasks of writing, compiling, executing, debugging, and analyzing the parallel computation. Central to HeNCE is an X-Window interface that the programmer uses to perform these functions [1].

5 Social issues

The social problems in distributed computing involve both policies and administration. The complexities arise when distributed computing cuts across both intra and inter administrative domains. Multiple computer centers each with their own system administrators, accountants, and security personnel become involved. Access and use of local and remote filesystems and I/O devices may be required by distributed applications but may be restricted by local policies. Bandwidth and access to remote databases are local decisions that can affect distributed applications.

One of the first concerns of local management when asked to make machines available to a distributed computing environment is the impact of the environment on internal priorities. While computers are often idle, they were purchased for a particular purpose by the organization. If they are not available when needed because of outside users, then there is a conflict between the external priorities of the distributed computing environment and the internal priorities of the organization's mission. The argument that they could reciprocate and accomplish their mission using the distributed environment may not be viable if the applications in question are not suited or have not been developed to work in a distributed environment.

Accounting is a complicated operational issue when a heterogeneous distributed network of computers and storage media are involved. First there is the issue of multiple organizations being involved, each with a potentially different charging algorithm and collection method. The user of the distributed environment does not want to receive 10 or 100 bills from different organizations because of how an automatic scheduler happened to distribute his parallel application. Part of the infrastructure of the distributed computing environment must be a consolidated and consistent accounting method.

Several operational issues are involved with scheduling. Does each organization manage the scheduling of jobs on their local machines or is there a master wide-area task scheduler? In the first case, tasks from one site might be distributed to another site, but their scheduling and priority would be handled locally. In the second case, questions arise about who controls the master scheduler. This person or group could potentially disrupt the operation of several organizations by a mistake or purposeful setting of the schedulers priorities.

The scheduler's task is to make good utilization of the entire distributed environment. A second task for the scheduler is to load balance parallel applications over a heterogeneous network with machine loads changing dynamically due to other users. This is a largely unexplored research area that must be addressed in the operation of the distributed computing environment.

Another operational issue involving scheduling is the types of machines jobs are sent to. Some machines will be personal workstations, while others will be shared resources like compute or storage servers at an organization. Different scheduling procedures need to be addressed for the personal workstations. A researcher's productivity may plummet if the scheduler keeps sending his machine new jobs every time he stops typing for a few seconds. But if the scheduler ignores this class of resource, then the overall utilization of the distributed environment decreases.

6   Conclusion

PVM is the de facto standard in distributed computing. All the major computer vendors have announced that PVM will be available on their systems. Thousands of users are solving their scientific and engineering problems using PVM. And several production software packages have been converted to PVM and many more are in the process of being converted. PVM continues to evolve to meet the needs of users and to keep up with the changing technology. For example, as gigabit networks become more common PVM will be modified to exploit the full potential of this technology.

If distributed computing is going to jump to the next level, which involves geographically distributed, multi-organization resources, then several social issues must be addressed and solved. The most important problems involve scheduling, accounting, and support.

Future research focuses on making PVM a high-speed, portable message-passing core that can be easily integrated into more complex software such as schedulers, performance monitors, debuggers, programming environments, large-scale scientific applications, distributed database applications, distributed multimedia programs, etc. The goal is to make it easier for users to exploit the resources made available by the world-wide computer network infrastructure.

Notes: The PVM source code, users guide, and reference manual are available without charge from the software server netlib@ornl.gov. For information on how to get this material send email to the above address with the message: **send index from pvm3**.

References

1. Beguelin, A., et al.: HeNCE Users Guide. Technical report University of Tennessee. (May 1992)
2. Bricker, A., Litzkow, M., Miron, L.: Condor Technical Summary. CS technical report No. 1069 University of Wisconsin, (Jan. 1992)
3. Green, T., Snyder, J.: DQS, A Distributed Queuing System. Preprint of SCRI technical report. Florida State University, (May 1992)
4. Sunderam, V.: An Inclusive Session Level Protocol for Distributed Applications. *Proceedings - ACM Sigcomm 90 (Computer Communications Review)*, **20**(4), pp. 307-316, Philadelphia, September 1990.
5. Stocks, M., et al.: Complete Solution of the Korringa-Kohn-Rostocker Coherent Potential Approximation: Cu-Ni Alloys. *Phys. Rev. Letters*, 41, 339, 1978.

The Design of the PACLIB Kernel for Parallel Algebraic Computation*

Wolfgang Schreiner and Hoon Hong

schreine@risc.uni-linz.ac.at hhong@risc.uni-linz.ac.at
Research Institute for Symbolic Computation (RISC-Linz)
Johannes Kepler University, A-4040 Linz, Austria

Abstract. This paper describes the runtime kernel of PACLIB, a new system for parallel algebraic computation on shared memory computers. PACLIB has been developed as a professional tool for the simple design and efficient implementation of parallel algorithms in computer algebra and related areas. It provides concurrency, shared memory communication, non-determinism, speculative parallelism, streams and a parallelized garbage collection. We explain the main design decisions as motivated by the special demands of algebraic computation and give several benchmarks that demonstrate the performance of the system. PACLIB has been implemented on a Sequent Symmetry multiprocessor and is portable to other shared memory machines and workstations.

1 Introduction

Computer algebra is that branch of computer science that aims to provide exact solutions of scientific problems. Research results of this area are e.g. algorithms for symbolic integration, polynomial factorization or the exact solution of algebraic equations and inequalities [6]. All these algorithms operate with arbitrary precision arithmetic; they are therefore more expensive with respect to time and space than the corresponding numerical methods. However, they always provide correct solutions and are not influenced by the stability properties of the given problem.

The parallel computation group at RISC-Linz has started a project that pursues the development of PACLIB, a new system for parallel algebraic computation on shared memory multiprocessors [20, 21]. Our goal has been to develop a professional tool for the simple and efficient implementation of parallel algorithms in computer algebra and related scientific areas. PACLIB is a combination and extension of two free software packages:

- SACLIB [5] is a library of C functions that is based on a list processing kernel with automatic garbage collection and supports all fundamental objects and methods of computer algebra: arbitrary precision integer and rational arithmetic, polynomial arithmetic, linear algebra, polynomial gcd and resultant

---

* Supported by the Austrian Science Foundation (FWF) grant S5302-PHY "Parallel Symbolic Computation".

computation, polynomial factorization, real root calculation and algebraic number arithmetic. Several algebraic applications have been implemented in this library such as the Partial Cylindric Algebraic Decomposition Method [10] and the Gröbner Bases Algorithm [4].

- μSYSTEM [7] is a library that supports concurrency on shared memory multiprocessors and UNIX workstations. The μSYSTEM kernel distributes *tasks* (light-weight processes) among *virtual processors* which are UNIX processes scheduled by the operating system. On a multi-processor, virtual processors are therefore executed by multiple hardware processors truly in parallel. The μSYSTEM task management is quite efficient and allows the utilization of rather *fine-grained parallelism*.

We applied and considerably extended the mechanisms of the μSYSTEM to develop a suitable parallel programming interface for SACLIB. In this paper, we will explain the design of the runtime kernel of this system that in particular supports the following features:

- **Concurrent Tasks:** Any function can be executed as a separate task; the scheduling of tasks and the balancing of load among processors is performed automatically.
- **Data Sharing:** All heap structures can be shared among tasks; arguments and results are passed by reference without any duplication of data.
- **Non-Determinism:** A task may simultaneously wait for the results of various other tasks. The further computation depends on which task delivers its result first.
- **Speculative Parallelism:** If by the result of one task the result of another task is not required any more, the superfluous task may be explicitly aborted.
- **Streams:** Tasks may be connected by streams of data and work in an overlapping fashion (pipelining).
- **Parallel Garbage Collection:** The automatic memory management is based on a mark and sweep scheme collector where both phases are efficiently parallelized.

The PACLIB kernel has been implemented on a SEQUENT SYMMETRY shared memory computer with 20 processors under the Dynix/ptx version of UNIX. The system is portable to any machine supported by the μSYSTEM package (a port to a multi-processor SILICON GRAPHICS is on the way). The PACLIB programming model is explained in large detail in [13]; a comprehensive description of the PACLIB kernel is given in [19]. The development of PACLIB applications is illustrated in [22].

2 Design Requirements

Systems for numerical computation in general do not meet the demands of algebraic applications. The main reason is that numerical programs operate on elementary objects (floating point numbers) and regular structures (vectors and matrices) whose size does not change during the computation. The memory demand of a task is therefore known in advance and its (relative) runtime can be predicted very precisely. Numerical applications can be naturally parallelized using the SPMD model of computation [29].

On the contrary, the objects of algebraic computation are symbolic expressions (arbitrary precision integers and rationals, polynomials, sets of polynomials, ...) that are dynamically allocated on a heap. These objects tend to grow very much in the course of the computation, which also increases the runtime of the operating tasks. The dynamic behavior of algebraic algorithms concerning time and memory is therefore very complex and often unpredictable even for known input values.

For parallelizing such algorithms, the SPMD model of parallelization is not suitable. We need the possibility to create concurrent tasks asynchronously and depending on the actual state of the computation. The task creation overhead should be very small since algebraic algorithms can be often parallelized at a medium- or fine-grained level only. Furthermore, flexible synchronization and communication constructs are required to minimize the runtime dependencies between tasks; in particular we need non-deterministic constructs that allow to select the first available result of a set of tasks.

By the dynamic nature of the basic objects, algebraic applications are at least as strongly bound by memory as by time. A garbage collector is required that reclaims no more used objects. In a parallel environment, the issue of garbage collection is even more important, since p processors in general allocate heap space at a rate that is p times higher than a single processor (provided that the total memory size is the same). In order to preserve the ratio of garbage collection time to the actual computation time, the garbage collector itself must be efficiently parallelized.

The high memory consumption also suggests that a distributed memory model of computation may be not appropriate. In such a model, all arguments of a remote task must be explicitly copied into the heap of the executing processor and the results must be copied into the heap of any requesting processor. Eventually, many duplicate structures will exist in the system and even within one heap (since initially shared substructures will be duplicated). The size of solvable problems is therefore drastically smaller than on a single processor machine with the same amount of memory. A global address space that allows the sharing of objects between processors is therefore preferred[2].

From the above discussion, we derive the following demands that we consider essential for systems for parallel algebraic computation:

- Dynamic task creation with low runtime overhead.
- Flexible synchronization constructs that support non-determinism.
- A shared heap with a global address space and parallel garbage collection.

---

[2] Currently, such a global address space is only efficiently supported by computers with few (≤ 32) processors. However, new *virtual shared memory* architectures promise to fulfill this demand also for massively parallel machines [17].

In the following sections, we will describe our approach to meet these demands and will give the reasons that led to the current design.

3 The Overall Structure

The PACLIB kernel consists of the following main components (depicted in Figure 1):

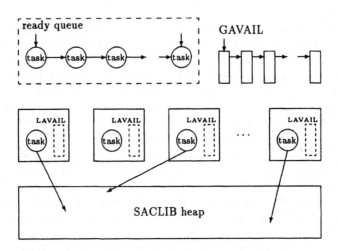

Fig. 1. The System Structure

1. **Ready Queue:** This queue contains all tasks that are *active* but not *running*. The μSYSTEM scheduler selects tasks for execution from the head of this queue; tasks that are preemptively descheduled are inserted at the tail.
2. **Shared Heap:** The SACLIB heap is an array of fixed-size list cells and serves as the only communication medium between tasks. There is no communication bottleneck since all PACLIB tasks may read all heap cells simultaneously.
3. **Virtual Processors:** Each virtual processor is a UNIX process that exclusively owns a local list LAVAIL of free heap cells. Each task executed on this processor allocates new heap cells from this list.
4. **Global Available List:** GAVAIL denotes a global list of free lists (of fixed but arbitrary length) in which the unused heap cells are linked together. Processors whose local lists run out of free cells receive their new LAVAIL from GAVAIL.

The next sections describe the task and the memory management in more detail.

4 Task Management

4.1 Functional Model

Algebraic algorithms are mostly based on purely mathematical functions that are entirely defined by their argument/result behavior. The PACLIB model of parallelism reflects this view. A PACLIB task receives certain SACLIB objects as input arguments and returns a SACLIB object as its result. This result may be retrieved later by a handle to this task.

task = pacStart(*fun*, *args*)

creates a new task that executes *fun(args)* and can be referenced via the handle *task*. *task* is a first-order SACLIB object i.e. it can passed to other functions or tasks or stored in a SACLIB object. The result of this task (which is the value returned by *fun*) may be retrieved (arbitrarily often) by any task that knows *task*.

value = pacWait(*tptr*, *tasks*)

returns the result *value* of one of the *tasks* and writes the handle of the delivering task into the location *tptr*. If all denoted tasks are still active, pacWait blocks until one task terminates and then delivers the result of this task. Of course, this non-deterministic construct also supports the deterministic subcase of waiting for the result of a single task.

It may happen that by the result of some task the results of the remaining tasks have become irrelevant (speculative parallelism). In this case, the superfluous tasks should be aborted such that they do not consume any more processor time and memory resources.

pacStop(*tasks*)

terminates the execution of all denoted *tasks* and of all subtasks created by these tasks. If some task has already delivered its result, it is not affected any more. pacStop can be considered as an annotation that does not influence the correctness of a program (modulo termination) but only its operational behavior.

What is the physical interpretation of a task handle? One possibility is to implement it as a *task descriptor* i.e. as a reference to the workspace. Before a task stops execution, it stores its result there for the later retrieval by other tasks. However, this approach has severe disadvantages: either the task descriptor is not deallocated after the corresponding task has terminated and the workspace is never reclaimed. The other possibility (implemented in the μSYSTEM) is to deallocate the task descriptor when the result is received by another task. But then the abstract view of task handles as promises for task results goes lost, since the result of a task may be retrieved only once.

Since we wanted to preserve our abstract view of tasks, we decided to split the description of a task into two separate entities: a *task descriptor* and a *result descriptor*. *task* is then a reference to the result descriptor which is a SACLIB list that essentially contains three items: a semaphore for mutual exclusion, a flag that signals whether the result is available and either the result value itself or a queue of the descriptors of those tasks that are waiting for the result.

For each new task, a result descriptor and a task descriptor are allocated and mutually linked. Actually, the task executes a function `pacShell` that calls *fun* with the corresponding arguments *args*. `pacShell` stores the function result in the result descriptor and awakes all tasks blocked on this descriptor. Finally, `pacShell` deallocates its task descriptor and the task terminates.

The large task descriptor therefore occupies space only as long as the task is actually alive. After the termination of the task, only the small result descriptor is left by which other tasks can receive the result. Since this descriptor is a SACLIB object, it is subject to garbage collection and is (together with the result) reclaimed when no task has the *task* handle any more. Hence, task results do not occupy memory longer than necessary.

4.2 Stream Model

There are several parallel algebraic algorithms (e.g. for *critical pair completion* [6]) for which the pure argument/result model is not adequate. These algorithms can be better described in terms of tasks that possess an internal state. Such a task receives a sequence of input objects, processes each object according to its internal state (which is changed by the computation) and forwards a sequence of results to other tasks.

Therefore PACLIB supports an additional form of task communication by *streams*: a stream is a buffered communication channel by which a task can transmit a sequence of values to another task (or even to a set of other tasks). A stream can have three states:

1. *empty*: no element is available in the stream.
2. ⟨*first*, *rest*⟩: the stream is a pair of an element *first* and another stream *rest*.
3. *closed*: no element will ever become available in the stream.

Usually, an *empty* stream s_0 is created and passed as an argument to two new tasks. One task (the *producer*) changes the state of the stream from *empty* to ⟨v_0, s_1⟩ where v_0 is the value to be transmitted and s_1 is a new and *empty* stream. The other task (the *consumer*) receives v_0 and s_1 that can be used for the transmission of another value. If the consumer tries to receive a value while s_i is still in the *empty* state, the task is blocked.

In this fashion, a sequence of streams $s_0, s_1, \ldots, s_n$ is generated that transmit the values $v_0, v_1, \ldots, v_{n-1}$. The producer finally sets the state of s_n to *closed*, which terminates the communication. Any task that has a stream handle s_i may receive the associated v_i and that v_i may be extracted from s_i arbitrarily often.

stream = pacOpen()

creates an *empty* stream and return its handle.

pacClose(*streams*)

sets the state of all *streams* to *closed*.

pacPut(*stream*, *value*)

sets the state of the *stream* to $\langle value, new \rangle$ where *new* is a new and empty stream. Then *stream* is replaced by *new*, i.e. any further application of *stream* will actually refer to *new*. Elements may be retrieved from a stream by

done = pacGet(*sptr*, *vptr*, *rptr*, *streams*)

If all *streams* are *closed*, pacGet returns FALSE. If some streams are *open* but all of them are *empty*, pacGet blocks the current task until the state of some stream has changed. If some stream s has the state $\langle v, r \rangle$, s is written into the location *sptr*, v into the location *vptr* and the rest stream r into the location *rptr*. pacGet then returns TRUE.

The implementation of streams is entirely based on the concepts introduced in the previous section. A stream is just a PACLIB result descriptor *without* an associated task descriptor. The result descriptor receives by pacPut a heap cell $\langle v, r \rangle$ where v is the value to be transmitted and r is a reference to a new result descriptor. pacClosed writes a NIL reference into the result descriptor, which terminates the stream. pacGet is implemented by the same algorithm as pacWait.

The definition of streams as result descriptors (i.e. synchronization points) without task descriptors (i.e. separate threads of control) again reflects the motivation for the introduction of this concept. The effect of a stream could be also simulated by a sequence of tasks in the following way: each task returns a result cell that is composed of an element and of a reference to a subtask computing the next cell. Actually, the concept of streams is orthogonal to that of function results i.e. the one can be based on the other.

4.3 Timings

The time overhead imposed by the PACLIB kernel is negligible i.e. a sequential program runs as fast as when linked with the SACLIB kernel. We now give several benchmarks that characterize the overall efficiency of the system. All timings were performed on a SEQUENT SYMMETRY with 128 MB main memory and 20 processors i80386 running at a clock rate of 20 MHz. A function call takes on this machine roughly 8 μs (including the passing of arguments on the stack). The creation of a corresponding PACLIB task by pacStart takes in average 230 μs i.e. approximately 30 times longer.

The time required for the reception of a task result by pacWait depends on whether the receiving task is blocked or not and how many results it waits for. We

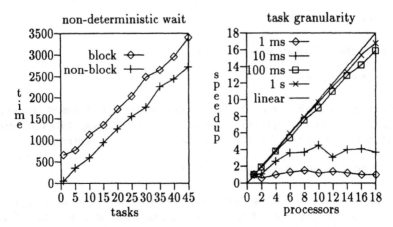

Fig. 2. Task Benchmarks

performed two benchmarks measuring the time that a task spends in pacWait with respect to the number of tasks m that it is waiting for (provided that the delivering task is the last one in the list). In the first test, the receiving task finds the result of the last task already available and is therefore not blocked. In the other test, none of the results is available yet; the current task is blocked and will be awaked by the last task in the list.

The results depicted in the left picture of Figure 2 show that the time t required for the delivery of a result is linear in the number of tasks m that are waited for. Roughly, we have $t = m * 60 + b$ μs where $b = 0$, if the receiving task is not blocked, and $b = 600$, if the task is blocked and awaked[3]. Waiting for a single task therefore costs 60 μs minimum.

In order to estimate the minimum granularities for PACLIB applications, we ran the following benchmark (see the right picture in Figure 2): a main task started 100 subtasks (that were calibrated to execute for a certain amount of time) and received the corresponding results deterministically in sequence. The time from the start of the first task until the reception of the last result was measured. This test therefore represented the worst case by including most of the synchronization overhead into a single sequential task.

Granularities up to 10 ms were to small to to outweigh the parallelization overhead. This shows that just considering the task creation time of 24 μs gives a too optimistic picture by neglecting the times for context switches, reception of results and other effects. However, for tasks running 100 ms, almost linear speedups were achieved that could be not significantly improved by larger granularities.

---

[3] Actually, these 600 μs include 260 μs cost for two context switches, since the benchmark was executed on a single virtual processor.

5   Memory Management

5.1   The Garbage Collector

The PACLIB memory subsystem is transparent with respect to parallelism, i.e. it provides the same interface as the sequential SACLIB. The operation COMP(h,t) allocates a new heap cell and fills the head field with h and the tail field with t. The new cell is allocated from the local available list LAVAIL of that processor that currently executes the task. If LAVAIL runs out of free cells, the processor picks the first available list in GAVAIL as its new LAVAIL. If GAVAIL is also empty, a global garbage collection is triggered. This two-level memory management scheme of PACLIB is a pragmatic compromise between two extremes that both have significant disadvantages:

1. **Global Available List Only:** In order to keep GAVAIL consistent, it must not be simultaneously updated by different processors. Without local available lists, each call of COMP would require a semaphore operation that would considerably increase the runtime overhead of the function. Moreover, due to the serial access to GAVAIL, this shared resource would represent a significant bottleneck for parallelization.
2. **Local Available Lists Only:** Without a global available list, there arises the danger of wasting heap space. Some processor might consume cells from its local available list LAVAIL faster than the other processors. It would then trigger garbage collection even if there were still plenty of free cells available (since these cells were attached to the local available lists of other processors).

In order to trigger garbage collection, the processor puts the currently executed task back into the ready queue and interrupts by a signal the execution of the other virtual processors (actually UNIX processes). After all processors have acknowledged the interruption, garbage collection takes place in two phases:

1. **Mark:** All cells that can be referenced by any task are marked. Since all user tasks are descheduled, all heap references are on the stacks of these tasks. Each virtual processor picks a task descriptor, scans the associated stack and marks all heap cells that can be reached.
2. **Sweep:** All unmarked cells are reclaimed to construct a new list GAVAIL. Each processor scans a different portion of the heap, unmarks the marked cells and reclaims the unmarked cell. When a new free list of the desired length is built, the list is linked into GAVAIL.

The work of the sweep phase is well balanced among all processors since they operate on different heap sections of the same size. The balance of load in the mark phase depends on the number of available tasks and the number of cells that can be reached by each task. The worst case is that of a single task (since its stack is scanned by a single processor). However, if we assume that there are substantially more tasks than processors, also this phase is performed in parallel.

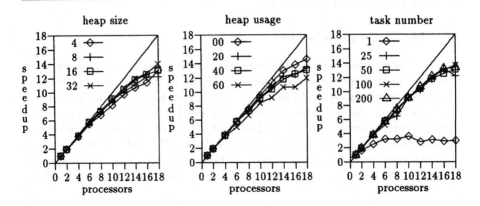

Fig. 3. Garbage Collection

5.2 Timings

We ran a set of benchmarks that measured the speedups that could be achieved for the garbage collector by starting a number of dummy tasks that evenly allocated heap cells. These programs tested the influence of three different parameters (see Figure 3):

- **Heap Size:** The larger the heap is, the longer the sweep phase takes (where all virtual processors can work independently in parallel). However, the total runtime differences are not very significant.
- **Heap Load:** The more heap cells are in use, the more time the mark phase takes. For an almost empty heap, a speedup of more than 14 could be achieved compared to a speedup of 12 for a heap with 60% cells in use.
- **Task Number:** The more tasks are active, the better the load balancing in the mark phase becomes. For a single task, only a speedup of 3 could be achieved; in all other cases a maximum speedup of 13 was possible.

Summarizing, in most cases the speedup is linear up to 10 processors and achieves a maximum of 14 with 18 processors. Each processor reclaims 1.5 MB of heap memory per second which is identical to the sequential SACLIB garbage collection rate. For typical applications, the garbage collection overhead is less than 15% of the total execution time.

6 An Application Example

As an example for the application of PACLIB, we sketch the implementation of a parallel algorithm for the exact solution of linear equation systems. Let A be a regular $n \times n$ matrix over $\mathbb{Z}$ and b a vector of length n over $\mathbb{Z}$. We want to find the vector x of length n over $\mathbb{Q}$ such that $A * x = b$. A and b may contain arbitrary integer numbers whose size is not limited by the word length of any computer; these numbers therefore have to be represented by sequences of computer words. Furthermore, the result vector x shall consist of rational numbers that are the *exact* solutions of the system; each rational has to be represented by a pair of integers (the nominator and the denominator, respectively).

Since we have to perform exact computations, the size of the involved integers steadily increases and arithmetic becomes more and more time-consuming. Thus the complexity of the Gaussian Elimination algorithm is $O(n^5 l^2)$ where l is the maximum length of the entries in A and b [28]. A more efficient approach is based on Cramer's Theorem saying that each x_i can be computed as $x_i = y_i/d$ where $d = \det(A)$ and $y_i = \det(A_i)$ (A_i is A with the i-th column replaced by b). Thus we may transform the problem of solving an equation system into the problem of computing determinants which can be efficiently done by *modular arithmetic*:

We take k prime numbers[4] p_j and map the system (A, b) into k systems (A^j, b^j) over the finite fields $\mathbb{Z}_{p_j}$. Provided that the p_j fit into single computer words, arithmetic can in these fields performed in constant time. Then we compute the determinant families $d^j = \det(A^j)$ and $y_i^j = \det(A_i^j)$ and apply the *Chinese remaindering algorithm* [1] to derive the original determinants y_i and d. Finally, we reduce the rationals $x_i = y_i/d$ to normal form. The total complexity of the algorithm is then $O(n^3 l^2 + n^4 l)$ [28]. The basic idea for the parallelization of this algorithms is as follows;

- **Mapping:** The k images (A^j, b^j) can be computed in parallel.
- **Determinants:** The k determinant families (d^j, y_i^j) can be computed in parallel.
- **Chinese Remaindering:** $n+1$ tasks may compute d and each y_i in parallel.
- **Reduction:** The n reductions $x_i = y_i/d$ can be performed in parallel.

The PACLIB program first creates k **det** tasks, one **cra_d** task and n **cra_y** tasks. Each **det** task maps the given system into a domain $\mathbb{Z}_{p_j}$ and computes the determinant family (d^j, y_i^j). The **cra_d** task takes the list of **det** tasks and receives in a non-deterministic order their results to compute d. In the same way, each **cra_y** task computes its y_i, waits for the result of the **cra_d** task and performs the final reduction y_i/d.

The first two pictures in Figure 4 visualize the profiling information that was generated by a program run solving an equation system of dimension 15 with 18 processors. In the left picture, each horizontal line represents the execution time of a task; the medium picture displays the utilization of the processors. The right picture in this figure shows how much the PACLIB program was faster than the sequential SACLIB program for three equation systems with various dimensions (5, 10 and 40) and maximum lengths of the matrix entries (30, 300 and 900 bit).

Since k is usually very large, all processors are saturated with work during the determinant computation phase. A significant part of this phase is overlapped

---

[4] An upper bound for k can be determined from the entries of (A, b).

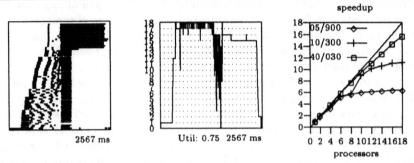

Fig. 4. Exact Solution of Linear Equation Systems

with the execution of the cra_d and the cra_y tasks, because the **det** results are delivered in a non-deterministic order. The final reduction of the solutions is performed by the cra_y tasks, therefore the maximum speedup is bounded by the dimension of the system. However, the speedup is very good, if if the dimension of the system is larger than the number of available processors. For the case of small dimensions, we have developed somewhat more efficient variants of the algorithm [22].

7 Related Work

Finally, we want to relate the concepts of PACLIB to other parallel systems:

Functional Programming: The PACLIB task model is influenced by functional programming [25] and related concepts as dataflow [16] and guarded horn clause languages [11]. PACLIB tasks are similar to the "futures" of MULTILISP [12]. However, PACLIB uses an explicit synchronization function to access task results, while futures are transparent to the program. This is possible since in MULTILISP all operand types are checked at runtime. The **eval** construct of LINDA [8] also resembles the functional model of parallelism.

Non-Determinism: There exist approaches to incorporate non-determinism into a functional framework [3]. Guarded horn clause languages [11] offer committed choice non-determinism. LINDA [8] allows the non-deterministic selection of tuples that match a given pattern. Message passing languages like OCCAM [14] offer the non-deterministic reception of messages from different sources.

Streams: Streams are a concept of non-strict functional languages [25], data flow languages [16] and guarded horn clause languages [11]. In contrast to message passing channels, streams are first-order objects that can be accessed by many tasks simultaneously. There also exist more general forms of non-strict data structures (e.g. I-STRUCTURES [2]).

Garbage Collection: There is a large amount of literature on garbage collection in a parallel environment (for a bibliography, see e.g. [18]). For the PACLIB garbage collector, we chose a relatively simple solution which is a natural extension of the SACLIB mark and sweep collector and provides a comparative efficiency.

Parallel Computer Algebra Systems: Most approaches to parallel computer algebra combine sequential computer algebra systems with parallel programming models:

- **PARSAC** [15] is a parallel variant of the computer algebra library SAC-2 based on MACH threads. The system supports a shared heap where each thread owns a set of memory pages from which it allocates new cells. A terminating thread copies its result into the page set of the parent thread and frees its own page set.
- **Linda-Maple** [9] is a combination of the computer algebra system MAPLE with the LINDA model. Each MAPLE process has a separate heap. Interprocess communication is based on the LINDA tuple space by character strings into which MAPLE arguments and results are converted.
- **||MAPLE||** [23] is a combination of MAPLE with the guarded horn clause language STRAND. Parallel programs are written in STRAND while sequential algebraic computations are performed by MAPLE processes (each with a separate heap). The communication between both layers is based on STRAND character strings.

Light-Weight Concurrency: Packages similar to the μSYSTEM are incorporated into MACH [26], the SUN version of UNIX [24] and the CHARM Kernel [27].

8 Conclusions and Further Work

PACLIB is now a reliable and efficient tool for the implementation of algebraic algorithms on shared memory multi-processors. Our current work concentrates on the extension of the PACLIB library that now includes parallel algorithms for resultant computation, the exact solution of linear equation systems, the Gröbner bases method and others. We will also continue to introduce new features (e.g. task priorities) into the PACLIB kernel. Furthermore, we work on the development of an X11-based performance analysis environment and on the design of a high-level programming interface that generates parallel PACLIB code from functional specifications.

9 Acknowledgements

The authors would like to thank Andreas Neubacher, Kurt Siegl, Hans-Wolfgang Loidl and Tudor Jebelean who helped to design the PACLIB concept. Volker Stahl, Werner Landerl, Wolfgang Stöcher, Mark Encarnacion, Carla Limongelli and others designed and implemented several PACLIB programs. This work was supported by the Austrian Science Foundation (FWF) grant S5302-PHY "Parallel Symbolic Computation".

References

1. A. V. Aho, J. E. Hopcroft, and J. D. Ullman. *The Design and Analysis of Computer Algorithms.* Addison-Wesley, 1974.

2. Arvind, R. S. Nikhil, and K. K. Pingali. I-Structures: Data Structures for Parallel Computing. Computation Structures Group Memo 269, Laboratory for Computer Science, Massachusetts Institute of Technology, Cambridge, MA, February 1987. Also in: Proceedings of the Workshop on Graph Reduction, Los Alamos, New Mexico, September 28 – October 1, 1986.

3. P. S. Barth, R. S. Nikhil, and Arvind. M-Structures: Extending a Parallel, Nonstrict, Functional Language with State. In *Functional Programming Languages and Computer Architectures,* volume 523 of *Lecture Notes in Computer Science,* pages 538–568, Harvard, Massachusetts, USA, 1991. Springer, Berlin.

4. B. Buchberger. Gröbner Bases: An Algorithmic Method in Polynomial Ideal Theory. In N. K. Bose and D. Reidel, editors, *Recent trends in Multidimensional Systems,* chapter 6, pages 184–232. D. Reidel Publishing Company, Dordrecht-Boston-Lancaster, 1985.

5. B. Buchberger, G. Collins, M. Encarnation, H. Hong, J. Johnson, W. Krandick, R. Loos, A. Mandache, A. Neubacher, and H. Vielhaber. A SACLIB Primer. Technical Report 92-34, RISC-Linz, Johannes Kepler University, Linz, Austria, 1992.

6. B. Buchberger, G. E. Collins, R. Loos, and R. Albrecht, editors. *Computer Algebra — Symbolic and Algebraic Computation.* Springer, Vienna, New York, 1982.

7. P. A. Buhr and R. A. Stroobosscher. The μSystem: Providing Light-weight Concurrency on Shared-Memory Multiprocessor Computers Running UNIX. *Software — Practice and Experience,* 20(9):929–964, September 1990.

8. N. Carriero and D. Gelernter. *How to Write Parallel Programs.* MIT Press, 1990.

9. B. W. Char. Progress Report on a System for General-Purpose Parallel Symbolic Algebraic Computation. In *Proceedings of the ISSAC'90, Tokyo, Japan, August 20–24,* pages 96–103, Department of Computer Science, University of Tennessee, Knoxville, TN 37996-1301, 1990. ACM Press, New York.

10. G. E. Collins and H. Hong. Partial CAD Construction in Quantifier Elimination. Technical Report OSU-CISRC-10/89 TR 45, Computer and Information Science Research Center, Ohio State University, Columbus, OH, 1987.

11. I. Foster and S. Taylor. *Strand — New Concepts in Parallel Programming.* Prentice-Hall, Englewood Cliffs, New Jersey, 1989.

12. R. H. Halstead, Jr. Multilisp: A Language for Concurrent Symbolic Computation. *ACM Trans. Prog. Lang. Syst.,* 7(4):501–538, October 1985.

13. H. Hong, W. Schreiner, A. Neubacher, K. Siegl, H.-W. Loidl, T. Jebelean, and P. Zettler. PACLIB User Manual. Technical Report 92-32, RISC-Linz, Johannes Kepler University, Linz, Austria, May 1992. Also: Technical Report ACPC/TR 92-9, ACPC Technical Report Series, Austrian Center for Parallel Computation, July 1992.

14. Inmos. *Occam 2 Reference Manual.* Prentice Hall, New York, 1988.

15. W. Küchlin. The S-Threads Environment for Parallel Symbolic Computation. In *Computer Algebra and Parallelism, Second International Workshop,* pages 1–18, Ithaca, USA, May, 1990. Springer, Berlin. Volume 584 of Lecture Notes in Computer Science.

16. R. S. Nikhil. ID (Version 88.0) Reference Manual. Computation Structures Group Memo 284, Laboratory for Computer Science, Massachusetts Institute of Technology, Cambridge, MA, March 1988.
17. J. Rothnie. Kendall Square Research Introduction to the KSR1. In H.-W. Meuer, editor, *Supercomputer '92 — Anwendungen, Architekturen, Trends (Applications, Architectures, Trends)*, pages 104–113, Mannheim, Germany, June 25–27, 1992. Springer, Berlin.
18. M. Rudalics. *Multiprocessor List Memory Management.* PhD thesis, Johannes Kepler University, Linz, Austria, 1988. Also: Technical Report 88-87, RISC-Linz, Johannes Kepler University, Linz, Austria, 1988.
19. W. Schreiner. The Design of the PACLIB Kernel. Technical Report 92-33, RISC-Linz, Johannes Kepler University, Linz, Austria, 1992. Also: Technical Report ACPC/TR 93-4, ACPC Technical Report Series, Austrian Center for Parallel Computation, February 1993.
20. W. Schreiner and H. Hong. A New Library for Parallel Algebraic Computation. In R. F. Sincovec et al., editors, *Sixth SIAM Conference on Parallel Processing for Scientific Computing*, volume II, pages 776–783, Norfolk, Virginia, March 22–24, 1993. SIAM. Also: Technical Report 92-73, RISC-Linz, Johannes Kepler University, Linz, Austria, 1992. Also: Technical Report ACPC/TR 93-9, ACPC Technical Report Series, Austrian Center for Parallel Computation, February 1993.
21. W. Schreiner and H. Hong. PACLIB — A System for Parallel Algebraic Computation on Shared Memory Computers. In H. M. Alnuweiri, editor, *Parallel Systems Fair at the Seventh International Parallel Processing Symposium*, pages 56–61, Newport Beach, CA, April 14, 1993. IPPS '93. Also: Technical Report 93-03, RISC-Linz, Johannes Kepler University, Linz, Austria, February 1993. Also: Technical Report ACPC/TR 93-12, ACPC Technical Report Series, Austrian Center for Parallel Computation, February 1993.
22. W. Schreiner and V. Stahl. The Exact Solution of Linear Equation Systems on a Shared Memory Multiprocessor. Technical report, RISC-Linz, Johannes Kepler University, Linz, Austria, 1992.
23. K. Siegl. Parallelizing Algorithms for Symbolic Computation Using ‖MAPLE‖. In *Fourth ACM SIGPLAN Symposium on Principles and Practice of Parallel Programming*, pages 179–186, San Diego, California, May 19-22, 1993. ACM Press. Also: Technical Report 93-08, RISC-Linz, Johannes Kepler University, Linz, Austria, February 1993.
24. Sun Microsystems. *System Services Overview, Lightweight Processes*, May 1988.
25. B. K. Szymanski, editor. *Parallel Functional Languages and Compilers.* Frontier Series. ACM Press, 1991.
26. A. Tevanian, Jr. and R. F. Rashid. MACH: A Basis for Future UNIX Development. Technical Report CMU-CS-87-139, Computer Science Department, Carnegie-Mellon University, Pittsburgh, PA, June 1987.
27. University of Illinois. *The CHARM (3.2) Programming Language Manual*, December 1992.
28. F. Winkler. Computer Algebra I. Technical Report 88-88, RISC-Linz, Johannes Kepler University, Linz, Austria, 1988.
29. H. Zima and B. Chapman. *Supercompilers for Parallel and Vector Computers.* Addison Wesley, New York, 1990.

Generating Parallel Code from Equations in the ObjectMath Programming Environments

Peter Fritzson and Niclas Andersson

Department of Computer and Information Science
Linköping University, S-581 83 Linköping, Sweden
E-mail: petfr@ida.liu.se, nican@ida.liu.se

Abstract. For a long time efficient use of massively parallel computers has been hindered by dependencies introduced in software through low-level implementation practice. This paper presents a programming environment and language called ObjectMath (Object oriented Mathematical language for scientific computing), which aims at eliminating this problem by allowing the user to represent mathematical equational models directly in the system. The system performs dependency analysis of equations to extract parallelism and automatically generates parallel code for numerical solution.

   The system is currently being used for industrial applications in advanced mechanical analysis, but is generally applicable to other areas. Using ObjectMath, it is possible to model classes of equation objects, to support inheritance of equations, and to solve systems of equations.

1   Introduction

The current state of the art in modeling and programming in scientific computing and advanced mechanical analysis is still very low-level. A designer often spends more than half the time and effort of a typical project in implementing and debugging FORTRAN programs. These programs are written to evaluate and optimize a mathematical model of the machine element and to perform numerical experiments. Numerical problems and convergence problems often arise, since the optimization problems usually are non-linear. A substantial amount of time is spent on fixing the program to achieve convergence. Feedback from results of numerical experiments usually lead to revisions in the mathematical model, which subsequently require reimplementing the Fortran program. This whole process is rather laborious and error prone.

   Thus there is a clear need for a higher level programming environment that would eliminate most of these low-level problems and allow the designer to concentrate on the modeling aspects. Such an environment would also allow better utilization of the *inherent parallelism* of scientific problems, which otherwise is hidden within the low-level FORTRAN code.

1.1 The ideal programming environment: programming in high-level equations

The ideal high level programming environment would automatically transform systems of equations into efficient symbolic and numerical programs. It would select optimization routines with good convergence properties for the given problem. The environment would also aid in formulating equations given geometrical constraints and transforming equations between different coordinate systems. However, fully automatic versions of some of these capabilities will be hard to achieve. It is more realistic to assume that the user will work in dialogue with the interactive system, and that the user can supply valuable hints and information that will guide the system in choosing the right algorithms and transformations. Another important advantage of an equational representation over a FORTRAN implementation is that more *inherent parallelism* of the problem is preserved. Thus better results can be expected when generating code for massively parallel machines. Some desired capabilities of the programming environment are listed below:

- Modeling support in expressing systems of equations, e.g. handling of geometrical constraints and coordinate transformations.
- Integration of object-oriented techniques for better structuring of equational models.
- Algebraic transformations of equations.
- Transformation of equations in to programs for computation on *massively parallel* hardware.
- Evaluation of numerical experiments.
- Graphical presentation and visualization.

2 The ObjectMath Language and Environment

ObjectMath is both a language and a programming environment. The programming environment is designed to be easy to use for application engineers (e.g. in the field of mechanical analysis) who are not computer scientists. It is interactive and includes a graphical browser, similar to the one found in the Smalltalk-80 system [8]. Support routines for generation of numerical code and visualization are also part of the environment as well as a class library containing general classes. This paper focuses on the language, but we will nevertheless give a short overview of the programming environment later in this section.

The ObjectMath language is an hybrid modeling language, combining object-oriented constructs with a language for symbolic computation. This makes ObjectMath a suitable language for implementing complex mathematical models, such as those used in machine element analysis. Formulae and equations can be written with a notation that closely resembles conventional mathematics, while the use of object-oriented modeling makes it possible to structure the model in a natural way.

An existing computer algebra language, Mathematica [18], was chosen as a basis for ObjectMath. Building an object-oriented layer on top of an existing language is not ideal, but this decision was taken in order that a prototype could be implemented quickly to test the feasibility of the approach. Thus the current ObjectMath language is a first prototype and the whole language is scheduled for reimplementation in a near future, making it independent of Mathematica.

Mathematica was chosen over other similar systems partly because it was already used by our industrial partner, and partly because of its excellent support for three-dimensional graphics. The relationship between Mathematica and ObjectMath can be compared to that between C and C++. The C++ programming language is basically the C language augmented with classes and other object-oriented language constructs. In a similar way, the ObjectMath language can be viewed as an object-oriented version of the Mathematica language.

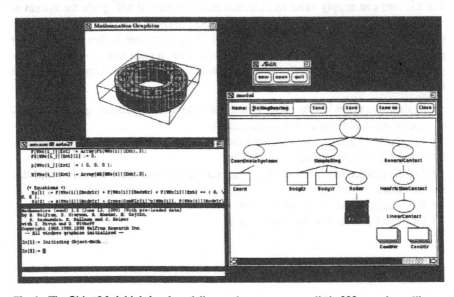

Fig. 1. The ObjectMath high-level modeling environment on a realistic 200-equation rolling bearing example. The three-dimensional view of the bearing has been automatically generated from equations expressed in ObjectMath.

2.1 Object-Oriented Modeling

Models used for analysis in scientific computing are inherently complex in the same way as other software. One way to handle this complexity is to use object-oriented techniques. Wegner [20] defines the basic terminology of object-oriented programming:

- *Objects* are collections of operations that share a state. These operations are often called *methods*. The state is represented by *instance variables* which are accessible only to the operations of the object.
- *Classes* are templates from which objects can be created.
- *Inheritance* allows us to reuse the operations of a class when defining new classes.

A subclass inherits the operations of its parent class and can add new operations and instance variables.

When working with a mathematical description that consists of hundreds of equations and formulae (e.g. a model of a complex machine element), it is highly advantageous to *structure* the model. A natural way to do this is to model machine elements as *objects*. Physical bodies, e.g. rolling elements in a bearing, are modeled as separate objects. Properties of objects like these might include a surface description, a normal to the surface, forces and torques on the body, and a volume. These objects might define operations such as finding all contacts on the body, computing the forces on or the displacement of the body, and plotting a three-dimensional picture of the body.

Abstract concepts can also be modeled as objects. Examples of such concepts are coordinate systems and contacts between bodies. The coordinate system objects included in the ObjectMath class library define methods for transforming points and vectors to other coordinate systems. Equations and formulae describing the interaction between different bodies are often the most complicated part of problems in machine element analysis. It is therefore practical to encapsulate these equations in separate *contact objects*. One advantage of using contact objects is that we can substitute one mathematical contact model for another simply by plugging in a different kind of contact object. The rest of the model remains completely unchanged. When using such a model in practice, one often needs to experiment with different contact models to find one which is exact enough for the intended purpose, yet still as computationally efficient as possible. The ObjectMath class library contains several different contact classes.

The use of *inheritance* facilitates *reuse* of equations and formulae. For example, a cylindrical roller element can inherit basic properties and operations from an existing general cylinder class, refining them or adding other properties and operations as necessary. Inheritance may be viewed not only as a sharing mechanism, but also as a concept specialization mechanism. This provides another powerful mechanism for structuring complex models in a comprehensive way. Iteration cycles in the design process can be simplified by the use of inheritance, as changes in one class affects all objects that inherits from that class.

Object-oriented techniques make it practical to organize repositories of reusable software components. All classes have a well defined interface which makes it possible to use them as black boxes. Inheritance allows us to specialize existing classes and thereby reuse them, even if they do not exactly fit our needs as they are. The ObjectMath class library is one example of such a software component repository. It contains general classes, for instance different contact classes and classes for modeling simple bodies such as cylinders and spheres.

2.2   ObjectMath Classes and Instances

A *CLASS* declaration declares a class which can be used as a template when creating objects. ObjectMath classes can be parameterized. The ObjectMath *INSTANCE* declaration is, in a traditional sense, both a declaration of class and a declaration of one object (instance) of this class. This makes the declaration of classes with singleton instances compact. It is possible to inherit from classes implicitly declared by an ObjectMath *INSTANCE* declaration, just as from classes declared with a *CLASS* declaration.

An array containing an as yet unspecified number of objects can be created from one *INSTANCE* declaration by adding an index variable in brackets to the instance name. This allows for the creation of large numbers of nearly identical objects, for example the rolling elements in a rolling bearing. To represent differences between such objects, functions (methods) that are dependent upon the array index of the instance can be used. The implementation makes it possible to do computations with an unspecified number of elements in the array.

The bodies of ObjectMath *CLASS* and *INSTANCE* declarations contain formulae and equations. Mathematica syntax is used for these. Note that the Mathematica context mark, `, denotes remote access, i.e. X`y is the entity y of the object X.

There are some limitations in the current prototype of the ObjectMath language for ease of implementation. Most notable is that a mechanism for enforcing encapsulation is missing. Encapsulation is desirable because it makes it easier to write reusable software since the internal state of an object may only be accessed through a well defined interface. When writing ObjectMath code we try to treat objects as black boxes, even if the language does not enforce this. Another limitation is that only single inheritance is allowed, though this has not been a problem so far. The next version of the ObjectMath language will provide both proper encapsulation and multiple inheritance.

A first prototype of the ObjectMath programming environment has been implemented using a combination of the languages Mathematica, C and C++. The ObjectMath modeling language supports single inheritance, grouping of equations and transparent integration of methods implemented in C++ into ObjectMath models. A translator expands the ObjectMath specification into Mathematica code, where algebraic transformations and simplifications are performed. Finally, C++ code can be generated for numerical solution of the parts of the problem which cannot be solved algebraically. A browser provides overview and editing of the class hierarchy. Very recently some capabilities for doing dependency analysis and generating parallel Modula-2* code has been added to the system. The first release of ObjectMath was able to handle a rather realistic 200-equation model of a rolling bearing. The latest 1992 release has been used to solve additional application problems.

2.3   Generating parallel code from equations

As mentioned previously, one of the main problems in extracting parallelism from application programs written in languages such as FORTRAN is the low level of abstraction. During the process of implementing a typical numerical simulation program, many unnecessary dependencies and constraints are introduced because of implementation choices. The program is thus, in a sense, *overspecified*. This means that many possibilities for parallelization are lost.

Force equilibrium

$$\vec{F}_{W_\rho,I}^{(WN_i)} + \vec{F}_{W_\rho,E}^{(WN_i)} + \vec{F}_{W_\rho,ext}^{(WN_i)} = 0$$

Moment equilibrium

$$\vec{M}_{W_\rho,I}^{(WN_i)} + \vec{M}_{W_\rho,E}^{(WN_i)} + \vec{M}_{W_\rho,ext}^{(WN_i)} +$$

$$\vec{p}_{W_\rho,I}^{(WN_i)} \times \vec{F}_{W_\rho,I}^{(WN_i)} + \vec{p}_{W_\rho,E}^{(WN_i)} \times \vec{F}_{W_\rho,E}^{(WN_i)} +$$

$$\vec{p}_{W_\rho,ext}^{(WN_i)} \times \vec{F}_{W_\rho,ext}^{(WN_i)} = 0$$

```
INSTANCE BodyW[i] INHERITS Roller(W[i])
...
(* Equations *)
Eq[1] := F[WNo[i]][BodyIr] +
    F[WNo[i]][BodyEr] +
    F[WNo[i]][Ext] == { 0, 0, 0 };
Eq[2] := M[WNo[i]][BodyIr] +
    ... == { 0, 0, 0 };
...
END BodyW[i];
```

Fig. 2. The The same equations for Moment and Force equilibrium in both mathematical syntax and in ObjectMath same equations for Moment and Force equilibrium in both mathematical syntax and in ObjectMath syntax

If instead the problem is represented at the highest level of abstraction, i.e. the mathematical model consisting of equations, it should be possible to extract essentially all parallelism from the application model. Low-level executable source code for solution of systems of equations should be automatically generated from the mathematical model and combined with high-quality parallel numerical algorithms to form the parallel application code. The whole process is depicted in Fig. 3. The dependency analysis is based around the standard algorithm for finding strongly connected components in a directed graph [1]. The equations are partitioned into sets of mutually dependent equations by this algorithm (i.e. separate system of equations) and the reduced, acyclic dependency graph is built. The reduced graph is then used to schedule the solution of the equation systems, i.e. to determine the order in which the systems has to be solved and which systems that can be solved in parallel.

2.4 Generating parallel code for a four motor servo example

There are many methods for solving ODE:s, but Runge-Kutta methods [9], [10] are rather stable when encountering discontinuities, which makes them a natural choice for rolling bearing applications. A simple test-problem that can be formulated as ODE:s is shown in Fig. 4. We use this test case as the main example of parallel code generation in this paper.

One of the languages we decided to use was Modula-2* [13]. It is developed at Karlsruhe University as a target language since it supports a rather machine-independent programming model. Programs written in Modula-2* can be compiled for execution on several parallel machines such as MasPar and CM2, and it is also possible to compile for single processor execution on Sun Sparcstations. We managed to run the single processor part of the compiler but we still have not been able to test it on the MasPar. Instead we used CONLAB [12], an extension to MATLAB with primitives for expressing parallelism and communication. By choosing appropriate communication

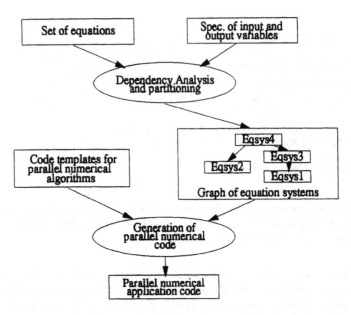

Fig. 3. Two sources of parallelism: application-dependent parallelism is extracted from the equation-based model by dependency analysis; algorithmic parallelism is obtained by inventing or using suitable parallel numerical algorithms for solution of each system of equations. The final application code uses parallelism from both sources.

times we simulated the solving of the test-problem on the Intel iPSC/2 hypercube. The simulation shows good correspondence between simulator and the real machine. Two levels of parallelism are shown in Fig. 5; equation level and equation system level.

If we use the fine grain level of parallelism, the utilization of processors becomes too low due to:

- *Communication takes too much time.* The communication time is greater than the computation for each equation.
- *Allocation of processors.* We have not considered the distance between different processors. This is not important in the CONLAB environment.
- *Size of equations.* If, in a more realistic setting, the equations are more complex, the communication time becomes negligible.

Fig. 6 shows the scheduling of solving the four systems of equations which were extracted from the four-motor example by the dependency and partitioning analysis. In this simple case, it was very easy to generate optimal scheduling. More complicated dependency graphs are handled by scheduling those equation systems whose results are needed for the computation of two or more other nodes.

In the case of parallel Runge-Kutta, the numerical algorithm allows parallelism in the form that all right-hand sides in equations can be evaluated in parallel. Fig. 7 shows the generated code which is inserted into the source code template of the Runge-Kutta solver.

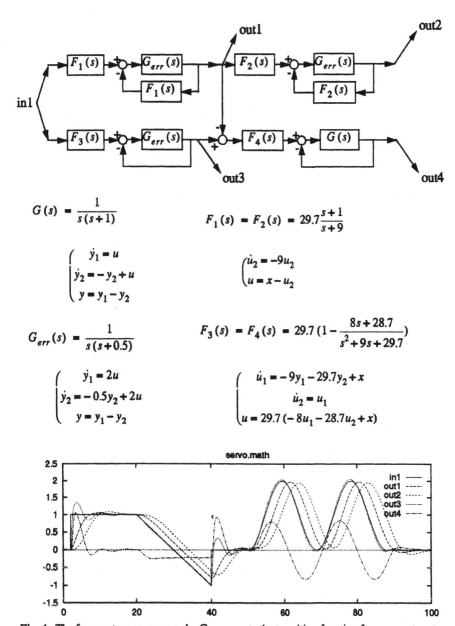

$$G(s) = \frac{1}{s(s+1)}$$

$$F_1(s) = F_2(s) = 29.7\frac{s+1}{s+9}$$

$$\begin{cases} \dot{y}_1 = u \\ \dot{y}_2 = -y_2 + u \\ y = y_1 - y_2 \end{cases}$$

$$\begin{cases} \dot{u}_2 = -9u_2 \\ u = x - u_2 \end{cases}$$

$$G_{err}(s) = \frac{1}{s(s+0.5)}$$

$$F_3(s) = F_4(s) = 29.7\left(1 - \frac{8s+28.7}{s^2+9s+29.7}\right)$$

$$\begin{cases} \dot{y}_1 = 2u \\ \dot{y}_2 = -0.5y_2 + 2u \\ y = y_1 - y_2 \end{cases}$$

$$\begin{cases} \dot{u}_1 = -9y_1 - 29.7y_2 + x \\ \dot{u}_2 = u_1 \\ u = 29.7(-8u_1 - 28.7u_2 + x) \end{cases}$$

Fig. 4. The four-motor servo example. G represents the transition function for a correct motor whereas the three G_{err} are motors with a problem, which means the response curve will deviate from the desired shape. This can be partly remedied through appropriate control. The response curves are computed by the parallel Runge-Kutta ordinary differential equation solver, which has been automatically generated (and combined with a Runge-Kutta algorithm template) from the equations expressed in the ObjectMath system.

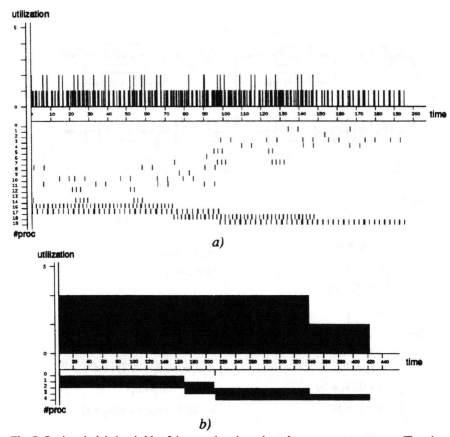

Fig. 5. In a) each right hand side of the equations is evaluated on a separate processor. Thus the communication overhead is relatively high compared to b) where each equation system is allocated to a single processor. In this case the utilization is much better in b) but consider the potential in a) when the complexity of the equations grows.

3 Some Applications of ObjectMath

So far the ObjectMath environment has been tested and evaluated by modeling and analyzing several different problems. Two of the first realistic problems were:

- A three-dimensional model describing a rolling bearing.
- An advanced surface description model, used for rolling bearing analysis.

The rolling bearing example was designed as a realistic but manageable test case for the ObjectMath language and environment. It consists of over 200 equations and can easily be extended, for instance with more realistic contact models. The mathematical model is described in [5] and the ObjectMath implementation in [7]. The bearing consists of an inner ring, an outer ring, and a number of rolling elements in between. The objects

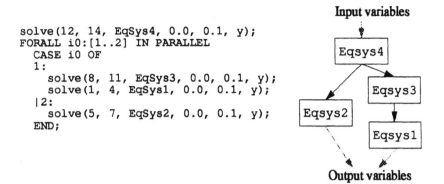

```
solve(12, 14, EqSys4, 0.0, 0.1, y);
FORALL i0:[1..2] IN PARALLEL
  CASE i0 OF
  1:
    solve(8, 11, EqSys3, 0.0, 0.1, y);
    solve(1, 4, EqSys1, 0.0, 0.1, y);
  |2:
    solve(5, 7, EqSys2, 0.0, 0.1, y);
  END;
```

Input variables

Eqsys4

Eqsys3

Eqsys2

Eqsys1

Output variables

Fig. 6. Generated Modula-2* code for scheduling of the of the solution, using the dependency graph obtained from dependency analysis of the equations. Equation system Eqsys4 is solved first, whereafter Eqsys2 is solved in parallel with Eqsys3 and Eqsys1.

modeling these bodies are called BodyEr, BodyIr, and BodyW respectively. Note that BodyW is an array of n rolling elements.

The rings and rolling elements have many properties in common and inherit most of their description from the class Ring in the ObjectMath class library. Ring in turn inherits from the class Body which defines properties that hold for all physical bodies, such as force and moment equilibrium, normal of the surface, the volume of the body, and a method for generating a plot of the body. The class Ring includes a definition of a parametric surface for rings and the class Roller specializes Ring by setting the inner radius to zero and eliminating the inner surface. The hierarchy of ring classes and instances can be seen in Fig. 8. In this figure, classes are drawn as ovals and instances (objects) as rectangles.

```
(* Eqsys1 *)
    FORALL i:[1..4] IN PARALLEL
      CASE i OF
        1: ydot[1] := (y[4] + (Value(0) * y[2])); |
        2: ydot[2] := y[3]; |
        3: ydot[3] := ((-y[3]) + (-y[2]) + (Value(29.7) * ((Value(-8)
           * y[4]) + (Value(-28.7) * y[1]) + y[9] + (-y[13])))); |
        4: ydot[4] := ((Value(-9) * y[4]) + (Value(-29.7) * y[1]) + y[9]
           + (-y[13]));
      END;
    END;
```

Fig. 7. Modula-2* generated for parallel evaluation of right-hand sides, to be inserted into a code template of a parallel Runge-Kutta method for the solution of ordinary differential equations.

The second implemented ObjectMath model is being used in the development of an advanced surface description model. If ObjectMath had not been available, this implementation would have been developed by hand and coded in FORTRAN.

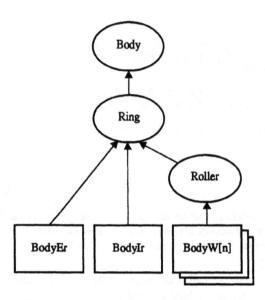

Fig. 8. Body classes and instances in the rolling bearing model

4 Related Work on Symbolic/Algebraic systems

Object-oriented modeling has been used for a number of different application areas. ObjectMath also has a lot in common with conventional computer algebra systems (in particularly Mathematica), but, as mentioned in the introduction, these systems usually lack capabilities that are important for advanced scientific computing, most notably good structuring support.

FINGER [15], [16] is a system for automatic generation of finite element analysis programs. This work differs from our primarily in that we are mainly interested in problems which cannot be solved using FEM.

Omola [2] is an object-oriented modeling language, primarily designed as a simulation modeling language for continuous time systems, especially in the application area of control engineering. The emphasis is on automatic extraction and solving of equations, rather than on permitting interactive manipulation as in ObjectMath. Parallel techniques are not implemented. Some simple symbolic transformations are used to increase efficiency. Automatic solving of sets of equations is applicable to many control engineering problems, but problems in the application area of machine element analysis are usually much more complex and still requires substantial human interaction for efficient solution.

Many systems do not generate numeric code from equation-based models. Of those that do generate code, we know of only one, a recent version of FINGER, which generates parallel code for specialized FEM computations.

4.1 Conclusions and future work

There is a strong need for efficient high-level tools and languages in scientific computing to enhance the programming process and to exploit the maximum parallelism of applications in scientific computing. We feel that the ObjectMath system is highly successful in satisfying part of this need. Complex mathematical equations and functions can be expressed at a high level of abstraction rather than as procedural code. Object-oriented features allow better structure of models and permit reuse of equations through inheritance. This conclusion is supported by the successful modeling and analysis of several realistic applications. Symbolic computation has proved to be a useful technique that can increase both productivity and quality in software development for mechanical analysis in an industrial environment.

We have also seen that the complexity of realistic sets of equations in mechanical analysis makes it essential that the environment allows the user to interactively supply extra information to guide the solution process. Even if it sometimes is possible to solve whole problems automatically, it is desirable to take advantage of the extensive application domain knowledge of the engineer using the system. Thus, advanced problems can be solved much more efficiently and we are less likely to run into convergence or efficiency problems. Once the extra solution and transformation steps have been supplied, the transformation from high-level model down to executable numerical code is largely automatic.

The capability of performing dependency analysis of equations and generating parallel code has recently been added to the ObjectMath environment. We have succeeded in generating code for CONLAB and simulating the Intel iPSC/2 hypercube. Due to practical problems with the Modula-2* compiler and the MasPar installation we have not been able to run anything on the MasPar machine. Hence we will switch to generating parallel Fortran code in the future. Also, substantial improvements in the generated parallel code are still possible, e.g. by using pipe-line parallelism between the Runge-Kutta solvers for ordinary differential equations. Other types of parallel equation-solvers should also be integrated into the system.

4.2 Acknowledgements

Henrik Nilsson implemented the dependency analysis and partitioning of equations necessary to schedule parallel solution of systems of equations. He also improved the English of this paper. Lars Viklund and Johan Herber implemented most of the sequential parts of the ObjectMath environment, e.g. the browser, the translator from ObjectMath to Mathematica, and integration of C++ into ObjectMath classes. Dag Fritzson at SKF ERC provided mathematical expertise and realistic application examples.

References

1. Alfred V. Aho, John E. Hopcroft, Jeffrey D. Ullman. *Data Structures and Algorithms*, 222-226, Addison-Wesley, 1983.

2. Mats Andersson. Omola – an object-oriented language for model representation. Licentiate thesis, Department of Automatic Control, Lund Institute of Technology, P.O. Box 118, S-221 00 Lund, Sweden, May 1990.

3. J.H. Davenport, Y. Siret, and E. Tournier. *Computer Algebra – Systems and Algorithms for Algebraic Computation*. Academic Press, 1988.

4. Richard J. Fateman. A review of Mathematica. Preliminary version. To appear in the *Journal of Symbolic Computation*, 1992.

5. Dag Fritzson and Peter Fritzson. Equational modeling of machine elements – applied to rolling bearings. Technical Report LiTH-IDA-R-91-05, Department of Computer and Information Science, Linköping University, S-581 83, Linköping, Sweden, March 1991.

6. Peter Fritzson and Dag Fritzson. The need for high-level programming support in scientific computing applied to mechanical analysis. Technical Report LiTH-IDA-R-91-04, Department of Computer and Information Science, Linköping University, S-581 83, Linköping, Sweden, March 1991. Accepted for publication in *Computers and Structures – an International Journal*.

7. Peter Fritzson, Lars Viklund, Johan Herber, and Dag Fritzson. Industrial application of object-oriented mathematical modeling and computer algebra in mechanical analysis. In Georg Heeg, Boris Magnusson, and Bertrand Meyer, editors, *Technology of Object-Oriented Languages and Systems – TOOLS 7*. Prentice Hall, 1992.

8. Adele Goldberg. *Smalltalk-80: The Interactive Programming Environment*. Addison-Wesley Publishing Company, 1984.

9. E. Hairer S.P. Nørsett G. Wanner. *Solving Ordinary Differential Equations I: Non stiff Problems*. Springer-Verlag, 1980.

10. E. Hairer G. Wanner. *Solving Ordinary Differential Equations II: Stiff and Differential-Algebraic Problems*. Springer-Verlag, 1991.

11. Thomas W. Page, Jr., Steven E. Berson, William C. Cheng, and Richard R. Muntz. An object-oriented modeling environment. In *OOPSLA'89 Conference Proceedings*, 1989.

12. Peter Jacobson. *The CONcurrent LABoratory: Algorithm Design for and Simulation of Parallel Architectures*. Licentiate thesis. Institute of Information Processing, Department of Computing Science, University of Umeå, Sweden,1992.

13.   Walter F. Tichy, Christian G. Herter. *Modula-2*: An Extension of Modula-2 for Highly Parallel, Portable Programs.* Technical report 4/90 - January 1990, Universität Karlsruhe, Fakultät fur Informatik, Postfach 6980, D-7500 Karlsruhe 1.

14.   Lars Viklund, Johan Herber, and Peter Fritzson. The implementation of ObjectMath – a high-level programming environment for scientific computing. To appear in *Proceedings of the 1992 International Workshop on Compiler Construction,* Springer-Verlag, 1992.

15.   Paul S. Wang. FINGER: A symbolic system for automatic generation of numerical programs in finite element analysis. *Journal of Symbolic Computation,* 2:305–316, 1986.

16.   Paul S. Wang. Graphical user interfaces and automatic generation of sequential and parallel code for scientific computing. In *IEEE CompCon Spring,* 1988.

17.   Peter Wegner. Concepts and paradigms of object-oriented programming. *OOPS Messenger,* 1(1):8–87, August 1990.

18.   Stephen Wolfram. *Mathematica – A System for Doing Mathematics by Computer.* Addison-Wesley Publishing Company, second edition, 1991.

The Paragon Performance Monitoring Environment

Bernhard Ries

Intel European Supercomputer Development Center (ESDC)
Dornacher Str. 1, 85622 Feldkirchen, Germany, e-mail: bernhard@esdc.intel.com

R. Anderson, W. Auld, D. Breazeal, K. Callaghan, E. Richards, W. Smith

Intel Supercomputer Systems Division
15201 N.W. Greenbrier Parkway, Beaverton, OR 97006
e-mail: {raya, auld, donb, karla, ericr, wds}@ssd.intel.com

Abstract. Parallel systems present a special challenge to debugging and performance analysis given the massive amounts of data and physically distributed state of the application. We describe an integrated toolset that provides an extensible and consistent programming environment for monitoring and visualizing the performance of parallel applications. It uses a scalable distributed monitoring system to gather performance data that drive profiling and graphical performance visualization tools. Performance data ara analyzed by both application and system oriented performance tools which are tied together by a common graphical interface.

1   Introduction

Modern scalable high-performance computing systems provide the high potential for sustained performance that is needed to solve Grand Challenge computing problems. To fully understand the performance behavior of such systems and to operate the machines near the high end of their performance range, new performance data-collection, analysis and visualization tools are needed. Some of the most challenging problems that have to be solved by an integrated performance environment are:

- Different categories of users require different types of performance tools. For example, system administrators are interested in observing the overall behavior of the system while application programmers need to focus on a specific application run. Thus, there is a need for both system and application performance analysis tools. The tools must be able to present information at different levels of detail: from low-level information on hardware and operating system statistics up to high-level metrics on program efficiency or speed.

- Monitoring the performance of massively parallel systems or applications can lead to very large amounts of performance data. Different techniques must be devised for the performance environment to be able to handle or reduce the amount of data that needs to be processed. Possible approaches include selective instrumentation techniques, data reduction and compression, and scalable presentation techniques. Many researchers agree that processors with at least the same processing power as those executing the application are needed to properly reduce and present performance data. This dilemma can be solved by using the high-performance computing system itself for performance analysis.

- The current trend towards multiprogramming in operating systems for scalable high-performance computers introduces new problems for application performance tools. In order to be an aid in tuning applications the tools must be able to distinguish system effects from application bottlenecks.

- Monitoring the performance of parallel applications necessarily introduces perturbation. The performance environment must strive to minimize the amount of intrusion and should try to filter out monitoring effects or provide the user with a measure of the intrusiveness of the measurements.

- The diversity of programming models available on scalable high-performance computing systems and the lack of programming model standards make it necessary for the tools to be highly flexible. Tools should be able to present the performance data in the context of the programming model being used but it should not be necessary to design a completely new performance environment for every new programming model.

This paper describes how these problems are addressed in the integrated performance monitoring environment developed by Intel and initially targeted for use on Intel Paragon systems. It consists of an instrumentation front-end, a distributed monitoring system and a set of graphical and command-oriented tools that can be used to analyze performance data.

The paper is organized as follows: in section 2 we describe related work, section 3 gives some background on the target system, an Intel Paragon running Paragon OSF/1. Section 4 gives a detailed description of the performance monitoring architecture. Section 5 describes future plans and extensions, and section 6 presents our conclusions.

2   Related Work

The field of performance monitoring and performance visualization for parallel machines has received a lot of attention lately. This has led to a large number of monitoring environments with different capabilities. The Pablo [16] project has implemented a system in which performance tools are built from individual modules that can be easily interconnected and reconfigured. The Pablo team has also developed a self-documenting trace-format that includes internal definitions of data types, sizes and names. The TOPSYS environment [3] is based on a distributed monitoring system that is used by multiple tools, including an on-line performance visualizer [4]. The IPS-2 system [11] takes a hierarchical approach to performance visualization and integrates both system and application based metrics. ParaGraph [10] is a tool that provides a large number of different displays for visualizing the performance of parallel application. We have tried to integrate the results of this work into our performance monitoring environment and will likely continue to exploit the results of this research.

3   The Paragon Multiprocessor

3.1   Hardware Architecture

The Paragon [6] hardware architecture consists of processing nodes based on the Intel i860XP microprocessor. Each processing node has one i860XP application processor, a second i860XP used for message-protocol processing and a Network Interface Controller (NIC) that connects the node to the communication network. Nodes are arranged in a two-dimensional mesh and are interconnected through a network that provides a full-duplex node to node bandwidth of 200 MB/s.

Each node board also contains hardware support for performance monitoring in the form of a special daughterboard that provides hardware counters. The counters are used to monitor bus ownership and information about communication traffic. In addition, the daughterboard implements a a 56-bit global counter that is driven from the global 10 MHz clock from the backplane. This counter is used to generate global time stamps that are accurate to 100 ns local to each node and 1 microsecond across all nodes in the system. This feature is of particular importance since many performance tools need highly accurate time stamps to generate correct results.

3.2   Operating System and Programming Model

The operating system and programming model supported by the target architecture have to be taken into account during the design of performance monitoring tools since the performance tools should be able to present the performance data in the context of the programming model being used.

The Paragon OSF operating system [19] is based on the Mach 3.0 microkernel technology and an extended OSF/1 server. Each node in the system runs a microkernel that provides core operating system functions like virtual memory management and task management. Other operating system services are handled by the OSF/1 server. The operating system provides a single system image with standard UNIX functionality. Multiprogramming is fully supported by the operating system - multiple users may log on to the machine and run applications at any time.

If all nodes in the machine were scheduled according to conventional UNIX scheduling policies, this would lead to non-deterministic load conditions for parallel application runs. To avoid this, partitions with different scheduling characteristics can be defined within the machine. In this way, the nodes in the system are logically divided into an I/O partition that contains nodes designated to communicate with peripheral devices, a service partition used for sequential jobs (shells, user commands etc.) and a compute partition that is used for parallel application runs.

The service partition normally uses conventional UNIX scheduling with dynamic load balancing through process migration. Gang scheduling is used within the compute partitions. This means that while a parallel job is executing, it has exclusive access to the set of nodes it uses. After a configurable time-interval, the entire job is suspended (rolled out) and a different job is resumed (rolled in). Thus, the perturbation of parallel application runs through other jobs in the system is minimized. Even so, the scheduling of applications must be taken into account when designing performance tools because the effects of gang-scheduling must be filtered out by application level tools.

The Paragon supports a message passing programming model that is compatible with the NX/2 programming model available on previous generation Intel machines [14]. This model is also supported by the application level performance tools. However, support for other programming models such as shared virtual memory, High Performance Fortran (HPF) or thread models may be added in the near future. Thus, the performance monitoring environment must be flexible enough to allow tools for new programming models to be added without undue implementation overhead.

4   Performance Monitoring Architecture

4.1   Overview

Figure 1 gives an overview of the Paragon Performance Monitoring Architecture. It consists of the following parts:

- The Tools Graphical Interface (TGI) is used as a front-end for instrumenting the parallel application and to visualize the performance data produced by the performance tools. It is based on X-Windows and the Motif toolkit.

- The Instrumentation Front End is used to parse user requests for performance instrumentation of a parallel application. It generates the commands that are then sent to the distributed monitoring system through an RPC interface.

- The Distributed Monitoring System consists of the Tools Application Monitor (TAM), the performance library that is linked with the application program, and the event trace servers. The TAM is responsible for instrumenting the application with jumps to the performance libraries. The libraries produce trace data that are sent to the event trace servers. The servers perform post-processing tasks and write the performance data to file or send them directly to the application performance analysis tools.

- The application performance analysis tools interpret the trace data they receive from the event trace servers. Currently, we have implemented three tools. A modified version of ParaGraph allows detailed graphical animation of processor activity and message passing. Profiling tools (prof and gprof) can be used to examine performance at the statement and procedure level.

- The System Performance Visualizer (SPV) is designed to monitor the overall system usage by displaying parameters such as CPU utilization, bus usage and network traffic. Since this tool is not application oriented, there is no need for instrumentation. Instead, the data are directly generated by the hardware performance monitoring board.

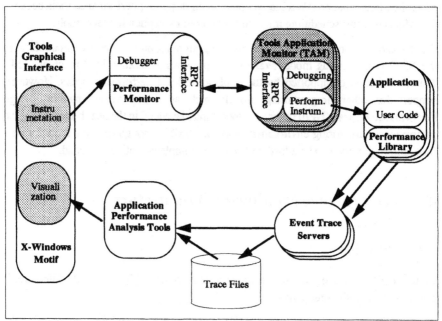

Fig. 1. Performance Monitoring Architecture

As can be seen, the performance monitoring environment is closely integrated with the debugging functionality since many of the tasks necessary for performance monitoring are also needed for debugging (e.g. accessing symbol table information, instrumenting the application). In the following discussion we will focus on the performance monitoring aspects of the Paragon tool environment. A detailed description of the debugging interface and the techniques used in the Tools Application Monitor can be found in [1].

4.2   Tools Graphical Interface

The Tools Graphical Interface serves two purposes. On the one hand it is used for loading, starting and instrumenting an application. On the other hand it provides a common interface through which the user can operate the performance tools and display performance data. The fact that all tools share a common user interface that is based on the Motif style guide standard makes the functionality of the tool environment easily and obviously available to the user. Operating and learning the interface is further facilitated by an on-line help system that provides context-sensitive help. Most tools also provide a command-line interface since this may be preferable to a graphical interface in some cases.

The tasks of instrumenting and starting application runs are closely integrated with the debugging functionality available on the Paragon. To instrument an application for use with a particular performance tool, the user starts the application using the debugger. The next step consists in defining a monitoring context, i.e. a part of the parallel application for which tracing is to be enabled. Such a context (a set of processes and start and stop locations for tracing within those processes) can be defined through a point-and-click interface (see Figure 2). This allows the user to focus on the part of the application that is limiting the performance and to reduce the amount of performance data that is generated, a feature that is of particular importance for detailed performance measurements. For example, the profiling functionality could be used to find the parts of the application that consume the largest percentage of time and these parts could then be analyzed in detail using the ParaGraph tool.

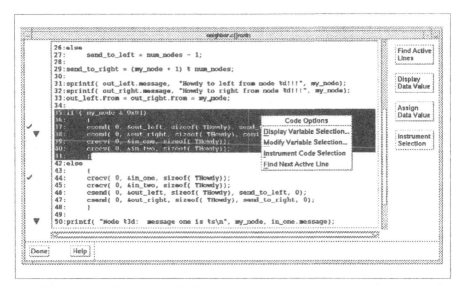

Fig. 2. Instrumenting an Application

4.3   Instrumentation Front End

The instrumentation front end parses commands it receives from the graphical or command-line interface and generates the commands that are then sent to the distributed monitoring system to instrument the application. In the first implementation, instrumentation is restricted to specifying a monitoring context and a tool (prof, gprof, ParaGraph) for which instrumentation is to be performed. The instrumentation front end then reads a file that contains a detailed description of what performance data is to be collected for the given tool. The instrumentation front end will be extended in future versions to allow users to specify in more detail what performance data should be gathered. For example, a user may want to focus on the message passing activity of a parallel application during a given application run. It may then be possible to restrict instrumentation to the message-passing functions thus once again reducing the amount of generated performance data.

4.4   Distributed Monitoring System

To overcome the difficulties associated with monitoring massively parallel applications with large numbers of processes, the Paragon performance monitoring environment uses a distributed monitoring system that is able to perform high-level operations in parallel. It consists of a network of TAM processes, a performance library and a network of event trace servers.

4.4.1   Tools Application Monitor

The Tools Application Monitor is made up of a network of TAM processes arranged in the form of a broadcast spanning tree with one TAM process for every node used by the application. This makes it possible to broadcast monitoring requests to all nodes in an efficient manner. The instrumentation front-end communicates with the TAM network through an RPC interface based on the Mach Interface Generator (MIG). Communication within the TAM network also occurs by message-passing over Mach ports. For the purposes of performance instrumentation communication within the TAM network is downstream only since the performance data are sent to the application performance tools by way of the event trace servers (see below).

4.4.2   Performance Library

To instrument an application for performance measurements, the TAM modifies the application code to vector to a performance library. To minimize the data collection perturbation, the performance library is automatically linked with every application so that event traces can be gathered without incurring the overhead of context switches. The performance data that can be captured include event traces and counters as well as profiling information:

Event traces and counters: The events that can be captured include function entry, function exit and arbitrary code trace points. In addition, simple, summing, and timing counters are supported. These mechanisms allow performance tools to reduce the amount of data that need to be forwarded to the tools. For example, the amount of messages exchanged between nodes could be measured by placing summing counters at message-passing functions without the need to analyze a complete event-trace. Similarly, timing counters can be used to collect the total time spent by the application between two points in the code.

To do event tracing of an application, the TAM instruments the application process in memory by replacing application code at the trace address with a branch to a new page of text. In the new text, a procedure call is made to the performance library with parameters specific to the event trace point. This procedure produces a trace record that contains the type of the event, a time stamp, information about who generated the event (e.g. node, process id) and additional data such as function parameters or data from a specified memory location. To minimize perturbation, the trace record is stored in a trace buffer that is periodically flushed to the event trace servers. In addition, the performance monitoring library can be configured to trace the time used to flush the event trace buffers in order to allow performance tools to determine the amount of perturbation introduced. Once the performance library procedure returns, the new text code executes the replaced instructions and jumps back to the event trace point and application execution continues.

Due to the complex programming model supported by the Paragon, tracing only events within the application code is not sufficient. Paragon applications may spawn multiple processes on every node. This means that context switch information has to be traced in spite of the fact that the gang scheduling policy ensures that an application has exclusive access to its processing nodes while it is scheduled. The context switch information is collected by the Mach kernel. Similarly, information about gang scheduling has to be gathered to enable the tools to correctly portray the application's performance information. This information is routinely gathered by the scheduler that is responsible for handling roll-in and roll-out events.

Profiling information: For profiling, a counter is set at each function exit and the performance library collects a statistical sample of the current program counter at each clock tick. To turn profiling on, the performance library sets up profiling buffers and then uses the OSF/1 AD profil() system call. When profiling is turned off, the performance library flushes and deallocates the profiling buffer. Profiling and event tracing can occur simultaneously. For example, the call graph information used by the gprof tool is derived from function entry/exit traces while the time spent within routines is measured through statistical profiling.

4.4.3 Event Trace Server

The Event Trace Servers perform post-processing tasks on the performance data they receive from the performance library. One event trace server services a number of performance libraries. The exact ratio of servers to performance libraries is configurable and depends on the type of performance measurement being performed. For example, for profiling, one separate file with profiling information is generated for each profiled process so it may be desirable to also have one event trace server per process. Other performance tools (e.g. ParaGraph) operate on a single trace file that contains event trace information from all monitored nodes in the application. In this case, the event trace servers must merge event trace information from multiple performance libraries, and information about context switches and gang-scheduling into one trace. ParaGraph also requires the trace to be sorted in time order. In this case, a network of event trace servers arranged in a tree configuration may be more appropriate.

In the normal case, the output of the event trace servers consists of one or many trace files that can be interpreted by the application performance analysis tools. However, the trace servers may also forward their output directly to a tool for on-line visualization of an application's performance.

The Paragon performance monitoring environment supports event traces in the Pablo Self-Defining Data Format[16]. SDDF is a trace description language that specifies both the data record structures and data record instances. The Pablo software supports both binary and ASCII trace representations and provides a flexible library of C++ classes to access and manipulate the data stored in SDDF files. It thus meets the goal to "standardize the interface routines to trace files and not the physical file itself" [12][13].

4.5   Application Performance Analysis Tools

The application performance analysis tools interpret the performance data gathered by the distributed monitoring system and report them back to the user. They either have a command-line interface that can be invoked from the graphical interface or directly use the functionality of the tools graphical interface to present graphical output. Currently, we have implemented three application performance tools but the design of the performance monitoring architecture makes it easy to integrate new tools into the framework.

4.5.1 ParaGraph

ParaGraph [10] is one of the most widely used tools for analyzing the performance of parallel applications. It can be used in a post-mortem fashion to visualize the performance data contained in a trace file generated during an application run. ParaGraph was originally written for use with the PICL Portable Instrumented Communication Library [7], which runs on a variety of message passing parallel architectures. In the mean time, many groups have adapted ParaGraph to other programming models and architectures [8][15][17]. The widespread use of ParaGraph was the prime motivation for providing the tool as part of the Paragon performance monitoring environment.

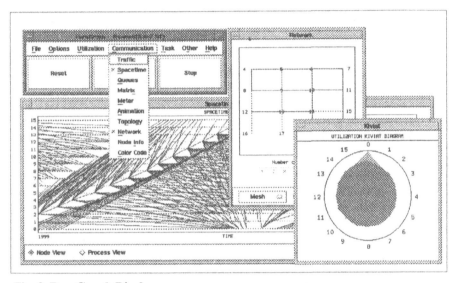

Fig. 3. ParaGraph Displays

ParaGraph is a graphical tool that provides a variety of displays to visualize the performance of a parallel application. The user can choose as many displays as will fit on the screen from three different types of displays. The utilization displays are concerned primarily with depicting processor utilization, communication displays can be used to visualize interprocessor communication, and the task displays provide a way of relating the events in the trace to source locations in the parallel programs. Figure 3 shows some of the displays generated by ParaGraph for a Householder transformation algorithm executed on 16 nodes. The general functionality of the tool has been left unchanged and will not be described any further. However, a number of important changes and enhancements have been made to the tool.

• ParaGraph has been integrated into the Tools Graphical Interface. Thus, the tool now has a standardized Motif interface that is easy to learn and consistent with the rest of the Paragon tool environment. As a side-effect, many new features were added to the user interface (e.g. the correct handling of expose and resize events, use of backing store, when available, to retain information when a window is obscured and re-exposed, customization of the interface through X-resources, the ability to interactively change the colors used for the visualization, an on-line help facility and extended support for saving ParaGraph's screen layout).

• ParaGraph now supports the major features of the Paragon/NX programming model such as synchronous, asynchronous and interrupt-driven message passing and probe operations. Since the distributed monitoring system allows tracing of system calls, we can also trace file I/O and display I/O activity in ParaGraph's utilization displays. ParaGraph also supports multiple processes per node and takes gang-scheduling and task switch information into account when displaying performance data. The mapping of logical application nodes to physical nodes is also available through the distributed monitoring system and is used by ParaGraph to visualize the routing of messages through the physical network.

• The instrumentation front-end allows the user to specify a monitoring context in an on-line fashion. This makes it possible to focus on subsets of nodes and parts of an application's code without the need to recompile. ParaGraph fully supports traces that come from subsets of an application's nodes. In addition, the user can select a subset of the traced nodes for visualization. This provides a primitive zooming mechanism and enhances the scalability of the tool.

• ParaGraph now supports traces in the Pablo Self-Defining Data Format [16] instead of the PICL trace format. One of the drawbacks of this approach is that the Pablo routines do not allow random-access to the trace file which forced us to drop ParaGraph's critical path analysis since it is based on scanning the trace file backwards. However, ParaGraph's critical path analysis seems to be of limited use since it provides little feedback as to where in the source-code the critical path is located. We plan to implement a true source-code oriented critical path analysis tool in the near future (see section 5.).

4.5.2 Prof and Gprof

For profiling, the Paragon performance monitoring environment provides slightly modified versions of the well-known UNIX tools prof and gprof [9]. The tools are fully integrated with the distributed monitoring system as has been described above. Thus, the tools graphical interface and the instrumentation front-end can be used to specify a profiling context in the usual way, which results in instrumentation of the appropriate part of the application.

One file containing profiling data is produced per instrumented application processes and the files are stored in a common directory for analysis by the profiling tools. In addition to the standard command-line interface, the profilers can also be invoked through the tools graphical interface (see Figure 4).

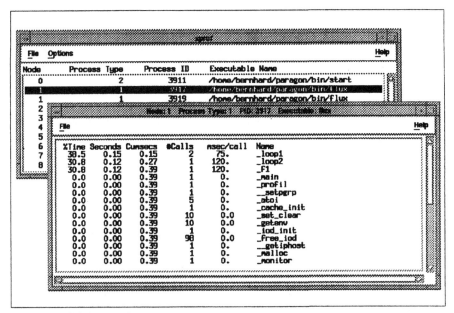

Fig. 4. Profiling Interface

4.6 System Performance Visualization

The application performance analysis tools described above allow the user to monitor the behavior and performance of parallel applications at different levels of granularity. They try to filter system effects out as far as possible. However, in many cases it is useful to monitor overall system usage without focusing on a specific application. The System Performance Visualization tool (SPV) serves this purpose.

One of the motivations for implementing this tool was the fact that the LED panel on previous generation Intel systems was often used as a primitive debugging and performance monitoring aid. SPV is a graphical tool that allows the user to visualize the Paragon front panel on a workstation but it also provides zooming capabilities that make it possible to display more detailed information such as CPU, mesh and memory bus utilization values. Colors that can be configured according to the user's wishes are used to represent different utilization values. Figure 5 shows some of the displays supported by SPV. The following displays are available:

- The CPU display shows the CPU utilization of all the nodes. Mesh utilization is not displayed.

- The Mesh display is a visualization of the Paragon front panel which shows both CPU and mesh utilization.

- The Values display adds the actual utilization values to the Mesh display.

- The Node display provides the greatest level of detail. It shows symbolic representations of the Paragon node boards (CPU, message passing processor, memory, bus and Network Interface Controller) and the mesh and displays the utilization values for all components.

The performance data displayed by SPV are generated by the hardware performance monitoring board and thus bypass the data collection mechanism used for the application performance analysis tools. The performance data collected by the hardware are sent periodically over the Paragon mesh to a daemon that forwards the information to the SPV tool. Thus, the display is pseudo real-time, i.e. the front panel information is displayed within a few seconds of the real Paragon front-panel.

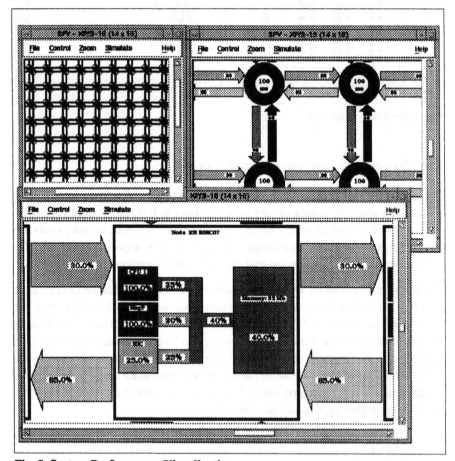

Fig. 5. System Performance Visualization

5 Future Directions

We plan to further improve our performance monitoring environment in the near future. Areas that will be investigated include:

- New tools: The design of the performance monitoring architecture makes it relatively easy to add new tools to the environment. We plan to add tools that help relate performance bottlenecks to locations in the user. In many cases, simple table of numbers may be more effective than sophisticated graphical displays. Thus, a good candidate for addition to the tool environment is a critical path analyzer such as the one implemented within the IPS-2 system [18]. As new programming models emerge, the tools will have to be modified to support these programming models.

- It is not feasible to cover all the needs users have for performance tools. The Pablo system is very flexible in that it allows tools to be configured out of existing modules. We plan to integrate parts of our tool environment completely into the Pablo software. This will allow users to add new tools and displays to the existing performance monitoring environment. It will also make it possible to run different modules of the performance analysis tools in parallel to fully utilize the power of the parallel machine for performance analysis. Selective instrumentation techniques can then be used to reduce the amount of performance data generated by tracing only the information needed for the displays the user has selected.

- We also plan to further modularize the tool environment. Currently, some of the features needed for performance analysis are implemented within the debugger (e.g. instrumentation, symbol table lookup). It would be desirable to implement these parts as separate modules that can be joined to form either performance or debugging tools.

6 Conclusions

The Paragon performance monitoring environment addresses many of the issues that make performance analysis for scalable high-performance computing a difficult task. It incorporates both system and application performance analysis tools which are able to present performance data at different levels of detail. The problems of monitoring massively parallel applications are addressed through a distributed monitoring system that is capable of using the power of the parallel system to perform performance analysis in parallel. At the same time we strive to minimize perturbation and measure the amount of perturbation introduced through monitoring. To some extent, the environment is able to support performance monitoring in a multiprocess and multiuser environment but this is a topic that needs further investigation.

Even though we have initially focused on implementing tools that support the NX message-passing programming model, we believe the monitoring environment is flexible enough to allow an easy implementation of tools for other programming models.

7 References

[1]   D. Breazeal, R. Anderson, W.D. Smith, W. Auld, and K. Callaghan. *A Parallel Software Monitor for Debugging and Performance Tools on Distributed Memory Multicomputers*. In *Proceedings of the Supercomputer Debugging Workshop 1992*, Dallas, Texas, October 1992. Los Alamos National Laboratory.

[2]   D. Breazeal, K. Callaghan, and W.D. Smith. *IPD: A Debugger for Parallel Heterogeneous Systems*. In *Proceedings of the ACM/ONR Workshop on Parallel and Distributed Debugging*, pages 216-218, Santa Cruz, CA, May 1991.

[3]   T. Bemmerl. *The TOPSYS Architecture*. In H.Burkhart, editor, *CONPAR 90 - VAPP IV*, volume 457 of *Lecture Notes in Computer Science*, pages 732-743. Springer-Verlag, Berlin, Heidelberg, New York, September 1990.

[4]   T. Bemmerl, O. Hansen, and T. Ludwig. *PATOP for Performance Tuning of Parallel Programs*. In H.Burkhart, editor, *Proceedings of CONPAR 90 - VAPP IV, Joint International Conference on Vector and Parallel Processing*, volume 457 of *Lecture Notes in Computer Science*, pages 840-851, Zurich, Switzerland, September 1990. Springer-Verlag, Berlin, Heidelberg, New York.

[5]   T.Bemmerl. *Programming Tools for Massively Parallel Supercomputers*. In *Proceedings of the CNRS-NSF workshop on Environments and Tools for Parallel Scientific Computing*, Saint Hilaire du Touvet, France, September 1992.

[6]   Intel Supercomputer Systems Division. *Paragon XP/S Product Overview*. Intel Corporation, 15201 N.W. Greenbrier Parkway, Beaverton OR 97006, 1992.

[7]   G.A. Geist, M.T. Heath, B.W. Peyton, and P.H. Worley. *A User's Guide to PICL, a portable instrumented communication library*. Technical Report ORNL/TM-11616, Oak Ridge National Laboratory, Oak Ridge, TN, October 1990.

[8]   I. Glendinning, S. Hellberg, P. Shallow, and M. Gorrod. *Generic Visualisation and Performance Monitoring Tools for Message Passing Parallel Systems*. In N.Tophan, R.Ibbett, and T.Bemmerl, editors, *Proceedings of the IFIP WG 10.3 Workshop on Programming Environments for Parallel Computing*, volume A-11 of *IFIP Transactions*, pages 139-149, Edinburgh, Scotland, April 1992. North-Holland.

[9]   S.L. Graham, P.B. Kessler, and M.K. McKusick. *gprof: a Call Graph Execution Profiler*. *ACM SIGPLAN Notices*, 17(6):120-126, June 1982.

[10]   M.T. Heath and J.A. Etheridge. *Visualizing the Performance of Parallel Programs*. *IEEE Software*, 8(5):29-39, September 1991.

[11]   J.K. Hollingsworth, R.B. Irvin, and B.P. Miller. *The Integration of Application and System Based Metrics in a Parallel Program Performance Tool*. In *Proceedings of the Third ACM SIGPLAN Symposium on Principles and Practice of Parallel Programming*, volume 26, no. 7 of *ACM SIGPLAN Notices*, pages 189-200, Williamsburg, Virginia, April 1991. ACM Press.

[12]   B.P. Miller and C. McDowell. *Summary of ACM/ONR Workshop on Parallel and Distributed Debugging*. *ACM Operating Systems Review*, 26(1):18-31, January 1992.

[13]   B. Mohr. *Standardization of Event Traces Considered Harmful or Is an Implementation of Object-Independent Event Trace Monitoring and Analysis Systems Possible?* In *Proceedings of the CNRS-NSF workshop on Environments and Tools for Parallel Scientific Computing*, Saint Hilaire du Touvet, France, September 1992.

[14]   P. Pierce. *The NX/2 Operating System*. In *Proceedings of the 3rd Conference on Hypercube Concurrent Computers and Applications*, pages 384-391. ACM, 1988.

[15]   D.T. Rover, M. B. Carter, and J. L. Gustafson. *Performance Visualization of SLALOM*. In *Proceedings of the Sixth Distributed Memory Computing Conference*, pages 543-550, Portland, Oregon, May 1991. IEEE, IEEE Computer Society Press.

[16]   D. A. Reed, R. D. Olson, R. A. Aydt, T. M. Madhyastha, T. Birkett, D. W. Jensen, B. A. Nazief, and B. K. Totty. *Scalable Performance Environments for Parallel Systems*. In *Proc. of the Sixth Distributed Memory Computing Conference*, pages 562-569, Portland,Ore, April 1991. IEEE.

[17]   M. van Riek and B. Tourancheau. *The Design of the General Parallel Monitoring System*. In N.Tophan, R.Ibbett, and T.Bemmerl, editors, *Proceedings of the IFIP WG 10.3 Workshop on Programming Environments for Parallel Computing*, volume A-11 of *IFIP Transactions*, pages 127-137, Edinburgh, Scotland, April 1992. North-Holland.

[18]   C.Q. Yang and B.P. Miller. *Critical Path Analysis for the Execution of Parallel and Distributed Programs*. In *Proceedings of the 8th International Conference on Distributed Computing Systems*, pages 366-375, San Jose, CA, June 1988. IEEE.

[19]   R. Zajcew, P. Roy, D. Black, C. Peak, P. Guedes, B. Kemp, J. LoVerso, M. Leibensperger, M. Barnett, F. Rabii and D. Netterwala. *An OSF/1 UNIX for Massively Parallel Multicomputers*. In *Proceedings of the Winter 1993 USENIX Technical Conference*, pages 449-468, San Diego, CA, January 1993. The USENIX Association.

Springer-Verlag
and the Environment

We at Springer-Verlag firmly believe that an international science publisher has a special obligation to the environment, and our corporate policies consistently reflect this conviction.

We also expect our business partners – paper mills, printers, packaging manufacturers, etc. – to commit themselves to using environmentally friendly materials and production processes.

The paper in this book is made from low- or no-chlorine pulp and is acid free, in conformance with international standards for paper permanency.

Lecture Notes in Computer Science

For information about Vols. 1–665
please contact your bookseller or Springer-Verlag